TRANSFORMING THE AMERICAN POLITY

REAL POLITICS IN AMERICA

Series Editor: Paul S. Herrnson, *University of Maryland*

The books in this series bridge the gap between academic scholarship and the popular demand for knowledge about politics. They illustrate empirically supported generalizations from original research and the academic literature using examples taken from the legislative process, executive branch decision making, court rulings, lobbying efforts, election campaigns, political movements, and other areas of American politics. The goal of the series is to convey the best contemporary political science research has to offer in ways that will engage individuals who want to know about real politics in America.

TRANSFORMING THE AMERICAN POLITY

THE PRESIDENCY OF GEORGE W. BUSH AND THE WAR ON TERRORISM

EDITED BY

Richard S. Conley
University of Florida

UPPER SADDLE RIVER, NEW JERSEY 07458

Library of Congress Cataloging-in-Publication Data

Conley, Richard Steven.
  Transforming the American polity: the presidency of George W. Bush and the war on terrorism/edited by Richard S. Conley.
     p. cm.—(Real politics in America)
  Includes bibliographical references and index.
  ISBN 0-13-189342-4
  1. United States—Politics and government—2001– .   2. United States—Foreign relations—2001– .   3. War on Terrorism, 2001—Political aspects.   4. September 11 Terrorist Attacks, 2001—Influence.   I. Title.   II. Series.
  E902.C655   2005
  973.931'092—dc22

                                                                    2004018738

Editorial Director: Charlyce Jones Owen
Acquisitions Editor: Glenn Johnston
Editorial Assistant: Suzanne Remore
Marketing Manager: Kara Kindstrom
Marketing Assistant: Jennifer Lang
Prepress and Manufacturing Buyer: Sherry Lewis
Cover Art Director: Jayne Conte
Interior Design: John P. Mazzola
Cover Design: Kiwi Design
Composition/Full-Service Project Management: Kari C. Mazzola and John P. Mazzola
Printer/Binder: Courier Companies, Inc.
Cover Printer: Phoenix Color Corp.

This book was set in 10/12 Palatino.

Real Politics in America
Series Editor: Paul S. Herrnson

Pearson Education LTD.
Pearson Education Singapore, Pte. Ltd
Pearson Education, Canada, Ltd
Pearson Education–Japan
Pearson Education Australia PTY, Limited

Pearson Education North Asia Ltd
Pearson Educación de Mexico, S.A. de C.V.
Pearson Education Malaysia, Pte. Ltd
Pearson Education, Upper Saddle River, NJ

10 9 8 7 6 5 4 3 2 1
ISBN 0-13-189342-4

CONTENTS

INTRODUCTION

RICHARD S. CONLEY

UNIVERSITY OF FLORIDA

The horrific events of September 11, 2001, fundamentally altered the course of American politics. As the symbols of the nation's economic and military power came under attack in New York and Washington, the presidency of George W. Bush was swiftly transformed into a wartime administration. Many factors—including Bush's use of prerogatives as commander in chief, Congress's delegation of broad authority to him, and his political skill—decisively shifted the balance in the constitutional order to the White House.

Throughout the history of the Republic it is in times of war that the institution of the presidency becomes the pivot point in the American political system. Chief executives are far less fettered by the typical constraints of constitutional checks-and-balances when crisis and war prevail. Grasping how Bush's presidency and consequently the American polity have been transformed by the war on terrorism must begin with this axiom. Evaluating Bush's use of constitutional and extraconstitutional power in the first wartime presidency of the twenty-first century, and the impact on governance, is the objective of the contributions in this volume.

Bush's actions, and his strategic exploitation of issues surrounding the war on terrorism, have had broad ramifications for relations between governing institutions and the public. The dynamism with which Bush has used the levers of the wartime presidency and the precedent-setting actions he has taken are nothing less than remarkable in such a short period of time. Bush's interpretation of the meaning of 9/11, and the ways in which he has framed the war on terrorism and homeland security, have provided political advantage at home and enabled him to reconstruct the basis of the nation's relations abroad. In just eighteen months after the attacks on the World Trade Center and the Pentagon, he moved from quick military action against the Taliban clerics in Afghanistan to armed confrontation with Iraqi dictator Saddam Hussein. With only a minimal international coalition in support of U.S. efforts to disarm Hussein by force, Bush shifted American foreign policy toward a doctrine of military preemption of perceived threats to the United States.

As the defining issue of Bush's presidency, the war on terrorism has entailed significant political calculations by the White House that must not be underestimated. In the 2002 midterm elections, Bush gambled that making homeland security a central issue would yield a substantial payoff for congressional Republicans. He has staked his reelection chances in 2004 on effecting successful regime change in Iraq in time to refocus attention on, and revitalize, the domestic economy. The war on terrorism has also provided essential insights into Bush's articulation of his own brand of conservatism. His penchant for unilateralism in foreign affairs, skepticism of international institutions, and willingness to expand the national security state while simultaneously limiting the growth of domestic programs is more consistent with the vision of Ronald Reagan than the legacy of moderate conservatives of yesteryear, such as Dwight Eisenhower. The war on terrorism has unquestionably replaced "compassionate conservatism" as the theme of his administration.

THE TRANSFORMATIONAL CONTEXT OF BUSH'S PRESIDENCY

The radical transformation of the strategic context of Bush's presidency appears most extraordinary when one considers the uncertain situation in which the president found himself in late summer 2001.

Having occupied the Oval Office for just a little more than eight months on 9/11, George W. Bush had been attempting to surmount lingering questions about his political leadership. He had become only the fourth president in U.S. history to lose the popular vote but win the Electoral College. The Florida recount controversy robbed Bush of any claims to a mandate, but seemingly did little to dissuade him from governing as though he had one, despite the risks. He pushed firmly ahead with his domestic agenda, the centerpiece of which was tax cuts that overshadowed other policy debates his first months in office.

Reviews of Bush's skill and leadership were quite mixed by summer 2001 and storm clouds were gathering on the horizon. The president had embarked on a "charm offensive" on Capitol Hill that enabled him to successfully push through tax cuts during his "honeymoon" period with Congress, and education reform by the end of the year.[1] But his faith-based initiative proposal had stalled as spring turned to summer.[2] And many blamed White House insensitivity for Vermont Senator Jim Jeffords's decision to leave the GOP, thereby allowing Democrats organizational control of the narrowly divided upper chamber and insuring a more difficult road for the president's agenda—and judicial appointments.[3] Moreover, there had been no wellspring of popular support for the president following the 2000 election. In fact, Bush's approval rating had drifted downward from the mid-to-high fifties from the time he took office to *its lowest point* just prior to 9/11. The Gallup Poll taken September 7–10, 2001, showed his job approval at just 51 percent.

Before 9/11, foreign affairs did not seem to be on the president's radar screen, perhaps not unexpectedly for a former Texas governor who had never held federal office. He made the routine trips to Mexico and Canada that are typical for a new chief executive. His only real "crisis" was an awkward one—reclaiming an Air Force plane held by the Chinese after the crew made an emergency landing.[4] Domestic affairs, including debates over how to spend projected budget surpluses and adjust entitlement programs, occupied much of the work of the White House and Congress.

Little could Bush anticipate how the murderous acts of nineteen hijackers on that September morning would thoroughly transform his institutional position, alter his focus of attention, and open up unprecedented opportunities to revive his presidency—and leave an indelible imprint on history. It fell to Bush, as the first president inaugurated in the new millennium, to wage a battle dissimilar in so many ways to the wars of his predecessors. The war on terrorism pitted the United States not against other nation-states, per se. Rather, the American *way of life* was under attack from an elusive enemy comprised of clandestine cells of Muslim religious zealots whose organization transcends borders and accountability. Samuel Huntington's controversial thesis of an impending "clash of civilizations" seemed to take on a certain prescience.[5]

In the eighteen months following 9/11, Bush began to articulate new doctrines and policies that set the compass of domestic politics and foreign affairs in decidedly new directions. Against the backdrop of renewed congressional bipartisanship and job approval ratings that soared to heights not seen since his father's victory in the Persian Gulf War a decade earlier, Bush led a military campaign in Afghanistan that successfully toppled the Taliban regime, which had given succor to members of Saudi-born Osama bin Laden's al Qaeda network. The victory led to the detention of hundreds of suspected operatives who were not identifiable "soldiers" of a national government. The administration used a contextually questionable precedent from World War II involving Nazi saboteurs to classify the captured Taliban and al Qaeda members as "enemy combatants." This classification limited detainees' legal rights and subjected them to military tribunals or indefinite confinement, drawing criticism from domestic and international human rights watch groups.[6]

Civil liberties seemed to come under attack frequently by the White House beginning with the military success in Afghanistan. Bush and some members of his cabinet, particularly Attorney General John Ashcroft, chastised members of Congress and the press who questioned administration policies.[7] Ashcroft intimated a lack of patriotism among Americans who, by expressing misgivings about government conduct, were abetting would-be terrorists. New domestic intelligence-gathering ventures by the federal government also alarmed civil libertarians. The most potentially draconian measures included one proposal by the Department of Defense for a "total information awareness" program linking personal and financial information on all Americans, and another by Bush to encourage average citizens to engage in surveillance of one another and to report "suspicious activities" to government authorities.[8]

In the aftermath of 9/11, Bush moved swiftly with independent action to combat terrorism at home. In October 2001, he created an Office of Homeland Security in the White House to coordinate federal counter-terrorism programs across agencies. Eight months later he seized the opportunity to call upon Congress for the largest reorganization of governmental functions since the presidency of Harry Truman. He won unprecedented latitude to structure a fifteenth Cabinet-level department—the Department of Homeland Security— that he argued would give the federal government the tools to fight terrorism at home and might serve as a template for an eventual overhaul of federal workplace rules in other agencies.

Homeland security was not simply an issue of bureaucratic reorganization. Bush used it strategically for partisan political advantage. He preempted Congress with his own proposal for a massive reorganization of the federal government, and when the Democrat-controlled Senate took issue with parts of his proposal, he used the stalled homeland security bill to Republican candidates' benefit in the 2002 midterm elections. By making homeland security a central feature of a personal campaign for fellow Republicans, casting blame on Democrats for refusing to cede to his demands for broad executive discretion, and putting his own credibility on the line, Bush reversed the long-standing trend of the president's party losing seats in off-year contests. With Bush's aid, House Republicans bolstered their majority and Senate Republicans regained the majority in the upper chamber.

Bush also articulated the basis of a new American foreign policy, the implications of which remain unclear. After victory in Afghanistan, he clarified his intentions to move from a policy of combating terrorist cells hiding at home and in various countries to preemptively confronting rogue nation-states that pose an imminent threat to the United States. In his first post-9/11 state of the union address in January 2002, Bush alluded to broadening the war on terrorism to tyrannical regimes that constituted an "axis of evil" stretching east from Iraq to Iran and North Korea. Indeed, in March 2003, the United States launched a military campaign to "liberate" Iraq, identify and destroy that country's putative cache of weapons of mass destruction, and precipitate regime change, despite staunch resistance by the international community and many of the permanent members of the United Nations Security Council, including France, Russia, and China.

Bush had reinterpreted the Founders' intent for defensive actions by commanders in chief to "repel sudden attacks" to meet perceived threats of the twenty-first century.[9] He argued that some prospective threats must be dealt with preemptively, contending repeatedly that the risks of inaction were far greater than the risks of military confrontation—at least in Iraq. Bush broke decisively with notions that dictatorial regimes like Iraq could be contained in the way the United States had attempted to do with the Soviet Union throughout the Cold War. He also clearly signaled a willingness to act unilaterally in the absence of international consensus, calling into question not only U.S. future relations with long-standing allies such as France but also the utility of the United Nations as a forum for dealing with international terrorist organizations and countries that sponsor terrorism. It is clear that Bush's intention was to avoid at all costs a future nuclear, biological, or chemical 9/11 by removing the ability of the bellicose dictator of Iraq to carry out such catastrophes. It is less clear how practicable such a policy will be vis-à-vis other threats, such as Iran and North Korea.

CHARTING THE POST-9/11 TRANSFORMATIONS

What perspectives can political scientists lend to explain the magnitude of changes in American politics since 9/11, and how Bush led the nation to war in Iraq by spring 2003? Any explanation must begin with the recognition that the war on terrorism has been a presidency-dominated undertaking made possible by the combination of constitutional flexibility, public and congressional support, and Bush's own convictions and advisory team. Like a pebble breaking the water of a serene pond, the centralization of power and influence in Bush's wartime presidency has had a rapid and significant ripple effect across the political system. Gauging the long-term and short-term impacts of presidential actions on American institutions, democratic processes, and civil liberties demands a close, detailed analysis.

It is the leitmotiv of *multiple transformations* catalyzed by the war on terrorism—with the presidency as the point of convergence for change in the American political system—that connects the nine essays that follow. This volume brings together original research by some of the foremost scholars of presidential and congressional politics. They convened on February 7, 2003, at the University of Florida to examine systematically how the seminal events of 9/11 have inalterably shaped the president's—and the American public's—basic frame of reference in domestic and foreign affairs at the beginning of the twenty-first century.

Together, the essays provide an interlocking set of vantage points on how the war on terrorism has fundamentally reoriented American national and international politics. They place into sharper view the consequences that are likely to endure well beyond Bush's administration—whether it is one term or two—relative to the balance of institutional power in our constitutional system, individual freedoms, and public judgments of the federal government and its role. Individually, each of the essays juxtaposes the unique context of the war on terrorism with established theories of presidential politics spanning leadership and crisis decision making, electoral strategy, civil liberties, and relations with Congress.

The essays are organized into four broad categories that emphasize the transformation of Bush's presidency and the impact of the war on terrorism across different segments of the American political system, including (1) the president's relationship with and leadership of the American public, as well as his campaign for Republicans in the midterm elections of 2002; (2) Bush's wartime decision making, advisory mechanisms, and cabinet relations; (3) civil liberties; and (4) dynamics within Congress and between the president and Congress. The final essay by Lawrence Dodd links these vital issues by examining how the wartime "narrative" has come to dominate American political discourse—and whether that is likely to change in the aftermath of 9/11 and the war with Iraq.

The first section features essays by Michael Genovese, Roger Davidson, and Andrew Busch. These three essays provide critical vantage points about the public dimensions of George W. Bush's crisis leadership. "Good leaders," Michael Genovese contends, "are astute enough to see what is needed, skilled enough to apply wisdom to the problem, and flexible enough to make appropriate alterations in style." In his essay "The Transformations of the Bush Presidency: 9/11 and Beyond," Genovese assesses how contextually appropriate Bush's leadership skills have been. He gives Bush high marks for his actions in the immediate aftermath of the World Trade Center and Pentagon terror attacks. Bush used the institutional and extraconstitutional bases of presidential power to reassure the American public, define the challenges of the war on terrorism, and act swiftly in Afghanistan. Genovese is far more critical of Bush's longer-term leadership and future potential. In particular, Genovese questions Bush's ability to grasp the complexity of foreign relations in a world in which change is the primary constant. He argues that the president too readily exchanges a multidimensional view of international conflict for oversimplifications—"good versus evil" or "us versus them" frameworks that are untenable in a world of regional and ethnic chaos where moral clarity is often dubious.

If Bush was indeed successful in articulating a vision of the war on terrorism shortly after 9/11, Roger Davidson's essay "Americans' Beliefs about Themselves, the World, and War: Before and After 9/11" suggests why. Davidson analyzes Bush's use of rhetoric and his role as "interpreter in chief" for the American public and shows how the president's post-9/11 rhetoric drew upon Americans' historical and cultural "myths" about themselves—deeply ingrained sets of beliefs about their "exceptional" status in the world, penchant for self-reliance and optimism, and peaceable, defensive nature. Bush sought to "frame" the war metaphor, make sense out of the tragedy of 9/11, and muster public support for appropriate governmental responses,

Davidson argues, by returning to Americans' traditional understanding of themselves and their relations with the larger world. A longer-term question Davidson poses is how Americans can reconcile their status as the world's only superpower with an unprecedented terrorist attack that accentuated new vulnerabilities to the homeland rather than global hegemony.

Whatever George W. Bush's worldview or scholarly critiques of his intellectual deficits, *public evaluations* of his job performance after 9/11 were extraordinarily positive over an extended period. As is typical in a time of crisis, Americans rallied around the commander in chief. As George C. Edwards has argued elsewhere, Bush faced the same dilemma as his predecessors insofar as he was unable to translate his *general* popularity into significantly stronger support for *specific* policy issues, particularly on the domestic front.[10] The public's basic policy preferences remain largely constant, even if presidential job approval is susceptible to wide variation in times of crisis. However, Bush's public presidency may have mattered much more in the midterm elections of 2002. Bush's high approval ratings and his steadfast campaigning for Republican candidates were central factors in key congressional races that broke in the GOP's favor.

In his essay "National Security and the Midterm Elections of 2002," Andrew Busch agrees that the president's job approval was a positive factor in Republican gains in Congress. The GOP regained control of the Senate with the addition of two seats and bolstered the House majority with an additional six seats. For only the third time since 1932, the president's party gained seats in Congress, reversing the historical trend of often significant losses— even during times when the United States was engaged in international conflict. However, Busch posits that the president's popularity was only one factor of many in explaining the 2002 electoral outcomes. Drawing upon theories of midterm elections dynamics, Busch argues that an intertwining of other factors contributed to the GOP's successes. Having sustained seat losses in the three prior elections, Republicans were "minimally exposed" to suffer further significant losses and recruited "quality challengers," such as Elizabeth Dole, who had strong name recognition and prior political experience. Moreover, with a majority of state legislatures under GOP control, redistricting in 2000 also favored Republican gains. The president's influence, Busch contends, was most visible in his fund-raising efforts for Republican candidates and his ability to make national security the central theme of the midterm contests that gave the GOP a common platform on which to campaign nationally.

The second section of the volume includes essays by Shirley Anne Warshaw and James Pfiffner. Together, the two essays emphasize how the war on terrorism transformed Bush's cabinet relations and highlight his decision making apparatus for military conflict in Afghanistan and Iraq. Warshaw's essay "Ideological Conflict in the President's Cabinet" accentuates conservative advisors' ultimate dominance in the Bush White House. The war on terrorism, Warshaw posits, did *not* affect domestic policymaking as conservatives had already assumed a position of preeminence in the administration beginning in the early days of Bush's presidency. The terrorist attacks of 9/11, did, however, alter Bush's advisory structures in foreign affairs. Bush, she argues, "had to pick and choose from his foreign policy advisors where there were deep personal and political divisions." In tracing Bush's emerging war cabinet after 9/11, Warshaw shows how key moderates, including Secretary of State Colin Powell and National Security Advisor Condoleezza Rice, were ostracized from the policymaking process. The marginalization of Powell, she concludes, was a product of Bush's willingness to exchange multiple advocacy for ideological harmony in the foreign policy decision-making process. An important question, then, is whether Bush's advisory structure closed off policy options.

In Chapter 5, "National Security Policymaking and the Bush War Cabinet," James Pfiffner further examines the consequences of Bush's advisory structure on decisions regarding the war in Afghanistan and the domestic and international campaign against Iraq through early 2003. Pfiffner emphasizes the lack of formal structures and the importance of personalities in Bush's decisions. Bush, he argues, sought unanimity in advisory meetings and did limit the range of options in policy discussions. But on the military action in Afghanistan, Pfiffner suggests that with the assistance of Rice, the president used disagreements constructively to steer his foreign-policy team back to consensus. Moreover, Pfiffner offers a positive assessment of Colin Powell's influence. Bush, he argues, *was* often uncomfortable with Powell's advice. But the Secretary of State was "the only person in the administration with sufficient stature and clout to be able to present an alternative perspective to the hard-line point of view of Cheney, Rumsfeld, and Wolfowitz." Pfiffner concludes that Powell's advice was a counterweight to the conservative tendencies of Bush's advisors and was instrumental in a number of early policy choices concerning Iraq—particularly in the president's decision to seek international support for military action in the United Nations and the adoption of Resolution 1441.

The third section of the volume takes up the question of the Bush administration's record on civil liberties. In "Challenges to Civil Liberties in a Time of War," Louis Fisher analyzes how fundamental freedoms for citizens and noncitizens have been affected by the president's policies since 9/11. Fisher is particularly concerned about the indefinite nature of the war on terrorism. In times past, the curtailing of civil liberties through expanded governmental powers ended with the termination of hostilities between the United States and other nations.

Fisher notes a number of precedent-setting actions with the potential of long-term consequences for constitutional freedoms. The Bush administration has sought to limit the disclosure of law enforcement information to Congress and reinterpreted the Freedom of Information Act (FOIA) to shield executive agencies from public access to government records deemed "sensitive." Attorney General John Ashcroft's controversial statements, as well as his elaboration of new guidelines on the Federal Bureau of Investigation's surveillance of domestic public events, pose challenges not only to free speech but to individual privacy. Fisher also argues that the administration's reliance on World War II precedents for military trials for noncitizen terrorists is dubious. Finally, the indefinite detention of "enemy combatants" as material witnesses, judicial decisions that limit detainees' access to legal counsel, and closed deportation hearings threaten the rights of noncitizens. On a positive note, Fisher does suggest that Bush has taken pains through his use of the bully pulpit to avoid singling out Arab Americans. The president's denunciation of discrimination may well have diminished violence against Muslims.

The fourth section of the volume assesses dynamics within Congress and the relationship between the president and Congress after 9/11. In Chapter 7, Barbara Sinclair considers the impact of the war on terrorism on bipartisan voting and presidential legislative success in Congress, and the extent to which members ceded prerogatives to the president. Sinclair argues that the events of 9/11 altered the legislative agenda on Capitol Hill, briefly suppressed partisan voting patterns, and benefited the president's victory ratio in both the House and the Senate. The effects, however, were ephemeral. As the legislative agenda reverted back to domestic issues by 2002, partisan voting patterns returned to the higher levels typical of the last two decades, and Bush's success ratio declined. In her analysis of specific legislation adopted by Congress in the immediate aftermath of 9/11—including emergency spending and the resolution authorizing the president's use of force to combat terrorism—Sinclair posits that Congress was careful to guard institutional power while striking a balance with the White House. "Congress," she argues, "was not willing to hand the president a blank check; yet the majority was also never willing to carry the challenge to Bush to a high-visibility public showdown" on most issues, the administration's Iraq policy notwithstanding.

The president and Congress did risk high-stakes, public politics on the issue of homeland security and the reorganization of the federal workforce. In Chapter 8, Richard Conley examines the "dual" politics of reorganization—Bush's campaign against Senate Democrats to win broad discretion to structure the new Department of Homeland Security and congressional efforts to revamp the committee system to insure adequate oversight of the new entity on Capitol Hill. Conley argues that Bush and Senate Democrats chose "strategic disagreement" and blame-game politics in lieu of negotiation on the specifics of the homeland security bill. Each jockeyed for political gain in the 2002 midterm elections, and Bush's use of the bully pulpit enabled Republicans to carry the day. With the Senate in GOP hands, the president ultimately won unprecedented latitude to structure the new department on his terms. Congressional leaders, fearing internal conflicts, have since been loathe to fundamentally reorganize committee structures to meet the challenge of oversight of the new department—a particular concern of civil libertarians who worry about infringement of individual privacy and domestic intelligence gathering activities. The absence of committee reorganization efforts, Conley suggests, may also hamper the department's effective functioning if budget processes on Capitol Hill are not rationalized.

The final essay by Lawrence Dodd, "Entrapped in the Narrative of War: Reflections, Questions, and Commentary," reconnects the broad themes emphasized in the individual essays and poses a series of critical questions about change in the American political system. In his concluding observations, Dodd discusses how the nation moved from concerns about domestic terrorism to a war narrative that has seemingly justified policies and actions that have taken the American polity into uncharted waters. "In adopting the narrative of world war," Dodd explains, "and connecting that narrative with the government's right both to preemptively invade other nations and to greatly expand domestic surveillance, the Bush administration has set in motion long-term dynamics that could have severe adverse consequences for the nation—and dynamics that may have been largely unnecessary to the uprooting of al Qaeda and the protection of the homeland." One of the most disturbing features of the war on terrorism is its quasi-permanent, or at a minimum, indefinite nature. World War II ended in the Allies' victory in Europe and Japan. The Cold War ended with the fall of the Berlin wall in 1989. At what point can the United States end the war on terrorism, restore the constitutional balance between institutions, and revert to peacetime protections of civil liberties?

On this score—as the country became engaged in military conflict in Iraq and faced the difficult road ahead to rebuilding the country by summer 2003, and as other possible threats such as Iran and North Korea loomed on the horizon—Dodd leaves us with a fitting caution: "The longer the narrative of war persists, and the more reliant on war our economics, our political calculations, our national unity, and our social fabric become, the more difficult it will be to find a sound political compass and peaceful democratic path once war recedes."

By spring 2004, Bush declared the end of offensive military operations in Iraq. Yet, as the nominal international coalition led by the United States prepared to transfer power to an interim Iraqi government on June 30, 2004, *more American soldiers had been killed or wounded in the post-war period than during the military invasion.* The chaotic situation in Iraq following the toppling of Saddam Hussein's brutal regime—punctuated by almost daily car bombings, cold-blooded murders of civilians, military scuffles between coalition forces and guerrillas loyal to Saddam Hussein, and assassinations of political figures set to lead a sovereign Iraq—clearly calls into question when, and if, the United States can disengage from Iraq in the foreseeable future. How, and if, George W. Bush and his successors can move the American polity beyond the war narrative, and come to terms with the broad repercussions of preemptive warfare in the Middle East, is undoubtedly the most critical challenge in coming years.

NOTES

1. "Mr. Bush's Smooth Start," *New York Times*, 4 February 2001, section 4, p. 16; Donald Lambro, "Bush's Legislative Accomplishments," *Washington Times*, 27 December 2001, p. A-15.
2. Dana Milbank, "DiIulio Resigns from Top 'Faith-Based' Post; Difficulties with Initiative in Congress Marked Seven Months at White House," *Washington Post*, 18 August 2001, p. A-4.
3. Michael Kelly, "Bush's Blunders . . .," *Washington Post*, 30 May 2001, p. A-19.
4. Thom Shanker, "U.S. Resumes Its Spy Flights Close to China," *New York Times*, 8 May 2001, p. A-1.
5. Samuel P. Huntington, *The Clash of Civilizations and the Remaking of the World Order* (New York: Simon & Schuster, 1996).
6. Steven Lee Myers with James Dao, "A Nation Challenged: Expected Captives: Marines Set Up Pens for Wave of Prisoners," *New York Times*, 15 December 2001, p. B-3; John Mintz and Bradley Graham, "U.S. Defends Prisoners' Treatment; Conditions Humane, Consistent with Global Pacts, Rumsfeld Says," *Washington Post*, 23 January 2002, p. A-9.
7. Neil A. Lewis, "A Nation Challenged: The Senate Hearing; Ashcroft Defends Antiterror Plan; Says Criticism May Aid U.S. Foes," *New York Times*, 7 December 2001, p. A-1.
8. "A Snooper's Dream," *New York Times*, 18 November 2002, p. A-18; Dan Eggen, "Under Fire, Justice Shrinks TIPS Program," *Washington Post*, 10 August 2002, p. A-1.
9. See Louis Fisher, "Invitation to Struggle: The President, Congress, and National Security," in *Understanding the Presidency*, ed. James P. Pfiffner and Roger H. Davidson (New York: Longman, 1997), pp. 262–271.
10. George C. Edwards III, "Riding High in the Polls," in *The George W. Bush Presidency: Appraisals and Prospects*, ed. Colin Campbell and Bert Rockman (Washington, D.C.: Congressional Quarterly, 2003).

THE TRANSFORMATIONS
OF THE BUSH PRESIDENCY

9/11 AND BEYOND

MICHAEL A. GENOVESE

LOYOLA MARYMOUNT UNIVERSITY

On September 10, 2001, George W. Bush, a man whom many believed did not actually win the presidency, was the object of more derision than respect. Bush's folksy verbal style, Texas accent, and penchant to invent words such as "strategery" made him an irresistible target for late-night comedians such as Jay Leno and David Letterman, who openly referred to Bush as "blockhead" and worse. Media portrayals of the president's bumbling, fumbling syntax and bland rhetoric made him more a national joke than admired leader.

But as the old American standard song, "What a Difference a Day Makes," suggests, twenty-four hours can be a political lifetime. The terrorist attacks of September 11, 2001, against the United States so dramatically changed political circumstances and public expectations of presidential leadership that the very (political) ground on which George W. Bush stood shifted dramatically. The tectonic plates of the political geography produced a crisis presidency and power shifted to the White House, and into the hands of George W. Bush.

This chapter examines the extent to which the altered political and personal positions of George W. Bush from his inauguration through early 2003 were a function of (a) changed conditions; (b) a changed Bush; and (c) the needs and demands of the public.

THE CRISIS PRESIDENCY

Leadership studies emphasize context as much, if not more, than skill. As circumstances change, the politically permissible levels of power also change. In times of peace and calm, the normal checks and balances of the Madisonian system—a strong Congress, for example—tend to bind a president and limit his range of political power. The separation of powers, and the sharing of power between the president and Congress, was designed to limit the potential for executive abuse of power, not to promote efficiency. It is a clumsy, burdensome system that proves frustrating, even maddening to presidents.

But in times of great upheaval, in war or crisis, the Madisonian checks intended to balance institutional power go into remission. In a crisis the public (and Congress) looks to the president as crisis manager, leader, problem solver, and savior.[1] The president's power increases in proportion to his responsibility. He becomes, in Clinton Rossiter's apt phrase, "A constitutional dictator."[2] For example, during the Civil War, Abraham Lincoln assumed and was granted extraordinary power to deal with the crisis at hand. Franklin D. Roosevelt, first during the Great Depression, then World War II, likewise, assumed and was granted powers that in normal circumstances would have been unacceptable.

GEORGE W. BUSH AND THE CRISIS PRESIDENCY

> "Some men are born great,
> Some achieve greatness, And some
> Have greatness thrust upon them."
>
> —William Shakespeare,
> *Twelfth Night*, Act 2, Scene 5

In the lives of presidents, replacing the word "greatness" with "opportunity" seems more appropriate. After all, presidents only rarely encounter opportunities for greatness, but they must still earn the title. Some, like Buchanan, squander the opportunity. Others, like FDR, seize the opportunity and turn it into greatness. George W. Bush, unlike his father and unlike his predecessor William Jefferson Clinton, was given the gift of opportunity. How he plays the opportunity card with respect to the war on terrorism will determine his place in history.

How best to explain the transformations of George W. Bush? While the president may have "grown" to meet the demands of crisis, the primary reason why Bush became a president of power is that circumstances changed—and changed dramatically. After the shocking terrorist attacks on New York and Washington on 9/11, the Democratic opposition in Congress fell nearly silent and the public rallied around the president. Once the United States launched a military assault on Afghanistan, the president's popularity soared. Much the same would have happened if Al Gore, Bill Clinton, or you or I were president. Bush benefited, not by a sudden infusion of skill and will, but as a function of changed domestic conditions and the imperative to combat terrorism. To evaluate Bush as president, we must understand the role of context in the achievement of power, but also examine the use of that power—that is, the skill the president applied to the circumstances and the purposes to which that skill was applied.

Not all presidents exercised skill, wisdom, or courage in the face of crisis. As the United States edged closer and closer to Civil War, and the southern states pulled out of the Union, President Buchanan had an opportunity to exercise leadership. But Buchanan, rather than being energized by the challenge, became paralyzed by it. He shrank in stature when he needed to rise.[3] When Abraham Lincoln took office, the crisis had deepened. But unlike his predecessor, Lincoln rose to meet the crisis and exercised skill, wisdom, and good judgment in the face of enormous pressure.[4]

Some officeholders have a narrow, limited repertoire of political skills, or can do but one or two things well. They tend to apply the same style of leadership to every political circumstance. But different circumstances require different styles of leadership. Times of war require authority and decisiveness. In peacetime, a softer, more collaborative style is often necessary in light of the American constitutional structure. In times of domestic or international upheaval, a president with vision might be needed. In times of grief, the president might need to be a national healer.[5]

The central lesson is that there is no one style that fits all circumstances. A good leader (a) recognizes what the circumstances require; and (b) chooses from a broad range of skills and applies the correct style to fit the demands of the problem. In short, *good leaders are astute enough to see what is needed, skilled enough to apply wisdom to the problem, and flexible enough to make appropriate alterations in style.*

Lincoln had it all; Buchanan did not. Franklin D. Roosevelt, known as "the juggler," had it. Winston Churchill did not. Churchill's style and skill were perfectly suited to the demands of war, but ill-suited to times of peace. And Churchill could not, did not, or would not "style-flex"—adjust his style to different circumstances. When Churchill's skills matched the times (war) he was extraordinary. But when circumstances called for a different style of leadership (domestic politics), he remained rigid and inflexible.

Effective leadership, then, is a function of (a) *context,* granting a president a wide or narrow opportunity; (b) *wisdom,* to see clearly and understand what is needed; (c) *skill* applied to circumstances that helps determine the level of resources and power available to a leader; and (d) a *vision* of a good and just outcome. Within this framework we can ask the following question: How well or how poorly did George W. Bush apply wisdom and skill to the circumstances following 9/11?

FOUR PHASES OF THE BUSH PRESIDENCY

Between inauguration and January 2003, the Bush presidency could be divided into four distinct phases: Phase I, inauguration to September 10, 2001; Phase II, September 11, 2001, to spring 2002, when the Palestinian-Israeli conflict erupted; Phase III, from spring 2002 to the November United Nations

(UN) Resolution on Iraq; and, Phase IV, the prelude to war with Iraq. Each phase presented very different demands and circumstances and required different skills and styles.

PHASE I

George W. Bush began his term with relatively weak "political capital." The 2000 presidential election was so close between Bush and his Democratic rival vice president Al Gore that no one could determine the "real" winner. Everything hinged on the outcome of the disputed results of the vote in Florida.

On election night, confusion reigned. The media, forgetting that a portion of Florida is in the Central Time Zone, prematurely declared Gore the winner in the Sunshine State while polls were still open in the Panhandle. Then that declaration was withdrawn, then the election was called for Bush, then it was too close to call . . . then it really got confusing! It took more than four weeks before, finally, the U.S. Supreme Court put an end to ballot recounts in Florida. In the controversial (and confounding) decision in *Bush v. Gore*, the high court effectively ensured Bush's victory in that state and subsequently in the Electoral College.[6]

Of course, the disputed nature of the 2000 election seemingly called Bush's legitimacy into question. Would the public accept Bush as president? Could Bush establish his legitimacy or would he forever be a tainted president? The American public, alas, accepted the Supreme Court's intervention in the election. And to his credit, Bush quickly asserted and established his authority. Still, governing after a closely contested election and managing a narrowly divided, partisan Congress would prove problematic.

Public expectations of Bush were relatively low, and Bush did not have an extensive policy agenda.[7] In Phase I, President Bush had ups (a tax cut, education reform) and downs (the defection of Republican Senator Jim Jeffords that led to the Republican loss of control of the Senate). Overall, his first eight months in office were, by most standards, rather ordinary. He was a poor-to-average communicator but an engaging politician; a delegating administrator and a moderate-to-conservative Republican; a superficial thinker, but a sincere person. He was not the kind of president who would lead a "revolution" like former House Speaker Newt Gingrich attempted, but a pragmatic conservative who might be able to accomplish incremental changes.

PHASE II

On September 10, 2001, George W. Bush looked like he might suffer the fate of his father as a one-term president. While the president had some early political successes, there were signs of trouble. The president's agenda was bogged down in Congress, Senator Jim Jeffords of Vermont left the Republican Party to become an independent and gave the Democrats a working majority in the Senate, the economy was faltering, and Bush seemed stalled.

   The terrorist attack on U.S. targets on September 11, 2001, utterly changed everything—politically—for George W. Bush. Radically altered domestic and international circumstances accorded him powers he had never dreamed of exercising. In a crisis, the president is typically granted a wide breadth of powers.[8] These emergency (or prerogative) powers assumed by the president have a variety of justifications. Clinton Rossiter laid out an elaborate rationale for emergency presidential power in *The Constitutional Dictatorship*,[9] as did Arthur M. Schlesinger, Jr., in *The Imperial Presidency*,[10] Richard M. Pious in *The American Presidency*,[11] and Robert E. DiClerico in *The American President*.[12] But, whatever the specific rationale, all agree that during a crisis the body politic turns to the president to "save" the political system.

   A crisis is meant to suggest a conflict that occurs suddenly and heightens tensions, where stakes are high (usually a threat to "vital" national interests), where there is little time to decide, and where decision makers are under intense pressure in an atmosphere of uncertainty containing expectations of hostile action. September 11 fits most of these standards.

   The attack of 9/11 changed the political arithmetic in the president's favor. While Bush's rhetorical acumen, per se, may have been less than inspiring, he squarely defined the threat, the challenge, and the initial steps for dealing with the terrorist attack. The 9/11 attack gave the administration a focus, a clear task. It also removed many of the obstacles that impeded presidential authority prior to the attack. The public rallied behind the president. The Congress overwhelmingly supported Bush. The Democratic opposition gave Bush nearly a free hand to act. Other nations gave their support. The president had POWER.

   How would Bush use this power? The president already had in place an experienced foreign-policy team. That team was given a clear goal: Stop terrorism. And the usually complex world was reduced to a simple equation: Call it revenge or justice, terrorists were the enemy, they had to be defeated! It was a single-minded goal and it gave drive and focus to the administration.

   Bush himself seemed to change as well. Presidential scholar Fred I. Greenstein noted "a dramatic transformation in his performance," arguing that Bush "became strikingly more presidential," and that "there has been an impressive increase in his political competence. . . ."[13] The public seemed to agree. Not surprisingly, for it typically happens that with every foreign, military, or national crisis, the president's popularity shoots up.[14] Bush's public approval exceeded and remained above 80 percent for quite some time.

   Had Bush grown? Did he rise to meet the challenge? A nuanced analysis suggests yes—in part. The 9/11 crisis did give Bush added power, and in the immediate aftermath of the attack, he performed quite competently. But, I would argue, more than Bush's growing, what took place was that we, the public, needed to believe that he had grown as president to meet the challenge.

   The United States was horrified, shocked, and frightened by the attacks of 9/11. The public had a deep psychological need for reassurance and comfort. We needed to believe that, in an out-of-control world, someone was in control and that everything would be okay. And while Bush did some of this, we chose to see him—because we needed to see him—as bigger, better, and different than he actually was.

The president is a "shaman in chief," a national healer (e.g., Reagan following the *Challenger* crash, and Clinton after the Oklahoma City bombing). Presidents fulfill a variety of psychological roles for us. They are "reassurer in chief," a kind of security blanket for the nation. Although Bush arguably lacked the rhetorical astuteness of, say, an FDR or a JFK, the public so needed to see him as a national reassurer, that we—for psychological reasons—made Bush something he was not. Yes, Bush grew, but more than his changing, the presidency became the rallying point for the public. We wanted to believe in him regardless of his performance or leadership defects. It was more about us than him.[15] As playwright Arthur Miller writes:

> What we want from leading men is quite the same thing as we demand of our leaders, the reassurance that we are in the hands of one who has mastered events and his own uncertainties. Human beings, as the poet said, cannot bear very much reality, and the art of politics is our best proof.[16]

In Phase II, Bush orchestrated the military assault on Afghanistan, the defeat of the Taliban regime, the damaging of the al Qaeda terrorist network, and the international effort to destroy terrorist cells. Yet, as the United States and its coalition began the process of rebuilding Afghanistan, critics began to charge that Bush, fearing a drop in his popularity, had decided to declare war on terrorism *and* lower taxes. The move bore a striking similarity to Lyndon Johnson's ill-fated effort to fund a domestic war on poverty and a military war in Vietnam while eschewing tax increases. Bush seemingly wanted a war on the cheap—a war that required no sacrifices—one that would not disturb the consumerism of the public. "Travel," he said; "Spend" he implored. This "war without sacrifice" effort marked, many suggested, a lack of political courage and failure of leadership on the part of the president.[17]

At the same time, the president's conservative lightning rod, Attorney General John Ashcroft, began a public counteroffensive designed to silence all criticism of the president and the administration's war on terrorism. He directly questioned the patriotism of the few critics of the war on terrorism and accused anyone who criticized the administration of aiding the enemy.[18] But critics questioned the tactics employed, arguing that it is precisely the right to dissent that is vital in a time of war!

Ashcroft also coordinated a narrowing of the civil and/or constitutional rights of U.S. citizens, empowering authorities to arrest citizens without charging them with a crime and refusing to allow them to see an attorney—all of which appeared to violate habeas corpus—in the name of fighting terrorism. A military commission was established that circumvented the standard judicial process. Military tribunals can disallow independent review, refuse appeals, employ different evidentiary standards than civilian courts, and hold trials in secret. The *New York Times* (November 15, 2001) editorialized that these tactics represented "a breathtaking departure from due process."

Bush's handling of elements of the war on terrorism at this juncture raised serious constitutional issues. Ashcroft's public comments seemingly contradicted the First Amendment (free speech, assembly). The military tribunals, based on dubious historical precedent (see Fisher, Chapter 6), challenged a host of constitutional protections, including the Fourth Amendment (prohibition against unreasonable searches and seizures), the Fifth Amendment (right to a prompt and public trial), the Eighth Amendment (protection against cruel and unusual punishment), and the Fourteenth Amendment (right to an attorney). The terrorist threat does pose difficult choices in the bid to balance liberty and safety. But whether Bush's tactics were justifiable or excessive became an important bone of contention between the administration and its critics. Some charged that the administration was using the war on terrorism as an excuse for resurrecting the "Imperial Presidency."[19] Even before 9/11, Bush and his coterie of advisors placed a premium on secrecy, appeared excessive in their application of executive privilege, and were miserly on their willingness to allow administration officials to testify before Congress (see Warshaw, Chapter 4).

To Bush's harshest detractors, the war on terrorism appeared as a pretext to promulgate an "administrative presidency" designed to obviate intrusions of Congress—in short, a "power grab" aimed at sustaining the president at the center of the political system.[20] But as the months passed and Bush continued to filter policy through the lens of war, other events intruded and began to crowd out the administration's steadfast focus on the war against terrorism. Economic scandals at home (Enron, Worldcom, Xerox), a crash of the stock market, and ethnic clashes, border disputes, and religious conflicts across the globe proved that the world was not static but dynamic. This messy, confusing reality conflicted with the administration's articulation of a unidimensional worldview. Bush's penchant to portray conflicts in simplistic terms—good versus evil, us versus them, freedom versus terrorism—arguably failed to capture the complexity of the post-9/11 world. Thus, planted in the heady days of Phase II amid military victory abroad and popular support at home were the problems that would soon reveal the dilemmas of an administration that had focused almost totally on the war on terrorism to the detriment of other important issues. Paradoxically, the seeds of Bush's problems in Phase III stem from what in Phase II appeared to be his success.

PHASE III

The war against terrorism, as important as it was, was not the only issue of importance to the United States and to the world. Phase III began, I would argue, with the Israeli-Palestinian clash that began in the spring of 2002.

The president had enunciated the "Bush Doctrine" in a September 2001 statement to Congress. "From this day forward," Bush declared, "any nation that continues to harbor or support terrorism will be regarded by the United States as a hostile regime." In the immediate aftermath of 9/11, the president's simplistic formulation could be viewed as an asset: focused, determined, single-minded. But in time, the asset turned into a liability. The "Bush Doctrine" deteriorated from doctrine to dilemma, from guiding vision to a political and moral quagmire—exemplified by the enormous complexities surrounding the Israeli-Palestinian conflict. *New York Times* columnist Frank Rich summed up the problem:

> Bush, who once spoke of rigid lines drawn between "good" men and "evil-doers," has now been so overrun by fresh hellish events and situational geopolitical bargaining that his old formulations—"either you are with us or you are with the terrorists"—have been rendered meaningless.[21]

Bush defended his perspective, contending that "moral clarity is important." Yet Bush's moral certitude toward the Taliban appeared to degenerate into hypocrisy when the Israeli-Palestinian conflict forced him to nuance or retreat. Indeed, the Palestine Liberation Organization (PLO) had been supporting terrorism. But making the PLO a "hostile regime," while satisfying a need for moral clarity, undermined a variety of other, more complex, and arguably more important, geopolitical and national security needs in the Middle East. Former Reagan administration Middle East expert Geoffrey Kemp suggested that applying Bush's simplistic formula to the Middle East conflict "reflects either appalling arrogance or ignorance."[22]

The Israeli-Palestinian conflict, which encompassed a complex set of historical and contemporary issues—from Palestinian suicide bombers to Israeli settlements on the West Bank—could not be reduced to a unidimensional "good versus evil" or "democracy versus terrorism" perspective, and did not fit with the administration's simplified foreign-policy rhetoric surrounding the war on terrorism. Resolution of the Israeli-Palestinian conflict would not come by condemning terrorist attacks, destroying the PLO, and supporting the government of Israel.

The Israeli-Palestinian conflict demonstrates how Bush defied an axiom of the public presidency articulated by Woodrow Wilson nearly a century earlier. While a young political scientist at Wesleyan University, Woodrow Wilson gave a lecture entitled, "Leaders of Men." Wilson pointed out how to persuade, or lead, opinion. "Men are not led by being told what they do not know. . . . Their confidence is not gained by preaching new thoughts to them. It is gained by qualities which they can recognize at first sight, by arguments which find easy and immediate entrance into their minds."[23]

Here, Wilson recognizes the dual role of leaders in a democracy: They must think in complex terms, but speak in simple terms. But in a crisis, the burden of persuasion shifts from a leader trying to gain support—in the crisis—to the leader already having support. Therefore, in a crisis, the leader need not take the people on a journey from point A to B (they are already at point B). Having that luxury means the job of a leader in crisis is to devise complex strategies to deal with complex issues and explain them in simple terms.

On the heels of the Israeli-Palestinian conflict came other regional and international conflicts that further undermined Bush's emphasis on "moral clarity": the India–Pakistan dispute, later the North Korea–South Korea hostilities, and finally the announcement that North Korea—one of the countries named by the president as constituting an "axis of evil"—had nuclear weapons. All of these clashes—and indeed all of international politics—suggest a complex, even contradictory, set of issues on the world stage in the post-9/11 era. Reducing the complexities of foreign policy down to a few absolutes may seem comforting, but contradicts reality. To recapitulate, then, Bush's major shortcoming was the inability to recognize the intricacy of foreign-policy problems and translate them into simple terms for the American public. In short, Bush failed to "style-flex." Instead, he simplified the problems themselves and rigidly adhered to his early post-9/11 stances.

Phase III for President Bush ended, however, on a light note. The result of the 2002 midterm elections in which the president's party gained seats in Congress and gave the Republicans control of both Chambers of Congress is testimony to Bush's political courage. He squarely put his reputation on the line by actively campaigning in a number of close races. The midterm elections also evidenced his political skill as he defied the historical odds and won over a number of swing voters (see Busch, Chapter 3). This substantial victory was followed by a UN Resolution (1441) calling for Iraq to disarm and readmit UN arms inspectors. It was less than the president wanted, but more than might have been expected.

PHASE IV

Phase IV conceptually, at least, began in the fall of 2002 with the release of the administration's new formulation of the basis of U.S. foreign policy, "The National Security Strategy of the United States of America."[24] The Bush administration document argued for a new strategy to meet the new demands of the post–Cold War world, calling for the United States to so dramatically outspend potential rivals on defense that adversaries cannot match the United States in terms of weaponry. It should be noted that the United States spends more on defense than any other country—in fact, more than the next fifteen-highest spending countries combined!

Most importantly, this document boldly announced the replacement of deterrence with preemption as the governing principle of U.S. policy and represented a *volte-face* for two centuries of American foreign policy. The document set forth the doctrine that the United States can—when policymakers determine that another nation might threaten us or our allies—attack that nation before it engages in any act of hostility or aggression. This breathtaking assertion of unilateral power has significant global and constitutional ramifications. It transforms the United States into the "policeman of the world," calling into question bilateral relations between the United States and other nations as well as multinational institutions. It also squarely contradicts interpretations of the Founders' intentions for the president to act as commander in chief in a defensive capacity.[25] The policy was ultimately put into action in March 2003, when the United States, backed by a minimal international coalition, invaded Iraq in the bid to oust Saddam Hussein from power and rid that country of alleged stockpiles of weapons of mass destruction.

CONCLUSION

In the end, presidents are judged by the size of the problems they must face and the skill with which they confronted these problems, the long-term impact of their actions, and the ends they sought. After 9/11, President Bush faced the enormous problem of waging the first war of the twenty-first century. But he was granted, and he used, extraordinary and extraconstitutional power to confront this challenge.

In part, President Bush grew to fit the demands of crisis; in part he was unable to grow to the proportions necessary to fully confront the problems he faced. As this analysis has demonstrated, at first Bush handled the post-9/11 crisis well. Later, his inability to articulate a coherent foreign policy that reflected the complexities of the post-Cold War and post-9/11 world exposed his leadership limits. Whether a product of his own personal characteristics, the advice of his closest counselors, or his penchant to view politics in terms of personalities rather than institutional, economic, or strategic forces, Bush's actions and rhetoric suggest a tendency to reduce complexity down to simple, one-dimensional terms. To an extent, we all do this. But a president, at one level, must be able to think in complex terms, oversee policy, and continually reexamine actions in light of new information. At another level, he must translate complex policy decisions into language the American public can readily comprehend.

In analyzing Bush's leadership in the war on terrorism, while it would be unfair to say "the emperor has no clothes," it is fair to say, I think, that the administration's inability to make the transition from unidimensionality to multidimensionality when events demanded such a transition represents the most significant shortcoming in the president's leadership in the eighteen months following 9/11. Crisis tends to paralyze some and animate others. Crisis paralyzed President Buchanan and energized President Lincoln. While George W. Bush is no Buchanan, he is no Lincoln either.

NOTES

1. See Michael A. Genovese, "Presidential Leadership and Crisis Management," *Presidential Studies Quarterly* (spring 1986).
2. Clinton Rossiter, *The Constitutional Dictatorship: Crisis Government in the Modern Democracy* (Princeton, NJ: Princeton University Press, 1948, p. 99).
3. See Michael A. Genovese, *The Power of the American Presidency, 1789–2000* (New York: Oxford University Press, 2001).
4. Philip Shaw Paludan, *The Presidency of Abraham Lincoln* (Lawrence, KS: University Press of Kansas, 1994).
5. Gary L. Gregg and Randall Adkins, "The Healer-in-Chief: Ronald Reagan and the Challenger Disaster," in *Reassessing the Reagan Presidency*, ed. Richard S. Conley (Lanham, MD: University Press of America, 2003).
6. James W. Ceasar and Andrew E. Busch, *The Perfect Tie: The True Story of the 2000 Election* (Lanham, MD: Rowman and Littlefield, 2001).
7. On the "low opportunity" nature of Bush's presidency, see William W. Lammers and Michael A. Genovese, *The Presidency and Domestic Policy: Comparing Leadership Styles, FDR to Clinton* (Washington, D.C.: CQ Press, 2000).
8. See: Michael A. Genovese, "Democratic Theory and the Emergency Powers of the President," *Presidential Studies Quarterly*, vol. IX, no. 3 (summer 1979).
9. Rossiter, *The Constitutional Dictatorship: Crisis Government in the Modern Democracy*, pp. 297–306.
10. Arthur M. Schlesinger, Jr., *The Imperial Presidency* (Boston: Houghton Mifflin, 1973), pp. 450–451.
11. Richard M. Pious, *The American Presidency* (New York: Basic Books, 1979), p. 84.
12. Robert E. DiClerico, *The American President* (Englewood Cliffs, NJ: Prentice Hall, 1979), pp. 309–310.
13. Fred I. Greenstein, "The Changing Leadership of George W. Bush: A Pre-and Post-9/11 Comparison," *Presidential Studies Quarterly* (June 2002), p. 387.
14. George C. Edwards III, *The Public Presidency: The Pursuit of Popular Support* (New York: St. Martin's Press, 1983).
15. Thomas E. Cronin and Michael A. Genovese, *The Paradoxes of the American Presidency* (New York: Oxford University Press, 1998), pp. 152–159.
16. Arthur Miller, *On Politics and the Art of Acting* (New York: Viking Press, 2001), p. 40.
17. See David Gergen, editor-at-large, *U.S. News & World Report*, series of editorials, 2001.
18. Robert Scheer, "The Job Has Become Too Big for Ashcroft," *Los Angeles Times*, 28 May 2002, p. B-11; for a defense of the Attorney General, see Edward Klein, "We're Not Destroying Rights, We're Protecting Rights," *Parade Magazine*, 19 May 2002, pp. 4–6.
19. Arthur M. Schlesinger, Jr., *The Imperial Presidency* (Boston: Houghton Mifflin, 1973).
20. Richard P. Nathan, *The Administrative Presidency* (New York: Macmillan, 1983).
21. Frank Rich, "The Bush Doctrine, R.I.P.," *New York Times*, 13 April 2002.
22. Quoted in Rich, "The Bush Doctrine, R.I.P.," 13 April 2002.
23. Woodrow Wilson, "Leaders of Men," in *Papers of Woodrow Wilson*, vol. 6, ed. Arthur S. Link (Princeton, NJ: Princeton University Press, 1966–1990), pp. 644–671.
24. Since 1986, the executive branch has been required by law to submit to the Congress a document stating the overall foreign policy approach of the United States. The Bush administration used this opportunity to institutionalize a "first strike" or preemptive war strategy. For further information, see http://www.defenselink.mil and http://www.state.gov.
25. Louis Fisher, *Presidential War Power* (Lawrence, KS: University Press of Kansas, 1995).

AMERICANS' BELIEFS ABOUT THEMSELVES, THE WORLD, AND WAR

BEFORE AND AFTER 9/11

ROGER H. DAVIDSON

UNIVERSITY OF MARYLAND

No doubt every American connects personally with the event now known as 9/11. My wife and I were traveling in China. After spending a glorious day walking along China's Great Wall, we had returned from a performance of the Beijing Opera. Flipping on CNN, we were suddenly gripped by a surreal scene twelve time zones away, as the two World Trade Center towers were struck and engulfed in flames and smoke.

Two months later we made our own pilgrimage to ground zero. (Part of me is New Yorker: There I learned to jaywalk and to adore opera and Broadway theatre, while nominally enrolled in doctoral studies at Columbia University—more than a hundred city blocks north of the Trade Center site.) The twisted wreckage of the lower floors was still visible, as was the army of heavy equipment engaged in scouring the site. For blocks around there was an odor of still smoldering fires; the air was rank with the smells of death. The thousands of people who turned out that bright fall Saturday afternoon were silent and respectful—not at all your typical noisy New York crowd!

It is unclear what the planners and perpetrators hoped to gain from their act. Terrorism has causes and antecedents, of course; but terrorist acts are rarely accompanied by manifestos or lists of grievances or explanations of any kind. In this instance, statements emanating from the cluttered and troubled mind of Osama bin Laden failed to provide much context for the events. Were the acts directed specifically at the United States? Or were they, more plausibly, a crime against civilization itself: a blow aimed at global modernization, including changes within the Arab world? Did the perpetrators expect nations to cower in fear of further terrorist acts? And could they have foreseen the kind of western-led *jihad* against them that was to follow?

Whether or not the United States was the sole target, the events of September 11 were seen by Americans as aimed directly at them as individuals and as a nation. They took the losses personally and were determined to respond accordingly. Those who have studied the American popular character should not be surprised. For the American mode of thinking has been shaped and manifested over nearly four hundred years of shared experiences, from the first permanent settlements of the early 1600s to the twentieth century's global conflicts. This essay demonstrates how George W. Bush used the bully pulpit and drew upon traditional American political myths to interpret the events of 9/11 for the American public, and rally support for and justify a war on terrorism that would fundamentally transform his presidency.

AMERICAN POLITICAL MYTHS

The American character embraces a series of myths concerning the nation, its people, and its relationship to the world. The term *myth* is used in a neutral, nonjudgmental sense: These are simply elements that Americans tend to believe about themselves. According to such objective measures as we might apply, these are no doubt neither wholly true nor wholly false. Yet they are enduring features of the nation's public rhetoric, its literature, its films and plays, its arts and crafts. American visitors to other countries are often instantly recognizable (these days, not because of their apparel); Europeans, who are perhaps most like us, are repeatedly reminded that they and we are *not* alike.[1] Many of these traits were identified by that parade of notable visitors who traveled to see the New World for themselves and write about what they found. Hector St. John de Crèvecoeur arrived in the eighteenth century, and over the next century came Alexis de Tocqueville, Harriet Martineau, Charles Dickens, James Bryce, and many others. Today, citizens of other lands appear to accept many of Americans' self-images, although they may regard others as wrongheaded or delusional. Thus these myths remain very real to those of us who manifest them, and to those who observe us; they profoundly, and predictably, shaped the American people's responses to the events of September 11.

MYTH NUMBER ONE: THE CHOSEN PEOPLE

"Who then is this American, this new person?" Crèvecoeur, who posed this question in 1782, was a Frenchman who settled in the New World for many years. His answer: An "American" was someone who,

> leaving behind all his ancient prejudices and manners, receives new ones from the new mode of life he has embraced. . . . Here individuals of all nations are melted into a new race of people, whose labors and posterity will one day cause great changes in the world.[2]

As a North American, Crèvecoeur exulted that "[w]e are the most perfect society existing in the world."

From the very beginning, Americans have seen their country as a "promised land." By extension the settlers viewed themselves as a people chosen by God for a special mission in the world. Exhorting his fellow Puritans in 1630, Governor John Winthrop of Massachusetts Colony likened the New World settlement to a "shining city on a hill." (This from the 1611 King James Bible's account of the Sermon on the Mount: "You are the light of the world. A city that is set on a hill cannot be hid."[3]) Speaking on the 1852 anniversary of the Pilgrims' landing on Plymouth Rock, pioneer clergyman Timothy Dwight Hunt told the New England Society of San Francisco that "[y]ou are the representatives of a land which is the model for every other. You belong to a family whose dead are the pride of the living. Preserve your birthright. . . ."[4]

Political figures have to this day echoed this expansive vision of the "shining city on the hill." In the wake of the Persian Gulf War, President George H. W. Bush declared in 1992 that "We are still and ever the freest nation on earth, the kindest nation on earth, the strongest nation on earth—and we have always risen to the occasion."[5] His successor, Bill Clinton, struck the same note five years later: "America is far more than a place; it is an idea—the most powerful idea in the history of nations, and . . . we are now bearers of that idea, leading a great people into a new world."[6] At the brink of a second Iraqi war in 2003, President George W. Bush affirmed that "the American flag stands for more than our power or interests. Our founders dedicated this country to the cause of human dignity, the rights of every person, and the possibilities of every life."[7]

Generations of Americans have agreed with these sentiments. Aside from Native Americans and African Americans, the United States is a nation of immigrants who, for a host of reasons, sought to transform their lives by emigrating to the New World. Even the slaves, who came involuntarily, showed little inclination to return to Africa after the Civil War won them their freedom. Once they become citizens—in the case of blacks, after a long struggle—Americans tend to be proud of their country. In his 1971 Pulitzer Prize–winning novel, *Angle of Repose,* Wallace Stegner describes the patriotism of his main characters, transplanted easterners who make their lives on the western frontier:

> One of the charming things about nineteenth-century America was its cultural patriotism—not jingoism, just patriotism, the feeling that no matter how colorful, exotic, and cultivated other countries might be, there was no place so ultimately right, so morally sound, so in tune with the hopeful future, as the U.S.A.[8]

Modern survey research confirms this American myth. Ninety-one percent of Americans questioned in a 1995 cross-national survey agreed with the statement that "I would rather be a citizen of [the United States] than any other country in the world."[9] (The corresponding figure for Britons was 72 percent; and just 50 percent of the Dutch held similar views of their country.) Americans are known for shaking the dust from their boots and moving on; but 73 percent of them said in the same survey that they would not want to leave their country even if they could improve their work or living conditions—about the median for citizens of major nations.

Americans reject chance as the shaper of their history. Asked what they believe accounts for their nation's success, Americans overwhelmingly credit governmental and economic arrangements, such as the Constitution (85 percent), free elections (84 percent), and the free-enterprise system (83 percent).[10] In no other country—not even Great Britain, home of the mother of parliaments—do citizens so often mention their form of government as a source of pride. Despite the much-touted ambivalence of the American public, from two-thirds to three-fourths of the respondents in a 2002 Gallup survey expressed trust and confidence ("a great deal" or "a fair amount") in the three branches of the federal government—nearly as robust as the support indicated in a similar survey thirty years earlier.[11]

Americans' unique pride in their special place in the world obviously fosters unique loyalty and patriotism. National self-esteem is a laudable quality, but in the American case it can also appear as a certain arrogance: the conviction that its motives are pure, that its way is the only right path to follow. Other nations' motives are often distrusted as insufficiently moral or even as evil. Throughout the nation's history there recurs the image of a befuddled Uncle Sam—the symbol of an open, guileless people—at the mercy of clever and brutal evildoers: the domineering British, the wily Spaniards, the worldly European powers, the Soviets and their "evil empire," and now Arab terrorists.

MYTH NUMBER TWO: INDEPENDENCE AND SELF-RELIANCE

In America, Lord Bryce observed, "everything tends to make the individual independent and self-reliant."[12] Birth or ancestry counted for little in the New World. In a pamphlet written for curious Europeans, Benjamin Franklin explained: "People do not enquire, concerning a stranger, *What is he?* But *What can he do?* If he has any useful art, he is welcome. . . ."[13]

The first great American fictional hero—Hawkeye, created by James Fenimore Cooper (*The Last of the Mohicans*, 1826)—embodies this new independence. A British officer is haranguing some buckskin-clad colonials, pushing them to fight against the French. When one of the colonials balks at this, the officer becomes furious. He shouts: "You call yourself a patriot and a loyal subject to the crown?" Hawkeye answers: "Don't call myself subject to much at all!"[14] One commentator remarked: Hawkeye is clearly going to be a political pain in the ass. He is a person in-between—between forest and settlement, between teepee and drawing room, between the old world and the new, a person who leads a life that is one long declaration of independence.

Americans are taught the values of personal initiative, persistence, self-reliance, and independence. These are the homely virtues that Benjamin Franklin extolled in *Poor Richard's Almanac*. They are repeated in popular literature: the *Horatio Alger* tales, the self-help manuals that flood the bookstores, and the persistent image of the lone hero—from Hawkeye to the Lone Ranger, from "Lucky Lindy" to Luke Skywalker. As early as the 1830s, de Tocqueville said of Americans: "They owe nothing to any man; they always expect nothing from any man. They acquire the habit of always considering themselves as standing alone."[15]

Although Americans are a uniquely religious people, they believe that people's success or failure in life flows from personal efforts—not from fate, or luck, or even God's will. One classic survey posed to a national sample the situation of two people with the same skill and training, one of whom had succeeded and the other not. Only 1 percent of the respondents volunteered that God's will or fate explained the situation. Another researcher asked this question in six developing nations: About 30 percent attributed personal success to luck and fate; in one country, the figure was 53 percent.[16]

The ethic of personal effort is not confined to the business and professional classes, but is expressed also by blue-collar workers. One study found that three-quarters of the workers in the United States affirmed the statement that "what happens to me is my own doing." Not surprisingly, Americans admire those who are successful and wealthy—like Bill Gates or Steve Forbes or H. Ross Perot. They don't resent such people; they want to be more like them. Indeed, many Americans see themselves as better off than they really are. A *Time* magazine survey in 2000 found that 19 percent of the people believed they have incomes in the top 1 percent, and a further 20 percent were convinced they would be in that category some day.[17] No doubt the rags-to-riches stories of popular celebrities disguise the true extent of social mobility; and the fact remains that the gap between rich and poor in the United States is wider than in any other nation in the industrial world, and has increased over the past generation.[18]

This independence and self-reliance—a trait that has served Americans well in the past—can manifest itself in go-it-alone policies and behaviors, reinforcing distrust of other nations' efforts and concerns, and antagonizing America's actual or potential allies.

The contemporary American public, interestingly, would rather support military interventions when they are multilateral efforts, in name if not necessarily in fact. (As de Tocqueville discovered, Americans are individualistic but also joiners.) This was true of both major twentieth-century wars, as well as the undeclared wars in Korea, Vietnam, and Iraq. During the Cold War, surveys indicated that, although the public was willing to go to war, they preferred to do so in concert with allies. Survey responses concerning a second, post-9/11 Iraqi war consistently reflected this inclination. Whereas a majority of citizens (55 percent) in a Pew survey in October 2002 favored an attack

on Iraq, only about half that number, 27 percent, would support action if allies failed to go along.[19]

MYTH NUMBER THREE: THE OPTIMISTIC TINKERERS

Mark Twain tells us that Huckleberry Finn, that quintessential American, became fascinated by the biblical story of Moses and the "bulrushes." But he
soon learned that, as he put it, "Moses had been dead a considerable long
time." With that, Huck informs us, "I didn't care no more about him; because
I don't take no stock in dead people."[20]

Americans are progressive, present- and future-oriented, and dedicated
to tinkering with things in order to make them better. At the core is a strong
sense of efficacy: the conviction that we can transform our world for our own
convenience. Efficacy requires *optimism.* Efficacy leads to trying; optimism
conveys the confidence that one can succeed and progress. Even in the depths
of economic depressions, most Americans express "quite a lot of confidence"
in the future of their country.

The terrorists' attacks challenged the very core of American self-confidence,
optimism, and future-mindedness. Terrorism, after all, involves unpre-
dictability and surprise, randomness in separating the doomed from the sur-
vivors, and a depth of evil that is to most people unfathomable and
inexplicable.[21] The nation's initial reaction, after all, could well have been to
lock its doors, shutter its windows, and adopt a view of the world more trag-
ic, more accepting (and more European, one is tempted to say). Some of these
behaviors indeed occurred. But in the wake of the attacks, nearly two out of
three Americans (63 percent) said that the resulting changes had been for the
better. As citizens contemplated the new year 2002, eight in ten said they were
more hopeful than fearful about what the coming year held for them personally; six in ten expressed confidence about what the year would bring for the
world in general.[22] In a global attitudes survey later that year, North Americans remained singularly satisfied about the quality of their individual lives,
although U.S. respondents were less sanguine about the state of their nation.[23]

If innovation can make things better, then Americans are open to try the
new and to experiment. Bryce observed that Americans'

> keenly competitive spirit and pride in their own ingenuity have made them
> quicker than any other people to adopt and adapt inventions: Telephones
> were in use in every little town over the West, while in the city of London men
> were just beginning to wonder whether they could be made to pay.[24]

So Americans have historically been pragmatists—short on theory and long on
common-sense observation, trial and error, and invention. This innovative spirit has led to a faith in machines and machinery—what today we call technology. North American inventions and conveniences are of course well known: the

reaper, the cotton gin, the sewing machine, electric lights, the phonograph, air conditioning, television, computer chips, lasers, and the Internet.

The American love affair with innovation goes beyond machines and conveniences. It extends to social arrangements—and maybe even human nature itself. From the first landing of the *Mayflower* to the present day, American history is full of contracts, covenants, constitutions, laws, and organizational plans. The eighteenth century's fascination with clocks and other mechanical marvels led the writers of the U.S. Constitution to devise what historian Michael Kammen has called "a machine that would go of itself."[25] Its elaborate system of checks and balances was intended, like the meshing of interlocking gears and wheels, to provide a self-regulating mechanism to guard against tyrannical power.

Even today, American leaders tend to believe that new devices—for example, new laws, government agencies, or regulatory procedures—can solve such complex problems as, say, campaign finance or immigration or healthcare benefits. One manifestation of this faith in man-made procedures is the Americans' extreme reliance upon law, lawyers, and courts to resolve the most complex and subtle of problems, from abortion policy and child abuse to affirmative action and genetic research.

The nation's innovation is displayed in its war-making. The Patriots adopted frontier modes of fighting against the orderly British troop formations. The Civil War brought such innovations as minie balls, iron clad ships, submarines, aerial reconnaissance, and a harbinger of the next century's total warfare: General William Tecumseh Sherman's devastating march through the South—sweeping past many of the cities while laying waste to the farms and the fields. World War II brought the Manhattan Project and the atomic bomb (proposed by Albert Einstein in a famous letter to President Franklin Roosevelt). The Cold War brought not only intercontinental ballistic missiles but surprising innovations originally designed to achieve military objectives—for example, rapid movement of military vehicles (the interstate highway system) and a communications system independent of conventional modes (the Internet).

Innovation continues as new threats are identified. Experts claimed that as many as thirty new technologies were deployed during the 2001 Afghanistan operations. These include—if one is curious—such things as: "foliage-penetrating radar sensors"; "microdrones" and "microwave guns" that stun rather than maim or kill; "nuclear quadrapole resonance sensors" to find explosive materials; and "thermobaric bombs" to penetrate cave networks with shock waves that destroy everything—and everyone—inside. The innovations go beyond technology: Americans are nothing if not organized, and so procedural and tactical advances may be at least as important as weapons.[26]

The nation's dedication to progress and invention—its pragmatic orientation to present conditions and its optimistic vision of the future—has led to historical successes. But Americans are willfully ignorant of history, and they naively believe that innovations—technological, military, or organizational—

can override complex cultural or religious barriers. This is an especially dangerous assumption when dealing with a complex problem like terrorism. Thermobaric bombs may eliminate some terrorists in caves, but they can hardly combat terrorism per se.

MYTH NUMBER FOUR: THE PEACEABLE KINGDOM

Americans have seen—and still see—themselves as a peaceable people who join international conflicts only when circumstances compel them to do so. Having left behind Old World prejudices and hatreds, its citizens—protected by 3,000 miles of the North Atlantic—soon resolved to maintain neutrality and nonalignment, especially toward the century-old struggle between France and Great Britain for European dominance. The most celebrated passage of President George Washington's Farewell Address of 1796, read dutifully in the chambers of Congress every year on his birthday, counsels that

> [t]he great role of conduct for us, in regard to foreign nations, is in extending our commercial relations to have with them as little political connection as possible. . . . 'Tis our true policy to steer clear of permanent alliances, with any portion of the foreign world.[27]

Neutrality was not an inevitable strategy to follow, especially in the nation's early years when partiality to either the British or the French was attached to the first factional divisions—between Federalists and Jeffersonian Republicans. Despite the help it had received from France, the new nation in 1795 concluded and ratified Jay's Treaty, in effect "a repudiation of the Franco-American alliance of 1778, which had been so instrumental in gaining French military assistance for the winning of the American Revolution."[28] Nor did a second war with the British (1812–1814) prevent the nation from recognizing that the British fleet provided a shield that would best protect its shipping and even enforce its hegemony in the Americas (in conformity with the Monroe Doctrine of 1823).

Although we have no direct public opinion data before the 1940s, surveys since then have shown that international conflicts produce a "rally-around-the-flag" effect that includes heightened support for the president, the military effort, and the national government in general. But if the hostilities drag on with no successful conclusion in sight, the public becomes impatient and the "rally effect" fades. This occurred during the Korean War, the Vietnam War, and after U.S. casualties in Lebanon, Somalia, and Angola.[29]

The September 11 attacks produced an immediate and sustained "rally" by the American people. President Bush's job support had been sagging before that date. Immediately after the disaster, his support soared to 92 percent. A year later, his job rating had declined to the mid-60s; not until early

2003 did his numbers approach pre-9/11 levels. Positive assessments of Congress peaked at 84 percent in the wake of the attacks, but eventually settled in the mid-50s—still far above historical averages.[30] This public support showed little sign of abating (eight in ten respondents believed the worst of the war was "yet to come"[31]) and lasted at least through the end of 2002.

Americans have historically been reluctant warriors. "This nation fights reluctantly," declared the second President Bush, "because we know the cost and we dread the days of mourning that always come."[32] The war for independence failed to inspire all the populace: Indeed, the dedicated patriots may well have been outnumbered by the British loyalists ("Tories") and those who were simply indifferent. The three nineteenth-century declared wars (1812–1814; 1845–1846; 1898) all evoked bitter opposition, as did several twentieth-century engagements (especially World War I and the undeclared wars in Korea and Vietnam). The Vietnam War (1965–1974) badly split the nation and toppled Lyndon Johnson's presidency. As for World War II, it was only the attack on Pearl Harbor in 1941 that silenced the powerful and vocal anti-interventionist movement of the interwar period. It became undoubtedly the most popular war in U.S. history: The "good war," journalist Studs Terkel called it in his Pulitzer Prize–winning oral history.[33] The brief Gulf War of 1991 enjoyed popular support, but the House and Senate votes authorizing it were fairly close. And the war was halted mainly because then president Bush and his advisors feared a popular revulsion against further military and civilian casualties (a decision later scorned by "war hawks" within the second Bush administration).

Thus a narrative theme of Americans' involvement in hostilities is their tendency to be reactive, albeit dedicated, fighters. Read the Declaration of Independence: Its brief but ringing assertion of popular rights is followed by a laundry list of British provocations, presented out of a "decent respect for the opinions of mankind." At the outset of the Civil War, President Lincoln understood the usefulness of having the Confederates assault the Union by firing the first shot, which they did against Fort Sumter in April 1861. The five declared wars were justified to respond to harassment of shipping and to protect U.S. interests in general. Post–World War II "peace actions" responded to attacks upon allies that threatened to destabilize their regions and hence jeopardize U.S. interests. To be sure, the Mexican and Spanish–American wars stretch the reactive rationale, although the latter case after all featured the mysterious sinking of the battleship *Maine* in Havana harbor. Nor should we forget the Gulf of Tonkin incident of 1964—in which two U.S. destroyers may, or may not, have been fired upon: This was the pretext for the infamous congressional resolution giving President Johnson virtually a blank check for taking action in Southeast Asia. In at least two twentieth-century cases—the two world wars—it could be argued that it was the nation's perceived vulnerability, its very lack of preparedness, that emboldened enemies to seize the opportunity and attack.

These principles—neutrality, peacefulness, and reactive military intervention—have for the most part characterized U.S. foreign policy, though with some notable exceptions. But the nation's post–World War II military machine has upset this historical pattern. This machine is a by-product of the Cold War. After each of its earlier wars, the United States quickly "sent the boys home" and shrank its armed forces; but the Cold War threat led to an unprecedented level of peacetime preparedness. By 1960, when retiring President Dwight Eisenhower—himself a career military man—warned against the "military-industrial complex," the new militarism had already infused the nation's economic and political systems, drawing support from elected officials, defense contractors, labor unions, and local communities, as well as from current and retired military personnel. Although this new military regime receives firm bipartisan support, the Republican party is its most loyal patron.

The entrenchment of the post–World War II military establishment has resulted in serious imbalances in U.S. policymaking. The Defense Department is the nation's largest employer, its largest customer, its largest procurer of equipment and services. No wonder it is treated with awe by politicians and claimants for government contracts. The State Department and its agencies, in contrast, have few strong domestic clients and political supporters. Its services and achievements are largely intangible, and in any event it spends much of its energy and money overseas. Since the end of the Cold War, the foreign policy agencies have been under almost constant siege from unilateralists on Capitol Hill. U.S. budgets thus display a striking imbalance between military spending and foreign representation or assistance (much of the latter being military rather than humanitarian). The nation spends nineteen cents of every federal dollar on the military, but only a penny on international affairs—less than half of which goes to foreign development and humanitarian assistance, the poorest record of any western industrialized nation.[34] Such an imbalance would seem especially inappropriate for a war against terrorism, in which military action can offer only limited solutions.

The economic and political entrenchment of this military establishment, not to mention the persistence of real or perceived threats, would seem to assure the preeminence of military might as the leading edge of U.S. power in the world. Unless they can be sold as elements of the war on terror, the less technologically attractive weapons of diplomacy—foreign aid, cultural exchanges, propaganda, and nation-building—will remain secondary aspects of U.S. policy.

DECLARING WAR ON TERRORISM

The Pearl Harbor attack, the "day that will live in infamy," is the closest parallel to the destruction of the World Trade Center. Although President Bush lacked Franklin Roosevelt's sense of the dramatic moment, no word picture was required this time: The visual image of the attack upon the nation's financial center went far beyond language. When Bush found his rhetorical footing three days later (in remarks at a National Cathedral prayer service), his frame of reference echoed the nation's perception of earlier conflicts:

> War has been waged against us by stealth and deceit and murder. This nation is peaceful, but fierce when stirred to anger. This conflict was begun on the timing and terms of others. It will end in a way and at an hour of our choosing.[35]

President Bush's declaration of war on terrorism was, as Kathleen Hall Jamieson and Paul Waldman have observed, a notable instance of "framing" a public issue: articulating and disseminating an interpretation, or way of thinking, that can be accepted by the press and the public.[36] From the perspective of the Oval Office, wartime rhetoric has payoffs both immediate and long-lasting. Especially in the immediate aftermath of a crisis event such as 9/11, a militant response on the president's part can be expected to evoke a "rally" response from the general public. And in history's longer frame, wartime presidents are more apt to be accorded the laurels of greatness than those who served in more benign times.

The very potency of the war metaphor, however, makes it a high-risk venture that can undo the executives who utilize it. If major military involvement is contemplated, opposition is likely to be heard not only from anti-war groups but also from bureaucracies within the government whose cultures encourage skepticism about military deployments. Despite President Bush's early and consistent embrace of the war metaphor, elements within his administration resisted such policies, sometimes through highly publicized leaks to the press.[37] Among these elements were: (1) the uniformed services within the Pentagon, which at least since the Vietnam era have been cautious about deployments that are not clearly winnable, or that risk eventual loss of public and political support; (2) State Department personnel, who are predisposed to prefer diplomatic methods of conflict resolution over arms, and who spend much of their time dealing with foreign governments that differ with the United States over such matters; and (3) the Central Intelligence Agency, whose personnel worried that war would prove a dangerous distraction from the global anti-terrorism campaign, especially compromising delicate but essential relationships with foreign intelligence services in the fight against al Qaeda.

In the long term, too, proclamations of war (of the extra-Constitutional variety) have been known to lose their potency over time. The first President Bush presided over a brief and putatively successful war on Iraq in 1991; but the rally effect did not survive economic worries the following year, when he failed to be reelected. The Korean and Vietnam wars dragged on without demonstrable victory, and so public support faded. One of the most famous remarks about Vietnam was Senator George Aiken's (R-VT) advice that the United States simply declare victory and pull out. This was in essence what

President Eisenhower effected in 1953 to end the Korean engagement, and what Congress finally got around to doing in 1974 about Vietnam. As for non-combat wars such as those against poverty and drugs, who can say how or when victory will be achieved, if ever? The same aura of narrative uncertainty surrounds the current war on global terrorism.

Several components of the post-9/11 "war" frame of reference are noteworthy: (1) Terrorism is an act of war, not a crime; (2) Terrorists are members of foreign-based organizations bent upon attacking nation states; (3) Terrorists target the United States not because of its government's actions but because of the nation's unique values, especially its freedom.[38] Each one of these assumptions rests at least in part upon precedents found in the American "mythology" I have discussed. Yet these assumptions are debatable at least, dubious at most.

"THERE'S A WAR ON"

The rhetoric of war is perhaps the most potent weapon of mass persuasion. It has the power to focus attention and mobilize action. Indeed, its value is so obvious that the metaphor has been extended from conventional war-making to other forms of national effort: for example, President Lyndon Johnson's war on poverty of the 1960s and the war on drugs, launched by President Ronald Reagan and sustained by succeeding administrations. Much of the power of the war metaphor lies in its familiar story line: It offers definable villains, a clearly demarcated field of battle, an identifiable foe in the garb of military troops, and an attainable objective.

Significantly, the leading U.S. responses to the terrorist attacks were to launch military invasions in Afghanistan, admittedly an incubator of terrorists, and then in Iraq, a terrorist regime with only tangential linkages to the 9/11 events. Wesley K. Clark, the retired NATO commander who led the 1999 war in Kosovo, characterized the response of U.S. leaders in the following way: "They picked war over law. They picked a unilateralist approach over a multilateral approach. They picked conventional forces over special-operations forces. And they picked Saddam Hussein as a target over Osama bin Laden."[39] General Clark blamed these choices on mistaken priorities, but the problem may lie more squarely in metaphor rather than motivation.

Indeed, the post-9/11 responses can be seen as an attempt to replicate traditional American mythological patterns. "Iraq," observed media commentator Neal Gabler, "provides a conventional narrative, like World War II, rather than a modern, unconventional narrative like the war on terrorism, which is precisely the point. The war on Iraq gives us the lineaments and the catharsis of a movie."[40] Indeed, President Bush's offhand remark about Hussein's behavior was to the effect that "[t]his looks like a rerun of a bad movie." What would a good movie look like? Applying various American cultural myths, one recalls such conventional plot lines as cowboys versus rustlers, GIs versus Nazis, or Luke Skywalker and Han Solo versus the Empire.

When applied to international conflicts, moreover, the war metaphor has the additional advantage of playing to the nation's strategic strength: its hegemonic military power. Nonetheless, the applicability of the war metaphor to the illusive foe of international terrorism is questionable. Senate Foreign Relations Committee chair Richard G. Lugar (R-IN) has observed,

> Military action will be necessary to deal with serious and immediate threats to our national security, but the war on terrorism will not be won through attrition—particularly because military action will often breed more terrorists. To win this war, the United States must assign to economic and diplomatic capabilities the same strategic priority we assign to military capabilities. What is still missing from American political discourse is support for the painstaking work of foreign policy and the commitment of resources to vital foreign policy objectives that lack a direct political constituency.[41]

SEEKING REVENGE AGAINST NATION-STATES

The second element of the post-9/11 frame was its emphasis on the actions of nation-states. This approach was not self-evident. Consider the reaction of a British observer who knows our country well: Baroness Shirley Williams, now leader of the Liberal Democrats in the House of Lords:

> Many of us hoped [she writes] the new Bush administration would declare this act a crime against humanity, thereby uniting the whole world not for a war between civilizations, but in a war for civilization itself. That was not to be. By declaring this act of terrorism as an act of war, the president pulled it back into the traditional conflicts of nation states.[42]

Such doubts were echoed by political philosopher Benjamin R. Barber, who lamented that "America has crafted anti-terrorist policies as if we still lived in the nineteenth-century world where the only enemies of states were other states."[43] The real foes, he contends, are nongovernmental organizations "hiding in the creases of the new global disorder." For such tasks, military might can only clear the playing field where the real game can be played out. In the wake of its decisive role after two devastating world wars, it is no accident that the United States became a chief architect of an international framework governing law, cooperation, and development.

Government and media emphasis on warfare against terrorist states made it difficult for citizens to disentangle highly publicized campaigns against rogue states such as Afghanistan and Iraq from less glamorous anti-terrorism activities here and abroad. At least initially, the American public seemed aware of the distinction: When asked in late 2002 which posed the greater threat to the United States, twice as many respondents cited al Qaeda and Osama bin Laden as mentioned Iraq and Saddam Hussein.[44]

AMERICA AS INNOCENT VICTIM

Finally, the post-9/11 frame embraced an explanation of terrorist activity that, consistent with American cultural mythology, reassured citizens that America was a blameless victim of the terrorists' attacks. In a strict moral sense, to be sure, no one injured by these heinous acts—the victims, their families, the workers at the sites, even those of us who looked on in horror—deserved in any way the fate inflicted upon them. The profoundest evil of terrorism is, after all, the very capriciousness of its targets and its victims. But that is not to say that terrorism lacks motivations or explanations, and that comprehending these contextual elements could help in planning future strategies and defenses.

According to the frame set forth by the president and echoed by other political leaders, terrorists attacked the United States not because of any of its government's actions but because of its western values, such as freedom and democracy. Such an interpretation pushed off the table any reasonable discussion of why the United States was the object of the terrorists' anger, or what might possibly be done to mitigate the situation. For one thing, America's global prominence alone makes it a magnet for terrorism. As Richard Betts argues, America's power "animates both the terrorists' purposes and their choice of tactics. . . . Political and cultural power makes the United States a target for those who blame it for their problems."[45]

"[L]urking behind every terroristic act is a specific political antecedent," writes Zbigniew Brzezinski.[46] The hatreds expressed toward the West—most virulently by the fanatics, but doubtless echoed by many of their compatriots in the region—are rooted in Arabs' historical encounters with western colonial powers, and more recently with U.S. interests. Such attitudes on the Arab "street," even if unfounded or prejudiced, need to be understood and taken into account in confronting the Middle East and its problems. In this light, a western public discourse that fails to acknowledge the antecedents and context of these hatreds will be impoverished—manifesting, in Brzezinski's words, "America's reluctance to focus on the political roots of the terrorist atrocity of September 11." As a German political scientist expressed it: "You think we are naive for resisting the use of force. We think you are naive for failing to understand how to dry up the sources of terror."[47]

Underlying the controversy over U.S. intervention in the Middle East is a debate on what is termed the nation's imperial prerogative. To what extent can or should the United States act alone in the international arena?[48] On the one hand, Americanists tend to urge unilateral action, on the strength of what they see as hegemonic military and economic power. They argue that the nation not only can but should act, preemptively if need be, to further its strategic interests, regardless of the objections of others, even of allies, who do not bear its unique responsibilities. One current manifestation of this independence is the unilateralist impulse on Capitol Hill and in the White House. These unilateralists have shown disdain for such international arrangements as the United Nations, the International Criminal Court, the Kyoto Protocol to the Climate Change Convention, and the network of arms control agreements including the Biological Weapons Convention and a revised ABM Treaty. In an effort led by unilateralists, the U.S. Senate in 1999 summarily rejected the Comprehensive Test Ban Treaty, a U.S.-spearheaded project that grew out of decades of bipartisan support for nuclear arms control.[49] Even proposals to deal with heavily indebted poor countries and limits on arms exports have been given scant attention.

Globalists, in contrast, hold that U.S. power is awesome but not unlimited. Other powers compete with the United States (the European Union, for example), and their respect and cooperation are crucial to the defense of common interests. Ironically, a superpower is the one nation most in danger when it spurns allies. In making this point, Owen Harries, former editor of the quarterly the *National Interest,* quoted Edmund Burke, who in the eighteenth century warned Parliament about the risks of British power:

> I must fairly say, [Burke remarked] I dread our own ambition, I dread our own being too much dreaded. . . . We may say that we shall not abuse this astonishing and heretofore unheard of power. But other nations will think we shall abuse it. It is impossible but that, sooner or later, this state of things must produce a combination against us which may end in our ruin.[50]

History suggests that great powers invite danger not only from terrorist bands that strike at their weakest points, but from rival powers that may unite against it.

Globalists insist that the United States as a superpower needs to respect the framework of international action that it helped to erect following World War II. Thus Benjamin R. Barber calls for "a new 'declaration of interdependence' that will embrace America's fully joining the world to which it is ever more seamlessly bound. . . . It involves strengthening international law, reinforcing multilateralism and spreading equality."[51]

PARADOXES OF AMERICAN POWER

The historical and cultural myths, or traits, discussed here—and others that could have been mentioned—suffuse Americans' political thinking and provide an intellectual framework for their reactions to terrorist attacks upon their homeland. These myths include the notions of American exceptionalism, independence and self-reliance, optimism and inventiveness, and peaceful intent. Together these ideas have supplied U.S. citizens with a reasonably coherent (if not always accurate) portrait of themselves and their relationship to the world at large. The most visible response—to wage war on nation-states alleged to nurture or harbor terrorists—is consistent with the mythic framework within which Americans think and act. It also fits with conventional narratives embracing challenge and revenge, forces in combat, and hoped-for resolution in victory.

What has yet to be fully incorporated into American myth is the nation's recently won status as the world's single superpower, a status undergirded by a military establishment that is vast (by its own historical standards) and demonstrably capable. This contemporary development raises a series of questions that are relatively novel in terms of the nation's past experiences. Does this superpower status imply global hegemony—not only military, but economic and political domination as well? Does this status suggest that the nation's multilateral initiatives of the post–World War II era could be trumped by reassertion of the more traditional national values of individualism and initiative? Finally, if American mythology shaped the nation's responses to the events of 9/11, will those events themselves in time transform that mythology in fundamental ways?

NOTES

1. See A. S. Byatt, "What Is a European?" *New York Times Magazine,* 13 October 2002, 46ff.
2. J. Hector St. John de Crevecoeur, *Letters from an American Farmer* (London, 1782), in *American Poetry and Prose,* volume I, ed. Norman Foerster (Boston: Houghton Mifflin, 1947), p. 177.
3. Matthew 5:14.
4. Quoted in Kevin Starr, *Americans and the California Dream, 1850–1915* (New York: Oxford University Press, 1986), p. 86.
5. George H. W. Bush, State of the Union Address, 28 January 1992.
6. Bill Clinton, State of the Union Address, 8 February 1997.
7. George W. Bush, State of the Union Address, 27 January 2003, text reprinted in *Los Angeles Times,* 28 January 2003, p. A-12.
8. Wallace Stegner, *Angle of Repose* (New York: Doubleday & Co., 1971), p. 319.
9. Survey by the International Social Survey Program, 1995. Reported in *Public Perspective* 10 (June–July 1999), p. 42.
10. Survey by Princeton Survey Research Associates for the Pew Research Center (April 6–May 6, 1999). Reported in *Public Perspective* 10 (October–November 1999), p. 4.
11. Cited in Karlyn Bowman, "POLLitics," *Roll Call,* 5 December 2002, p. 8.
12. James Bryce, *The American Commonwealth,* vol. II, ed. Louis Hacker (New York: Capricorn Books, 1959), p. 308. Bryce spent much time in the United States and viewed Americans benignly, but students of the American character would profit from reading his chapters on public opinion, especially Chapter 4 from Volume II of his 1888 work.
13. Benjamin Franklin, *Information to Those Who Would Remove to America.* Reprinted in: Richard E. Amacher, ed., *Franklin's Wit and Folly: The Bagatelles* (New Brunswick, NJ: Rutgers University Press, 1953), pp. 77–88.
14. James Fenimore Cooper, *The Last of the Mohicans* (New York: Bantam Books ed., 1989), p. 100. Cited in www.digitallyobsessed.com/showreview.php3?D=849. The independent bent of Cooper's hero, here called "Hawkeye," is discussed in Donald A. Ringe, *James Fenimore Cooper* (New York: Twayne Publishers, 1962), pp. 44, 86–88, 92, and 113.
15. Alexis de Tocqueville, *Democracy in America,* vol. 2, ed. Phillips Bradley (New York: Vintage, 1956), Book 2, Chap. 3.
16. See the discussion in Everett Carll Ladd, "Every Country Is Unique, but the U.S. Is Different," *Public Perspective* 6 (April–May 1995), pp. 14–26.
17. Cited by David Brooks in *New York Times,* 28 December, 2002, p. A-15.
18. Luxembourg Income Study, UNICEF, reported in "Poverty and Plenty," *Washington Post,* 29 March 1997, p. A-14.
19. Paul Richter and Doyle McManus, "Fewer Americans Back War in Iraq, Surveys Find," *Los Angeles Times,* 31 October 2002, p. A-8.
20. Mark Twain, *Adventures of Huckleberry Finn* (New York: Modern Library edition, 1985), p. 18.
21. Here I am indebted, as I often am, to the acute observations of media commentator Neal

Gabler, although in this case I take exception to his conclusions. Neal Gabler, "In Hannibal Country," *Los Angeles Times*, 10 November 2002, p. M-1.

22. Richard Morin and Claudia Deane, "Sept. 11 Changes Were for Better, Poll Majority Says," *Washington Post*, 1 January 2002, p. A-1.

23. Brian Knowlton, "A Global Image on the Way Down," *International Herald Tribune*, 5 December 2002, pp. 1, 8.

24. Bryce, *The American Commonwealth*, vol. II, p. 313.

25. Michael G. Kammen, editor, *A Machine That Would Go of Itself: The Constitution in American Culture* (New York: Alfred A. Knopf, 1986).

26. See Vernon Loeb, "Afghan Conflict a Lab for Honing Military Technology," *International Herald Tribune*, 22 March 2002, p. 8.

27. Quoted in Joseph J. Ellis, *Founding Brothers: The Revolutionary Generation* (New York: Alfred A. Knopf, 2000), p. 152.

28. Ellis, *Founding Brothers*, p. 136.

29. John Mueller, *Wars, Presidents and Public Opinion* (New York: Wiley, 1973); Paul Brace and Barbara Hinckley, *Follow the Leader: Opinion Polls and the Modern Presidents* (New York: Basic Books, 1992), pp. 92–94, 111–113.

30. Dana Milbank and Claudia Deane, "President's Ratings Still High, Poll Shows," *Washington Post*, 22 December 2002, p. A-4; Karlyn Bowman, "Like Bush, Congress Sees Approval Rating Decline Since Sept. 11," *Roll Call*, 8 August 2002, p. 8.

31. Morin and Deane, "Sept. 11 Changes Were for Better."

32. President George W. Bush, State of the Union Address, January 27, 2003.

33. Studs Terkel, *The Good War: An Oral History of World War II* (New York: New Press edition, 1997).

34. *Budget of the U.S. Government, Fiscal Year 2003, Historical Tables* (Washington, D.C.: Government Printing Office, 2002), Table 3.2; Robin Wright, "Don't Just Fund the War, Shell Out for Peace," *Washington Post*, 10 March 2002, p. B-5.

35. Quoted in Kathleen Hall Jamieson and Paul Waldman, *The Press Effect: Politicians, Journalists, and the Stories That Shape the Political World* (New York: Oxford University Press, 2003), p. 150.

36. Jamieson and Waldman, *The Press Effect*, pp. 151–152.

37. David Ignatius, "Doubt in the Ranks," *Washington Post*, 1 November 2002, p. A-35. Ignatius's analysis accords with much of what we have learned over the years about defense and foreign policy bureaucracies.

38. The first and third of these assumptions are discussed in Jamieson and Waldman, *The Press Effect*, pp. 152–154.

39. Quoted in David Ignatius, "A General's Doubts," *Washington Post*, 31 January 2003, p. A-27.

40. Neal Gabler, "Plotting a Story, Plotting a War," *Los Angeles Times*, 29 September 2002, p. M-6.

41. Richard G. Lugar, "Beating Terror," *Washington Post*, 27 January 2003, p. A-19.

42. Shirley Williams, "Please, America, Listen to Your Foreign Friends," *International Herald Tribune*, 29 March 2002, p. 7.

43. Benjamin R. Barber, "Mutual Aid Society on a Grand Scale," *Los Angeles Times*, 17 November 2002, p. M-2.

44. Associated Press survey cited in Will Lester, "Poll Finds Americans Wary of Tax Cuts, War," *Santa Barbara News Press*, 31 December 2002, p. B-1.

45. Quoted in Ivo H. Daalder and James M. Lindsay, "The Globalization of Politics: American Foreign Policy for a New Century," *Brookings Review* 23 (winter 2003), p. 15.

46. Zbigniew Brzezinski, "Confronting Anti-American Grievances, *New York Times*, 1 September 2002, p. D-9.

47. Quoted in Ethan Bronner, "Why Today's Europeans Object to America's Worldview," *New York Times*, 31 January 2003, p. A-26.

48. A thoughtful summary of the debate between Americanists and Globalists is presented by Daalder and Lindsay in their *Brookings Review* essay, "The Globalization of Politics," pp. 12–17.

49. The Senate debate on the CTBT is recounted in Roger H. Davidson, "Senate Floor Deliberation: A Preliminary Inquiry," in *The Contentious Senate*, ed. Colton C. Campbell and Nicol C. Rae (Lanham, MD: Rowman & Littlefield, 2001), pp. 22–29.

50. Quoted by William Pfaff, "Thatcher's Advice: Britain Should Give Up on the EU and Rely on the U.S.," *International Herald Tribune*, 23–24 March 2002, p. 4.

51. Barber, "Mutual Aid Society on a Grand Scale."

NATIONAL SECURITY
AND THE MIDTERM ELECTIONS OF 2002

ANDREW E. BUSCH

UNIVERSITY OF DENVER

The midterm election pattern has been one of the most firmly established features of American electoral politics. In the twenty-seven midterm elections from 1894 through 1998, the president's party had suffered net seat losses twenty-five times in the House and eighteen times in the Senate. The average midterm election in this period saw a loss of thirty-five House seats and three Senate seats by the president's party. These losses have typically extended to state government, as well, with the president's copartisans losing governorships and around 350 state legislative seats.

Consequently, the November 2002 midterm elections, in which Republicans gained six seats in the U.S. House, two seats and a majority in the U.S. Senate, and about 250 legislative seats around the country, surprised many, if not most, political observers. The results were widely labeled a broad Republican victory and, by some, even a mandate for President Bush. This outcome called out for an explanation, and one was quickly offered by analysts and partisans on both sides: National security issues were responsible.

And, indeed, the sudden salience of national security after 9/11 is the most plausible single explanation for Republican gains in 2001. With the end of the Cold War, American politics in the 1990s was consistently focused on domestic affairs. In 1992, Bill Clinton attacked George H. W. Bush for paying too much attention to foreign policy, and Americans seemed to agree; not only did they turn Bush out of office, but only 8 percent of voters cited foreign policy as the most important issue. In 1996, only 4 percent said foreign matters were primary. Even in November 2000, with the Middle East in renewed turmoil and the bombing of the *USS Cole* fresh in the memory, only 12 percent focused on nondomestic issues. Except for a few forays into missile defense and defense readiness, neither candidate had much to say about the world abroad. In short, the *Pax Americana* of the 1990s resulted in both an electorate and a political elite who were less concerned with security than at any time since the early 1930s.

That all changed on September 11, 2001. The electoral environment in America was drastically transformed as a result of the terrorist attacks and the Bush administration's response. One effect was obvious and direct, and three more were indirect, sometimes difficult to measure, but nevertheless impossible to ignore. First, national security issues regained a position at the top of the list of Americans' concerns. Second, as a result of the war on terrorism, Bush's stature increased considerably, and with it his approval ratings, which started the crisis at about 90 percent and remained in the mid-60s for the last half of 2002. Third, the attacks placed a premium on stability and made Americans less likely to seek drastic change at the ballot box. Finally, the terrorist attacks activated a potentially decisive set of interlocking attitudes and values among Americans that tilted the playing field to the right. Indeed, national security turned out to be the powerful undertow that shaped the election by its force even when it was not visible.

However important these 9/11 effects might have been, one cannot ascribe the outcome of the midterm elections simply to national security. To understand that further explanation is required, all one must do is review the record of other midterm elections held in periods of wartime or heightened concern over security. Even in times of global war or great danger, the midterm pattern has endured. For example, Franklin D. Roosevelt's Democrats lost fifty-five House and nine Senate seats in the World War II midterm of 1942. Days before the November 1918 armistice ending World War I, Woodrow Wilson's Democrats lost nineteen House seats and six Senate seats, giving Republicans control of both chambers. Harry S. Truman's Democrats lost twenty-nine in the House and six in the Senate in 1950, at a time when U.S. and allied troops had nearly cleared North Korea of communist forces. Lyndon Johnson's Republican opponents gained forty-seven in the House and four in the Senate in 1966, before popular opposition to the war in Vietnam had ballooned. In all of these cases—and most of the remaining cases of presidential loss—the president's position was seriously undermined both within his own party and across the aisle.[1]

Of all the midterm elections between 1894 and 1998, only three could be considered presidential victories: 1934, when FDR's New Deal majority was strengthened measurably in both houses; 1962, when John F. Kennedy lost only four seats in the House and gained three seats in the Senate; and 1998, when Bill Clinton's Democrats held their own in the Senate and gained five House seats. Of those three, only the 1962 elections—the campaign for which coincided with the Cuban missile crisis—came in a time of war or national security emergency. It is, perhaps, this last example—that of 1962—that provides the best model for understanding 2002, for reasons that will become clear in this chapter (see Table 3.1 on page 42).

Table 3.1 Presidential Party Seat Shifts
in Midterm Elections with National Security Focus

Year	President	Event	House	Senate
1918	Wilson	WWI	–19	–6
1942	Roosevelt	WWII	–55	–9
1950	Truman	Korea	–29	–6
1962	Kennedy	Cuba	–4	+3
1966	Johnson	Early Vietnam	–47	–4
2002	Bush	War on Terrorism	+6	+2

Structural Context of the 2002 Elections

The difference between the losses presidents typically suffer in wartime and the gains made by Republicans in 2002 must hence be explained by factors outside of national security alone. (As something of a microcosm of both the influence and limitation of the national security factor, at least five House candidates were political newcomers driven to run by 9/11, but all lost in the face of large structural disadvantages.)[2] In this respect, the "structural context" of the 2002 elections was crucial. This context established the boundaries within which the election would operate, and gave Republicans good reasons to be hopeful that they would be highly competitive in 2002, before introducing any specific issue into the equation. Those reasons were grounded in a variety of explanations that political scientists have offered for the pattern of presidential party losses through history, as well as in circumstances specific to 2002. The explanations include the following.

Coattails

In the presidential year, the winning candidate's party gains seats in Congress as a result of his "coattails." In the midterm years, that help at the top of the ticket is removed and the weakest winners from two years before lose their congressional races. However, George W. Bush had no national coattails in 2000, as Republicans lost two House seats (see Table 3.2 on page 43).

Surge-and-Decline

The typical 15–20 percent decline in midterm voter turnout comes disproportionately at the expense of weak partisans or independents who were stirred to vote for the winning presidential candidate (and his congressional allies) but who lose interest in the lower-profile midterm year.[3] However, Al Gore obtained more popular votes nationally than Bush, and won his small plurality—despite trailing by 3–5 percentage points the week before—on the

TABLE 3.2   PRESIDENTIAL COATTAILS IN PRESIDENTIAL
ELECTION YEARS PRECEDING NATIONAL SECURITY MIDTERMS

YEAR	PRES. WINNER	HOUSE COATTAILS	SENATE COATTAILS
1916	Wilson	−21	−3
1940	Roosevelt	+5	−3
1948	Truman	+78	+9
1960	Kennedy	−20	−2
1964	Johnson	+38	+2
2000	Bush	−2	−4

basis of last-minute decisions by undecided and marginal voters. These are precisely the sort of voters the surge-and-decline model would expect to drop out of the electorate in the following midterm election. As with coattails, there was no Republican "surge" in 2000 to "decline" in 2002 (see Table 3.3).

EXPOSURE

The more seats the president's party holds relative to a past baseline, the more seats it will stand to lose in the next election.[4] However, the congressional parties were nearly even in both the House and the Senate and neither was far from the baseline of the new congressional era begun in 1994. As a result, Republicans were not exposed in 2002. Indeed, Republicans had lost House seats in the previous three elections, leaving fewer vulnerable seats; not since the Democratic realignment of 1930–1936 had any party lost House seats in four straight elections (see Table 3.4 on page 44).

TABLE 3.3   PRESIDENTIAL POPULAR VOTE "SURGE":
PLURALITY IN PRESIDENTIAL ELECTION YEARS
PRECEDING NATIONAL SECURITY MIDTERMS

YEAR	PRES. WINNER	POP. VOTE PLURALITY
1916	Wilson	+3.1%
1940	Roosevelt	+9.9
1948	Truman	+4.4
1960	Kennedy	+0.1[*]
1964	Johnson	+22.5
2000	Bush	−.5

[*]This plurality is based on the conventional calculation awarding all of the votes for Kennedy's top elector in Alabama to his national vote total. In fact, since only five of Alabama's eleven electors were Kennedy Democrats, it is reasonable to argue that he should only be credited with 5/11 of the vote of his top elector. In that case, his national popular vote plurality would be −1%.

TABLE 3.4   GOP EXPOSURE IN 2002:
HOUSE AND SENATE TOTALS AND AVERAGE, 1994–2000

ELECTION	GOP HOUSE	GOP SENATE
1994	230	53
1996	227	55
1998	223	55
2000	221	50
Avg., 1994–2000	225	53
Pre-election, 2002	223	49

NATIONAL CONDITIONS (OR "REFERENDUM")

In this view, key indicators of national political conditions, especially measures of economic well-being and presidential popularity, determine midterm
election results. This can occur directly, through voter intent, or indirectly,
through the strategic calculations of potential candidates, parties, and con-
tributors.[5] The worse the national conditions in the year of the midterm election, the bigger one can expect the presidential party's losses to be. In 2002, the
national conditions model argued against large Democratic gains, as presidential approval ratings remained historically high and the economic picture
was, at worst, mixed.

PRESIDENTIAL PENALTY

Voters seek to punish the president's party simply because they want to hurt
the president.[6] This desire may be driven by an attempt to balance the government, or because negative appraisals are a more powerful motive than
positive appraisals.[7] This effect, which might have been heightened by Democratic rage over the contested outcome of the 2000 election, was arguably
softened by post-9/11 bipartisanship.

Additionally, the relative lack of truly competitive seats was a barrier to
large House gains for either party. Most analysts argued that no more than
thirty to fifty House districts were seriously in play, in comparison to approx-
imately 150 a decade before. Many analysts also predicted that Republicans
would gain three to six seats due to the post-2000 redistricting. And in the Senate, while twenty of the thirty-four seats up for election were held by the GOP,
several potentially vulnerable Democratic incumbents were running in the
"red states," the swath of "Bush Country" stretching across middle America.

Thus, it was clear months before election day that the structural context
of the 2002 elections, barring unforeseen catastrophe for the Bush administration, placed a sturdy floor under probable Republican losses in a way
that Roosevelt in 1942, Truman in 1950, or Johnson in 1966 were not protected.[8] Yet it still remained to Bush and Republicans to turn this favorable

structural situation into actual gains. This outcome was not inevitable, and national security did indeed play the central role in that process.

THE NATIONAL SECURITY ISSUE

It was clear after 9/11 that national security could not help but play an important role in the 2002 elections. However, several questions remained open. For example, how much would the issue fade over time? How would it affect specific demographic groups (i.e., would focus on war alienate women voters)? Would other issues arise to supplant it? And would national unity turn to recriminations that could harm Republicans in the end?

For his part, Bush strategist Karl Rove told Republican candidates early in the campaign season to "run on the war." For their part, many Democrats assumed that the template for 2002 was laid in the handful of odd-year elections held in November, 2001—for the mayor of New York and governors of New Jersey and Virginia—when Democrats won two of three races. Surveying the results, D.N.C. Chairman Terry McAuliffe predicted that in 2002 national security would be a secondary issue and Bush would "be of no benefit to any Republican candidate in the country."[9] However, there were reasons to question whether such broad lessons could be drawn from the odd-year elections. First, the aftermath of 9/11 *was* the primary factor in the one Republican win, the New York mayoral race, where Mayor Rudy Guiliani's handpicked successor Michael Bloomberg owed his victory to the post-9/11 popularity of Guiliani himself. Second, the two Democratic victories were in gubernatorial races, where national security issues play a limited role. Finally, there was a somewhat different dynamic at work in 2001. The spirit of bipartisanship on national security had not yet broken on issues like Iraq or homeland security, and as part of that atmosphere the president himself refrained from engaging seriously in any of the campaigns. While the New Jersey governor's race was probably beyond reach for the Republicans, it is plausible to believe that Bush's engagement on behalf of the Republican running for governor of Virginia might have averted his relatively narrow defeat, thus transforming a 2–1 Democratic day into a 2–1 Republican day. By 2002, the nonpartisan aura of American politics had worn off; issues had arisen to divide the parties, and there was much less risk that presidential campaigning would appear unseemly.

Not until election day could it be answered whether the assumptions of Rove or of McAuliffe were closer to the mark. Even in late September, 2002, it was not obvious what role national security would play in the vote; National Republican Congressional Committee chairman Representative Thomas M. Davis III observed that almost all campaign ads in close races had a domestic theme and declared that, from his perspective, "There is no one overriding issue. There is a matrix of issues."[10]

By November, 2002, the national security issue had developed three distinct areas. Republicans benefited because each of the areas remained prominent and because Democrats failed to achieve superiority in any of the three. Those three were the ongoing threat of al Qaeda terrorism most directly associated in the public mind with 9/11, issues surrounding the president's proposal for a cabinet-level Department of Homeland Security, and Iraq.

Fears of terrorism remained high throughout 2002. In the spring, an American al Qaeda sympathizer (Jose Padilla) was arrested as he returned to the United States from Pakistan, where he had allegedly volunteered to carry out a radiological "dirty bomb" attack on a major U.S. city. Several Yemeni Americans were also arrested as part of an al Qaeda cell in Buffalo, New York. Democrats tried to seize the initiative by focusing on failures in intelligence processing and analysis leading up to 9/11. Senate hearings were held in May and June, and for a time much of the media was transfixed on the questions of how much the administration knew and why preventive measures were not taken. However, in the end, it seemed that the worst that could be said was that a great deal of information had been available, but that none of it had pointed explicitly to 9/11. The administration survived relatively unscathed. It also survived intermittent attempts by select Democrats to attack on the issue of civil liberties. In September, Al Gore accused the Bush administration of waging "an attack on civil liberties."[11] The issue was never pursued consistently, and was not a major factor in the November vote.

Yet the reality of the terrorist threat continued to manifest itself. On September 11, the nation commemorated the one-year anniversary of the attacks, reminding voters of the danger and reviving dormant emotions. Within just the last month before election day, four events kept the war on terrorism fresh in the public mind: the assassination in Jordan of U.S. diplomat Laurence Foley, a devastating al Qaeda bombing of a club in Bali, the takeover of a Moscow theater by Chechen terrorists, and a CIA missile attack (launched from an unmanned Predator drone) that killed a key al Qaeda leader and five minions in Yemen. A picture of the burned-out hulk of their vehicle could be seen on the front pages of newspapers across America on the morning of election day.

The second issue, the creation of a homeland security department, was originally a product of Democratic probing on intelligence failures. For some time, Senator Joseph Lieberman and other Democrats had been pressing Bush to propose such a department in order to put the relevant domestic security operations under one bureaucratic roof. For some time, the president resisted on the grounds that the nondepartmental "Office of Homeland Security" was sufficient. In the summer of 2002, Bush reversed course, agreed to a cabinet level department, and sent a proposal to Congress. The White House immediately sought, with considerable success, to make the issue its own.

However, the parties quickly came to loggerheads over personnel provisions in the president's proposal that allowed him to bypass civil service rules for the employees of the new department. Bush and Republicans argued that the chief executive needed such flexibility in order to improve efficiency and defend the nation; Democrats refused to yield, despite the entreaties of moderates like Senator Zell Miller of Georgia. Thus, for several months the reorganization languished in the Senate. Democrats actually tried to bring their version of the bill up for a vote on the floor, but Republicans filibustered on behalf of the president's bill.

The issue, which was largely out of public view for months, exploded into the open in late September. While campaigning for New Jersey Republican Senate candidate Douglas Forrester, Bush went on the offensive, saying "the Senate is more interested in special interests in Washington, and not interested in the security of the American people." Senate Majority Leader Tom Daschle took the floor of the Senate to denounce Bush's charge as "outrageous" and to demand a presidential apology for unduly politicizing national security.[12] In turn, Republicans argued that it was Daschle who had been driven by political calculation on homeland security and national security more generally. The tone was set, and Bush even repeated his charge late in the campaign season.[13] Daschle's defensiveness was an indication that he feared the potency of Bush's attack, and rightly so: Karl Rove would later point to two Democratic Senators—Jean Carnahan of Missouri and Max Cleland of Georgia—whose defeats were traceable primarily to a public impression that they were placing the demands of organized labor ahead of national security.[14] In Cleland's case, the issue brought down a triple-amputee Vietnam veteran, who could not shake the image of being soft on defense; even the Georgia Veterans of Foreign Wars endorsed his opponent, Congressman Saxby Chambliss.[15]

This issue became intertwined with debate over the prospect of war in Iraq; indeed, Daschle, by accident or design, treated Bush's September comments as if they were directed at the pending Iraq resolution rather than the Homeland Security bill. While Iraq was a frequent topic of discussion throughout 2002, it began to dominate the news on September 12, the day George Bush went to the United Nations to make the case against Saddam Hussein. In the following weeks, the administration pursued a two-track strategy, asking for a congressional resolution of approval for the use of force against Iraq and asking for a tough new Security Council resolution. While there was little movement in particular races or in nationwide generic congressional preference polls that was directly traceable to the Iraq debate, it dominated the news for weeks during which Democrats had hoped to make their case on the economy and issues like prescription drugs.

Indeed, Democrats found themselves outmaneuvered by Bush on Iraq. With most polls showing that around three of five Americans favored action against Iraq, Democrats could neither oppose the president indiscriminately, appearing weak on security, nor embrace him without reservation, alienating their base on the left. Consequently, most of the Democratic leadership waffled but agreed with Bush in the end; a bare majority of Senate Democrats supported the Iraq use-of-force resolution while a majority of House Democrats (most with no significant electoral opposition) voted against it. Just as Democratic leaders were positioning themselves to adopt the administration's tough stand, a trip to Baghdad by three House Democrats—Jim McDermott of Washington, David Bonior of Michigan, and Nick Rahall of West Virginia—brought back images of George McGovern (or perhaps Jane Fonda). When McDermott asserted that Bush would "mislead" Americans on Iraq and implied that the president was less trustworthy than Saddam, a firestorm ensued.[16] While the comments were repudiated by top Democrats, they undoubtedly contributed to the difficulties of the party on this issue.

Bush came under a great deal of criticism, both before and after the election, that he was manipulating the Iraq situation for electoral gain. Only days after the election, Senator John Kerry (D-Mass.) spoke for many on the left when he attacked "the timing, the cynicism of it, the raw political exploitation of it."[17] However, Bush had agreed to a congressional debate only after being pressured by Democrats and some Republicans to allow one. It was Democrats who preferred that the debate come earlier rather than later, in hopes they could put national security issues behind them and move on to domestic issues well before election day. Furthermore, American war planners reportedly preferred to initiate war in early 2003; congressional authorization had to come in the previous fall to allow for the necessary buildup of forces around Iraq. In any event, the administration's continued focus on Iraq long after election day must cast considerable doubt on the suggestion that Bush's policy had its foundation in electoral calculation. To whatever degree the Iraq resolution and the midterm elections were connected, the connection was likely the reverse of what critics feared: Rather than using the resolution to affect the elections, the Bush administration used the elections as leverage to gain support for the resolution.

It is likely that opponents of military action in Iraq would have criticized Bush no matter how he handled the delicate interplay of policy and politics. Indeed, his father was attacked by Democrats in late 1990 when he waited until *after* the midterm elections to begin a buildup in the Persian Gulf of the armored forces needed for offensive operations to free Kuwait. The timing of the decision, they argued, did not give Americans an opportunity to fully take war into account in their midterm vote.

Democrats, recognizing Bush's advantage on national security issues, attempted to shift attention to other areas where they believed they had the upper hand. Foremost among these were economic issues—both the corporate corruption scandals of summer and the perceived sluggishness of economic conditions. Indeed, in July, House Minority Leader Richard Gephardt declared that Democrats could gain thirty to forty seats in the House on the strength of the corporate corruption issue. However, Republicans protected themselves against Democratic attempts to link them to the scandals when Bush signed on to the Senate reform measure, which then passed 97-0. For their part, Democrats were saddled with ties to Global Crossing and the questionable financial record of Democratic National Committee chairman Terry McAuliffe.

The overall state of the economy did not bear fruit for Democrats, either. The Democratic appeal was limited by the obvious effects of 9-11 on the economy, perceived obstructionism by the Senate, and the fact that the slowdown had clearly begun in the final months of the Clinton administration. On Bush's key economic policy—the tax cut of 2001—Democrats wavered, as they did on war with Iraq. While most opposed it, few were willing to call for its repeal, a contradiction that "rendered incoherent their criticism of [Bush's] economic management."[18]

Working against Democratic efforts to run on the economy was also the fact that the economic picture was mixed, but hardly catastrophic. The Dow Jones Industrial Average declined from nearly 12,000 when it peaked in January of 2000 to around 7,000 at the end of September 2002. Unemployment had increased, bankruptcies were up, and the federal budget deficit had returned. At the same time, however, the economy was growing at around 3 percent a year, personal income was growing at around 2 percent a year, and the pre-election unemployment rate stood at 5.7 percent, lower than the annual average in Bill Clinton's first term (6.0 percent). By some measures, including GDP growth, the economy in the third quarter of 2002 was actually stronger than it had been when Bush took office in January of 2001. And in the last month before election day, the stock market gained back around 1,500 points. In the last Gallup pre-election poll of likely voters, 28 percent called the economy excellent or good, 45 percent called it fair, and only 26 percent deemed it poor. Republicans won among those rating the economy excellent or good (by 70–27) and those who rated the economy merely "fair" (by a narrower margin of 49–46); Democrats won only among the quarter of voters who deemed the economy "poor." Altogether, Republicans and Democrats split the votes of those who considered the economy the number one issue.[19] In November, 2002, another Gallup poll showed that 55 percent of all Americans approved of the president's handling of the economy.[20]

Democrats were also unable to capitalize on other favorite issues like health care, education, and even Social Security. On each of these they were preempted and outmaneuvered by Bush and House Republicans. Ultimately, Gallup polls showed that substantial majorities of Americans supported the Republican position on the key issues: not only national security and Iraq, but also permanent tax cuts, judicial appointments, and Social Security.[21]

All of this meant that on election day national security had remained front and center, and Republicans had retained an advantage over all three components of that issue. Unlike past years, no national exit polling data was available, but some conclusions can be reached by reference to several national polls taken immediately before and immediately after the election. In open-ended surveys, Americans placed security issues higher than the economy by varying margins in Gallup polls and by a 41–17 margin in a poll conducted by consultant Richard Wirthlin. Indeed, Gallup polls showed economic issues clearly ahead of national security only for a brief moment in late July, at the height of the corporate corruption scandals. Fox News election-day polls in key Senate races also showed security outpacing the economy in six of nine states among voters and likely voters.[22] According to Gallup, Americans in November 2002 viewed Democrats as "too weak" on security by a 57–34 percent margin; conversely, Republicans were seen as "tough enough" by a 64–27 percent margin.[23] A post-election poll of voters taken by Democratic consultant Stanley Greenberg and Republican pollster Bill McInturff found that while the economy and jobs were listed by respondents as their top issue concern, more voters said their vote decision was more influenced by Bush's performance against terrorism than by his economic performance, by a 53–39 percent margin; given an opportunity to make a direct comparison, 57 percent said Bush's performance on "foreign affairs and international issues" had more influence on their vote than his performance on "the economy, tax cuts, and corporate corruption." Altogether, according to Greenberg and McInturff, "Foreign affairs and security issues—particularly homeland security—played an unprecedented role in this year's midterm elections."[24]

Furthermore, while the "gender gap" persisted, Republicans nearly erased their disadvantage among women, who were actually more likely than men to cite terrorism as a key concern.[25] This finding supported Wirthlin's contention that 9/11 had brought an important qualitative change in the nature of the national security issue, which became as well a matter of personal security.[26] Among another key demographic group—seniors—Republicans regained an edge they had lost in 2000, with McInturff arguing that in 2002 "there was a fair amount of evidence that they were most focused on terrorism and national security."[27]

To parse out the three strands of the national security debate, it seems likely that the terrorism and homeland security issue benefited Republicans more than did Iraq. Voters who listed terrorism as their number-one priority voted Republican by a wide margin, while the much smaller number of voters who cited Iraq split 48–46 for Democrats, according to Gallup polls.[28] This more-or-less even split, however, did not tell the whole picture. On the other side of the Iraq ledger, Republicans probably gained both by controlling the agenda for over a month and by standing unambiguously on the majority side of the issue while the Democratic position was harder to rally around. Numerous Democratic missteps on Iraq, not least the waffling on the Iraq resolution and the pronouncements of "Baghdad Jim" McDermott, may have cost the party dearly by contributing to its more general image of weakness. And it is worth recalling that central to the Bush administration's argument on Iraq was the contention that the issue of Saddam and the issue of terrorism were inextricably linked. It is thus possible that the 48–46 split was somewhat deceptive, since many Bush supporters may have folded Iraq into their answer on terrorism while Bush opponents—more skeptical of the president's argument of linkage—were more inclined to view it separately. Indeed, when Greenberg asked respondents in his own post-election survey whether they voted to "support President Bush's position on Iraq" or to "oppose President Bush's position on Iraq," supporters had a nineteen-percentage-point lead.[29] The net overall effect was probably a modest Republican advantage on Iraq, while they prevailed overwhelmingly on the terrorism/homeland security combination. What this meant, in sum, was that Republicans owned the cluster of issues that were most likely to actually drive voters.

GEORGE W. BUSH'S POPULARITY

In the aftermath of September 11, President Bush's job approval rating approached 90 percent, and he started the year around 80 percent. Though some slippage inevitably occurred, he still retained a level of support from the mid-to-high 60s to the low 70s from May through election day. Just prior to election day, Bush's approval rating was 63 percent in the Gallup poll (the midterm average is below 50 percent), and was 68 percent in the first post-election poll in November. In addition, Bush and Republicans were rated decisively higher than Democrats on most leadership qualities and for having a clear plan to deal with problems.[30] There is no question among analysts that 9/11 and Bush's response to it were the cause of that high level of public support; indeed, even before Bush had done anything to respond on September 11, 78 percent indicated that they had confidence in his ability to respond.[31] As Marc J. Hetherington and Michael Nelson observed, Bush's post–September 11 "rally effect" included the largest jump in approval (thirty-five percentage points), the single highest approval level (90 percent), and the longest duration of any presidential rally effect in American history.[32] This effect—and, through it, one must say national security—had several distinct consequences for the 2002 election.

First, by most accounts, Republicans won the crucial recruitment war for potential candidates. Even before September 11, Bush began recruiting strong candidates and clearing the primary fields for key challenges and open seats. These candidates included Elizabeth Dole in North Carolina, Norm Coleman in Minnesota, Saxby Chambliss in Georgia, and John Thune in South Dakota.[33] As importantly, numerous potential Democratic candidates were discouraged from running by Bush's popularity. As Gary C. Jacobson has shown, much can be explained about ultimate election outcomes by this early and invisible phase of the campaign.[34]

Second, Bush was a very successful fund-raiser for Republican candidates and the Republican Party. He headlined seventy Republican fund-raisers and raised $140–$150 million. This figure broke the previous record for presidential fund-raising set by Bill Clinton, who brought in $50 million in his first midterm year of 1994 and $105 million in 2000. Because of Bush's fund-raising success, the Republican National Committee had $30 million on hand at the beginning of October to only $5 million for the Democrats.[35] This money allowed Republicans to continue frequent polling to help make resource allocation decisions in the late stages of the campaign. It is impossible to know how much of this record-breaking performance can be traced to Bush's popularity, especially among Republicans, as the commander in chief. He had already established himself as a very successful fund-raiser in 2000, and he might well have shattered records even without the aid of the national security issue. However, it is also difficult to believe that the new environment did not aid him in this task at all.

Third, Bush translated his popularity into votes for Republican candidates, both by mobilizing the Republican base and by swaying some undecided voters in close races. After wrapping up fund-raising efforts in late October, Bush continued visiting states with crucial House and Senate races such as those in Colorado, Georgia, Minnesota, Missouri, and North Carolina. Altogether, Bush made ninety campaign visits to key congressional races.[36] In the last five days of the campaign, he traveled 10,000 miles on a fifteen-state, seventeen-city blitz, the most intense campaigning by a president for his party in recent memory.[37] One Bush rally in Georgia the weekend before the election reportedly produced 500 volunteers who knocked on 30,000 doors over the next three days[38] After the votes were counted, Saxby Chambliss, the beneficiary of that effort, said, "Our base was more fired up than any campaign I have ever seen."[39] Overall, Republicans were much more motivated and more successful at turning out their vote—by an estimated rate of 43 percent to 36 percent of Democrats[40]—and a large part of that success was owed to the support of Republican voters for the commander in chief in wartime. In October 2002, Bush had the approval of 95 percent of Republican voters.

More than in recent midterm elections, support for the president himself was an explicit issue for voters. According to CBS polls, in 1990, only 30 percent of voters said they were basing their congressional vote on their opinion of the president; in 1998, only 37 percent said so; in 2002, 50 percent said they were voting on the basis of their views of the president. Of those, three of five supported Bush. Likewise, a pre-election Gallup poll indicated that 53 percent would use their vote to send a message to George Bush, and his supporters outnumbered his opponents by a 2–1 margin. By comparison, in 1998, the 46 percent who said they would use their congressional vote to "send a message" were split exactly evenly between supporters and opponents of the president.[41]

PREMIUM ON STABILITY

A less-noted feature of the national security–conscious 2002 election environment was the degree to which the crisis atmosphere made Americans relatively risk-averse. This general tendency had two features. First, it made Americans less likely to seek major turnover or to adopt any "throw out the bums" mentality, a feature of public opinion that presented both a reassurance and a challenge to Republicans. This phenomenon showed itself in a low desire by poll respondents to effect wholesale change and in a relatively high

50-percent approval rating for Congress; in contrast, prior to the tumultuous 1994 midterm elections, Congress had a 23 percent approval rating.[42] Another manifestation of this desire for stability could be seen in polls showing that a plurality of 46 percent of Americans preferred that divided government continue.[43] This tendency of public opinion signaled a reluctance to disrupt the status quo very much in any direction, thus comforting Republicans that they had little reason to fear becoming victims of the full force of the midterm pattern. General satisfaction with Congress meant that incumbents would be hard to dislodge, and in the House—where the midterm pattern is most consistent over time—most incumbents were Republicans. On the other hand, this desire for continuity presented a challenge for Republicans, for whom success was defined as overcoming the status quo to reestablish unified government under their control. Democrats consequently made their electoral case in terms of their ability to serve as a check on the "far right." Republicans sought to redefine the Democratic "check" as dangerous "gridlock," pointed to homeland security (as well as Senate obstruction of judicial appointments) as evidence, and asked voters to end that "gridlock." To some degree, on election day, this counterargument prevailed. At the least, the message clearly resonated with Republican voters, and may have been partly responsible for higher GOP turnout.[44] Democratic analysts Tom Freedman and Bill Knapp later argued that the Republican strategy worked, saying, "The most obvious lesson of the election for Democrats is that voters do not want gridlock—they want results."[45] Perhaps voters valued continuity per se less than the smooth operation of government in time of crisis, for which continuity was a proxy.[46]

While neither party benefited unambiguously from the above factor, the public desire for stability arguably played to the strength of Republicans in another way, by putting a premium on a certain type of leadership that Republicans sought to represent through the medium of George W. Bush. It has been noted elsewhere that a key factor leading to the victory of Bill Clinton in 1992 was the end of the Cold War, which not only vitiated foreign policy as a key concern but also fundamentally transformed the nature of the "character" issue in presidential elections. In many respects, "character" before 1992 had to do with judgment and temperament, with steadiness, resolve, trustworthiness, and an even temper.[47] In the 1990s, as foreign threats subsided, "character" was supplanted by "compassion" and "empathy." In the post-9/11 world, it seemed possible that the pendulum had moved back again, and once again favored the sterner character touted by Republicans and the steady, grounded style of George W. Bush as president. An early sign of this new public sobriety came in the Georgia primary election, when two congressional firebrands—Republican Bob Barr and Democrat Cynthia McKinney—were turned out in favor of less polarizing alternatives. This was a concern for stability on a different level, less amenable to measurement, and it almost certainly worked to aid the GOP on balance (though it could work against particular Republicans).

MORE CONSERVATIVE ENVIRONMENT

Finally, 9/11 and the renewed concern with national security established a general electoral environment that provided more fertile ground for Republicans than for Democrats. In many cases, the specific issues involved were only peripherally related to security, if at all. However, a cluster of these issues worked together to place boundaries around the course of the general election.

To some extent, this new atmosphere revolved around values. For example, patriotism was undoubtedly strengthened considerably. No one could fail to notice the sudden outpouring of patriotic sentiment after 9/11 manifested in ways as diverse as displays of flags on homes and automobiles, an abundance of patriotic clothing, and a revival of patriotic music. Many Americans who had given little thought to the question in recent years took stock of how much, as Americans, they had to lose. There was also some revival of religious sentiment and observation. Churches were filled after 9/11, and it is likely that faith was deepened even for many who had never left the pews. Though much of the revival of church attendance was short-lived, it is unlikely that its effects were completely spent only a year later. While no one would argue that patriotism or religion are monopolies of the right—indeed, a noticeable feature of the new environment was the degree to which Americans participated across the political spectrum—it is hardly deniable that the critique of American society from the left has more often seen them as obstacles to overcome than as resources to treasure. Large elements of the agenda of the left require the reconception, if not repudiation, of those values, from increased reliance on international organizations to advancement of a secular social agenda emphasizing the "self-actualization" of individuals free from the constraints of "bourgeois morality." For their part, many conservatives clearly appreciated the coalitional significance of the post-9/11 change. *National Review* called patriotism "both the cement that unifies the [conservative] movement and the key to electoral victory. In 2002, as in the days of Nixon's 'silent majority' and the Reagan years, it was an emphasis on the nation, national security, and patriotism (rather than on the market or morality) that proved crucial to conservatism's success."[48]

This new environment, driven by 9/11, was not confined to the realm of values. Americans also grew more hardheaded about a variety of ancillary issues ranging from gun control to ethnic profiling to missile defense. To cite just a few examples:

- When the Bush administration announced that it would withdraw the United States from the Anti-Ballistic Missile Treaty of 1972—a policy fraught with controversy—few voices were raised to object. Support for missile defense ultimately worked its way into several Republican Senate campaigns.
- When the Air Line Pilots Association demanded that qualified pilots be allowed to arm themselves for defense—an idea that would have brought

significant organized protest from some quarters a short time before—Congress agreed, and pulled a reluctant administration along.

- Concerns about lax immigration enforcement—most closely associated with Pat Buchanan prior to 9/11—became a mainstream fear. In response, the administration was forced to suspend consideration of a plan to grant amnesty to illegal aliens from Mexico.

- The climate on law enforcement changed enough that when black Americans were polled in the fall of 2001, 71 percent said they supported racial profiling of Middle Easterners in order to prevent future terrorist attacks.[49]

Though few voters would place any of these issues as primary on election day, this subterranean attitudinal shift did not bode well for the liberal party. Like changing tastes in leadership qualities, it was often difficult to measure—indeed, phenomena like patriotic and religious sentiment were inherently averse to precise measurement—but it tilted the playing field to the right nevertheless.

RESULTS AND INTERPRETATIONS

In the end, Republicans gained two seats in the Senate and six in the House. Republicans won almost every close race (one exception was South Dakota, where incumbent Democratic Senator Tim Johnson beat John Thune by 527 votes). Democrats gained four governorships—as in 2001, in races little affected by national security—but Republicans still controlled a majority there, too. Republicans made a net gain of about 225 state legislative seats, compared to an average midterm loss of 350—putting them into the national lead for the first time since 1952—and went from an 18–17 deficit in legislative chambers to a 21–16 lead.[50] The Republicans beat Democrats in the nationally aggregated House vote by 52 to 46 percent, a narrow win but much improved over the 49–48 margin they held in 1996, 1998, and 2000.[51] Most analysts agreed that the key to Republican success was the "nationalizing" of the elections behind Bush's themes of national security and, to a lesser extent, tax cuts.[52] Three schools of thought quickly emerged.

One, consisting primarily of liberal Democrats, argued that national security was central to the election outcome because Bush had successfully (and perhaps unfairly) manipulated the issue. In this view, Bush and Republicans should be chastised for politicizing national security and distorting the record of the Democrats. Columnist E. J. Dionne, for example, called the debate over homeland security "one of the sorriest episodes in the history of partisanship. . . . By turning domestic security into a divisive and partisan issue, President Bush helped win his party an election."[53] To Dionne, "Bush succeeded brilliantly in hiding partisanship and ideology behind the determined face of national unity. He used his standing after 9/11 to intimidate his opposition."[54] *Newsday* likewise attributed the Democratic defeat to Bush's cynical use of homeland security, saying, "Democrats were right on the policy; the Republicans were masterful on the politics."[55] Senator Dianne Feinstein (D-Calif.) blamed the defeat on the ability of Bush to "obfuscate on the whole issue of the economy with his pre-election push for national security issues."[56] An unnamed Democratic staffer, reflecting on the role of homeland security, simply said "We were played. We got totally played."[57]

A second interpretation, voiced most frequently by Republicans and moderate Democrats, held that national security was central to the election because Bush was simply better on the issue than the national Democratic leadership. In this view, that Democratic leadership should be chastised for not taking national security seriously enough. Predictably, *National Review* argued that "[v]oters were concerned about national security, and they trusted President Bush and the Republicans on the issue. . . . The natural Republican advantage on the issue was augmented by the Democrats' frittering away of their credibility" with offensive calculation and obstructionism.[58] A surprising number of moderate Democrats agreed. To Elaine C. Kamarck, the Democratic strategy of trying to change the subject away from national security was "a recipe for political irrelevance."[59] To Gregory Michaelidis, a veteran of the Gore/Lieberman 2000 campaign, "getting serious about foreign policy is one of the first things Democrats need to do as they sift the post-election ashes."[60] Al From, head of the Democratic Leadership Council, echoed that Democrats needed to "get serious about national security."[61] Even Democratic officeholders like Senator Zell Miller, Senator Evan Bayh, Representative Steve Israel, and Representative Harold Ford offered versions of this critique. Ford, who challenged Representative Nancy Pelosi for the position of House minority leader when Richard Gephardt stepped down, declared, "If we want the American people to trust us to govern, we cannot take a dismissive or defeatist attitude toward issues of national security."[62]

Third, a common academic interpretation held that national security was key simply because the new environment favored Republicans naturally. Since at least the McGovernization of the Democratic Party, Americans have trusted Republicans more than Democrats on national security issues. Consequently, it automatically aids Republicans when those issues rise to the forefront. In this view, no one need be chastised; Republicans were simply being Republicans, Democrats were being Democrats. It just happened that in 2002, what the nation cared most about matched up fortuitously with what voters perceive Republicans do best. Writing in the *New York Times*, professors Donald Green and Eric Schickler argued that Republicans won because the election played to their pre-existing strength on national security, not because they grew fundamentally stronger.[63]

What these post-election interpretations had in common was the centrality they placed on national security. There was a remarkable degree of consensus on that basic point among both domestic and foreign observers. Some even claimed for Bush a "mandate" on terrorism or Iraq. James Pinkerton, former advisor to President George H. W. Bush, wrote: "Asked to give Bush a mandate for military action, [voters] gave him one."[64] Newspaper headlines claimed "Republican Victory Spells Support for President's Foreign Policy," "GOP Win Seen as Go-Ahead on Iraq Agenda," "A Republican Electoral Victory Has Opened Up the Road to Iraq," and "President Now Has a Mandate, Especially on Matters Relating to National Security."[65] Wisely, the president himself refrained from making such claims, which political scientists know are generally questionable owing to mixed voter motivations. Like a rare bird, the presidential mandate is more often talked about than sighted.

Nevertheless, the election outcome and the degree to which national security was important to that outcome had immediate consequences in the world of policy. The logjam on homeland security was broken in the 2002 lame-duck session of Congress, with a more-or-less total capitulation by Senate Democrats. Furthermore, Bush's midterm election victory translated almost immediately into a strengthened position in the world. Within hours of the election results, France relented in its opposition to a tough new Security Council resolution on Iraq. Though it later became clear that the French retreat was only temporary, the unanimous passage of Resolution 1441 proved to be a crucial step on the road to war.

CONCLUSION

In some ways, the effect of national security on the 2002 elections was direct indeed. It was, to a plurality of Americans, issue number one. It was an issue that Bush owned due to his post-9/11 response, and that Republicans as a party had owned for years before. Democrats could not gain the confidence of Americans on national security, and in the post-9/11 environment they could never succeed in changing the subject for long. Their dilemma was not an easy one to avoid, as the party that identifies itself by domestic activism and that, moreover, is heavily influenced by the remnants of the anti–Vietnam War movement with its longstanding antipathy to things military.

In other ways, the influence of national security, though powerful, was routed through intermediary forms. George Bush's popularity—a function of the rise of the national security issue—was crucial to the election outcome through candidate recruitment, fund-raising, and voter mobilization. The desire of voters for stability—another function of the national security issue—either benefited Republicans or put a floor under their potential losses. And what one might call "the return of public seriousness"—a recognition that politics can be about life and death, and an associated conviction that posturing must give way to realism—was itself a result of the return of national security as a key concern.

It must be recalled that a careful review of the explanations offered for the midterm election pattern of presidential loss indicated that Republican losses were likely to be slim regardless of the issue content of the election. Of course, some of those explanations—like lower turnout for the president's party and national conditions focusing on presidential approval—were themselves impacted by national security. Altogether, national security effects combined with a context that already indicated the probability of minimal presidential party losses to produce an historic victory for the presidential party. It was this combination that helps explain why Bush won his midterm when so many other wartime presidents—who enjoyed larger coattails and surge effects two years earlier, and whose parties were overexposed—did not.

All of which brings us back to 1962. After election day, analysts like Michael Barone explicitly compared 2002 to 1962, focusing on the way that the surprising results of both midterm elections cleared away questions about the presidents' legitimacy owing to the nature of their victories two years before.[66] There are also other reasons, more germane to our discussion here, for such a comparison. In both years, national security was central. Like Democrats in 2002, Republicans in 1962 were at the mercy of events, with the Cuban missile crisis and its favorable resolution the focus of attention. As well, the structural context was amazingly similar. Like Bush in 2000, Kennedy in 1960 had no coattails; Democrats lost twenty seats in the House. Like Bush in 2000, Kennedy in 1960 experienced no voter "surge," and either held a tiny popular vote lead or trailed slightly in the popular vote.[67] Indeed, of all the national security presidents listed in Table 3.1 on page 42, Kennedy and Bush are the only two to have experienced *both* negative congressional coattails and no significant popular vote "surge" in their presidential election year. And national conditions in 1962 included a slowly recovering economy and high presidential approval ratings, which Kennedy resolved to put on the line by undertaking an extensive travelling campaign for Democratic candidates. His planned 19,000-mile campaign trip was cut well short by the onset of the missile crisis, but his point was made.[68] In both cases, an American president dismissed by many as a "lightweight" defeated the expectations of history with the help of national security combined with a structural floor that put him within reach of that result.

NOTES

1. See Andrew E. Busch, *Horses in Midstream: U.S. Midterm Elections and Their Consequences, 1894–1998* (Pittsburgh, PA: University of Pittsburgh Press, 1999).
2. Malia Rulon, "Inspired by Sept. 11, Political Newcomers Jump In," *Denver Post*, 1 November 2002, p. 6-A. The five included a flight attendant, a pilot, an attorney, a single mother, and, in the most notable case, a New York fireman who had responded at Ground Zero on September 11 (Joe Finley). Despite receiving considerable attention for their connection to 9/11, all lost to well-financed incumbents in tough districts.
3. Angus Campbell, "Surge and Decline: A Study of Electoral Change," *Public Opinion Quarterly* 24 (1960), pp. 387–419; James E. Campbell, *The Presidential Pulse of Congressional Elections* (Lexington, KY: University Press of Kentucky, 1993).
4. Bruce I. Oppenheimer, James A. Stimson, and Richard W. Waterman, "Interpreting U.S. Congressional Elections: The Exposure Thesis," *Legislative Studies Quarterly* 11 (1986), pp. 227–247. This theory can apply to both presidential and midterm year congressional elections.

5. Gerald H. Kramer, "Short-Term Fluctuation in U.S. Voting Behavior," *American Political Science Review* 65 (1971), pp. 131–143; Howard S. Bloom and Douglas H. Price, "Voter Response to Short-Run Economic Conditions: The Asymmetric Effect of Prosperity and Recession," *American Political Science Review* 69 (1975), pp. 1240–1255; James E. Piereson, "Presidential Popularity and Midterm Voting at Different Electoral Levels," *American Journal of Political Science* 19 (1975), pp. 683–702; Edward R. Tufte, *Political Control of the Economy* (Princeton, NJ: Princeton University Press, 1978); Gary C. Jacobson and Samuel Kernell, *Strategy and Choice in Congressional Elections* (Boston: Little, Brown, 1981); Gary C. Jacobson, *The Politics of Congressional Elections*, 3rd ed. (New York: HarperCollins, 1992).
6. Robert S. Erikson, "The Puzzle of Midterm Loss," *Journal of Politics* 50 (1988), pp. 1011–1029.
7. Alberto Alesina and Howard Rosenthal, *Partisan Politics, Divided Government, and the Economy* (Cambridge, MA: Cambridge University Press, 1995); Samuel Kernell, "Presidential Popularity and Negative Voting: An Alternative Explanation to the Midterm Decline of the President's Party," *American Political Science Review* 71 (1977), pp. 44–66.
8. For a similar argument regarding the context of the 2002 elections, see James E. Campbell, "The 2002 Midterm Election: A Typical or an Atypical Midterm?" *PS: Political Science and Politics* 36, no. 2 (April 2003), pp. 203–207.
9. Dan Freedman, "Top Demo Sees Bush Loss in '04; McAuliffe Says Economy Is Key to Victory," *San Antonio Express-News*, 10 November 2001, p. A-21.
10. Adam Clymer, "G.O.P. Is Seen Ahead by Nose in House Races," *New York Times*, 27 September 2002, p. A-1.
11. "White House Disputes Gore's Criticisms," *Milwaukee Journal Sentinel*, 28 September 2002, p. A-10.
12. "Bush and Daschle Comments on Security and Politics," *New York Times*, 26 September 2002, p. A-15.
13. At a campaign stop in Cedar Rapids, Iowa, the day before the election, Bush said the Senate "is more interested in special interests, which dominate the dialogue in Washington, D.C., than they are in protecting the American people." Mike Allen, "Bush Urges Bipartisan Relations," *Washington Post*, 8 November 2002, p. A-12.
14. Howard Fineman, "How Bush Did It," *Newsweek*, 18 November 2002.
15. See Tatsha Robertson, "War Stance Influencing Close Races; Even Veterans Face Queries on Patriotism," *New York Times*, 1 November 2002, p. A-3. The Georgia race occasioned much bitterness among Democrats, who felt Republicans were questioning Cleland's "patriotism." Republicans countered that they were focusing on Cleland's liberal voting record and judgment on national security issues, which were legitimate targets.
16. See John H. Cushman, "Democratic Congressman Asserts Bush Would Mislead U.S. on Iraq," *New York Times*, 30 September 2002, p. A-8.
17. Joan Vennochi, "Kerry Walks a Fine Line," *The Boston Globe*, 19 November 2002, p. A-23.
18. George Will, "Bush Seals Mandate by Just a Few Key Votes," *Washington Post*, 7 November 2002, p. 39.
19. David W. Moore and Jeffrey M. Jones, "Higher Turnout among Republicans Key to Victory," Gallup News Service, http://www.gallup.com/poll/releases/021107.asp (accessed November 7, 2002).
20. David W. Moore, "Bush Approval at 68%," Gallup News Service, http://www.gallup.com/poll/releases/021115.asp (accessed November 15, 2002).
21. Frank Newport, "New Poll Measures Support for Issues on GOP Legislative Agenda," Gallup News Service, http://gallup.com/poll/releases/pr021113.asp (accessed November 13, 2002).
22. Unlike the Gallup and Wirthlin polls, these Fox News polls were not open-ended but rather prompted voters to choose between the economy and jobs or terrorism and national security as the issues that should be "the highest priority for the nation." The nine states were Arkansas, Colorado, Georgia, Minnesota, Missouri, New Hampshire, New Jersey, South Dakota, and Texas. While there was not a complete correlation between Republican victories and states that chose national security, two of the three states that represented Republican takeaways did so. See http://www.foxnews.com/story/0,2933,69084,00.html (accessed November 8, 2002).
23. On security versus economy, see Wirthlin Worldwide, November 7, 2002, and Jeffrey M. Jones, "Economy, Terrorism Continue to Top List of Most Important Problems," Gallup News Service, http://www.gallup.com/poll/releases/pr021118.asp (accessed November 8, 2002). The Gallup poll showed a 51–37 split in favor of national security in mid-October and a 40-37 split in mid-November. on Democrats, see Lydia Saad, "Democratic Party Image Takes a

Post-Election Hit," Gallup News Service, http://www.gallup.com/poll/releases/pr021114. asp (accessed November 14, 2002).

24. This joint survey was commissioned by the Vietnam Veterans of America Foundation to examine the role of national security in the 2002 election. When ranking issues, voters placed the economy in their top two issues 43 percent of the time to 31 percent for national security. See http://www.greenbergresearch.com/publications/reports/vvafpostM.pdf.

25. Gallup post-election polls indicated that Democrats had won a four-point advantage among women voters, Republicans a sixteen-point advantage among men. David W. Moore and Jeffrey M. Jones, "Higher Turnout among Republicans Key to Victory," Gallup News Service, http://www.gallup.com/poll/releases/021107.asp. (accessed November 7, 2002). See also Jones, "Economy, Terrorism Continue to Top List."

26. Wirthlin Worldwide, November 7, 2002.

27. Miles Benson, "GOP Now Has Edge with Senior Voters," http://www.newhouse.com/ archive/benson012103.html.

28. David W. Moore and Jeffrey M. Jones, "Higher Turnout among Republicans Key to Victory," Gallup News Service, http://www.gallup.com/poll/release/021107.asp (accessed November 7, 2002). Greenberg and McInturff concurred that homeland security was the greatest single issue within the war on terrorism. This general conclusion is confirmed by the nine state Fox News polls, which uniformly showed two interlocking phenomena. First, voters who listed terrorism as their top issue voted Republican; a smaller group listing Iraq voted Democratic. In another poll question, two-thirds to three-fourths of voters supported military action against Iraq, and those voted Republican; but the smaller group opposing war with Iraq voted Democratic by much wider margins.

29. See http://www.greenbergresearch.com/publications/reports/nprn110602fq.pdf.

30. Wirthlin Worldwide, November 7, 2002; Moore, "Bush Approval at 68%."

31. George C. Edwards III, "Riding High in the Polls," in *The George W. Bush Presidency: Appraisals and Prospects*, ed. Colin Campbell and Bert Rockman (Washington, D.C.: Congressonal Quarterly, 2003).

32. Marc J. Hetherington and Michael Nelson, "Anatomy of a Rally Effect: George W. Bush and the War on Terrorism," *PS: Political Science & Politics* 36, no.1 (January 2003), pp. 37–42.

33. See Howard Fineman, "How Bush Did It," *Newsweek*, 18 November 2002, p. 28.

34. Jacobson, *The Politics of Congressional Elections*, 3rd ed. (New York: HarperCollins, 1992).

35. See "Bush in Campaign Mode," CNN Allpolitics, http://www.cnn.com/2002/ALL POLITICS/10/22/elec02.bush.campaigning.ap/index.html (accessed October 22, 2002).

36. Wirthlin Worldwide, November 7, 2002.

37. Elisabeth Bumiller and David E. Sanger, "Republicans Say Rove Was Mastermind of Big Victory," *New York Times*, 7 November 2002, p. B-1.

38. David M. Halbfinger, "Bush's Push, Eager Volunteers, and Big Turnout Led to Georgia's Sweep," *New York Times*, 10 November 2002, p. A-24.

39. Jeffrey Gentleman, "Senator Cleland Loses in an Upset to Republican Emphasizing Defense," *New York Times*, 6 November 2002, p. B-1.

40. David W. Moore and Jeffrey M. Jones, "Higher Turnout among Republicans Key to Victory," Gallup News Service, http://www.gallup.com/poll/releases/021107.asp (accessed November 7, 2002).

41. See Hetherington and Nelson, Note 7. Data originally from CBS News pre-election poll cited in Adam Nagourney and Janet Elder, "In Poll, Americans Say Both Parties Lack Vision," *New York Times*, 3 November 2002; David W. Moore and Jeffrey M. Jones, "Late Shift toward Republicans in Congressional Vote," www.gallup.com/poll/releases/pro21104.asp?Version=p (accessed November 4, 2002).

42. By election day 2002, that possibility was confirmed by polls showing higher approval ratings for Congress and no desire by the public for a wholesale cleaning out of incumbents. See "Voters in No Mood to 'Throw the Bums Out,'" Gallup News Service, http://www.gallup. com/poll/releases/pr021106.asp (accessed November 6, 2002).

43. The Wirthlin Report, November 7, 2002.

44. Senator George V. Voinovich (R-Ohio) ventured that this message "ignited the Republican base to come and vote for the president so he could get the job done." Jack Torry, "Democrats Still Can't Fathom Why They Were Routed," *Columbus Dispatch*, 10 November 2002, p. C-5. Evidence for this proposition can be seen in a Gallup poll taken days before the 2002 election, in which adults nationwide preferred a Democratic Congress over a Republican Congress by a 27-25 margin but *likely voters* preferred a Republican Congress over a Democratic

one by a 38-29 margin. "Voters in No Mood to 'Throw the Bums Out,'" Gallup News Service, http://www.gallup.com/poll/releases/pr021106.asp (accessed November 6, 2002).

45. Tom Freedman and Bill Knapp, "How Republicans Usurped the Center," *New York Times*, 8 November 2002, p. A-31.

46. It is also worth noting that a Gallup poll taken shortly after election day showed Americans by a 2-1 margin saying that it was a "good thing" that most of the president's judicial appointments would now be approved by the U.S. Senate. Newport, "New Poll Measures Support for Issues on GOP Legislative Agenda."

47. See James Ceaser and Andrew Busch, *Upside Down & Inside Out: American Politics and the Election of 1992* (Lanham, MD: Rowman & Littlefield, 1993).

48. John Fonte, "Homeland Politics," *National Review*, 2 June 2003, p. 27.

49. For a more complete exposition on this subject, see Andrew E. Busch, "The Return of Public Seriousness," *Claremont Review of Books* (Fall 2001), pp. 4–5.

50. See Fineman, "How Bush Did It"; Timothy Noah, "Democrats 36,000: Where's That Emerging Democratic Majority?" *Slate*, http://www.slate.msn.com/?id=2073779&device= (accessed 11 November 2002).

51. Michael Barone, "No More 49% Nation," *U.S. News & World Report*, 18 November 2002, p. 33.

52. Todd S. Pardum and David E. Rosenbaum, "Bush's Stumping for Candidates Is Seen as a Critical Factor in Republican Victory," *New York Times*, 7 November 2002, p. B-4.

53. E. J. Dionne, "Brilliant Politics, At a Price," *Washington Post*, 22 November 2002, p. A-41.

54. E. J. Dionne, ". . . With No Battle Plan," *Washington Post*, 12 November 2002, p. A-25.

55. "How GOP Whipped Democrats on Homeland Issue," *Newsday*, 12 November 2002, p. A-26.

56. Philip Matier, Andrew Ross, "Feinstein to Demos: Time to Get Tough," *San Francisco Chronicle*, 24 November 2002, p. A-23.

57. Marc Sandalow, "Bush Made Democrats' Tune His Own," *San Francisco Chronicle*, 25 November 2002, p. A-17.

58. "Agony and Ecstasy of the Election; On the Right: President 'Earned Our Gratitude,'" *Baltimore Sun*, 17 November 2002, p. F-1. For similar analyses, see Zev Chafets, "It's the War, Stupid," *New York Daily News*, 17 November 2002, p. 41; "Disingenuousness Contributed to Huge Democratic Disaster," *Tampa Tribune*, 7 November 2002, p. 18; David Sarasohn, "Ailing Democrats Must Discover the World," *New Orleans Times-Picayune*, 30 November 2002, p. 7.

59. Elaine C. Kamarck, "Democrats Lost the Power of Ideas," *Newsday*, 8 November 2002, p. A-41.

60. Gregory Michaelidis, "The Wrong Lessons on Foreign Policy," *San Diego Union-Tribune*, 21 November 2002, p. B-13.

61. Al From, "What's Next for the Democrats? Our Party Needs to Embrace Tax Cuts . . . and Get the Big Things Right," *Wall Street Journal*, 14 November 2002, p. A-14.

62. Harold Ford, Jr., "Why I Should Be Minority Leader," *Washington Post*, 13 November 2002, p. A-27. See also "Party Fault Lines," *Newsday*, 11 November 2002, p. A-14; Steve Israel, "Path of Moderation Is Democrats' Best Road," *Newsday*, 20 November 2002, p. A-32; Jim Tharpe, "Zell Miller Rips His Party's Leaders," *Atlanta Journal-Constitution*, 9 November 2002, p. A-1.

63. For example, see Donald Green and Eric Schickler, "Winning a Battle, Not a War," *New York Times*, 12 November 2002, p. A-31.

64. James P. Pinkerton, "GOP Victory Is a Mandate for War," *Newsday*, 7 November 2002, p. A-39.

65. *Ottawa Citizen*, 7 November 2002, p. A-16; *San Francisco Chronicle*, 7 November 2002, p. A-1; *London Independent*, 10 November 2002, p. 27; *San Antonio Express-News*, 7 November 2002, p. B-6.

66. Michael Barone, "No More 49% Nation," *U.S. News & World Report*, 18 November 2002, p. 33; Michael Barone, "Party Like It's 1962," *Wall Street Journal Opinion Journal*, http://www.opinionjournal.com/editorial/feature.html?id=110002599 (accessed November 9, 2002).

67. Conventional wisdom holds that Kennedy had a national popular vote plurality of 114,673 votes out of almost 69 million cast. However, this calculation assigns all of the votes for the top Kennedy elector in Alabama to Kennedy as his official vote from Alabama, despite the fact that only five of the state's eleven electors were Kennedy electors; the remainder ran as "unpledged" Democrats. If one adjusts the Kennedy total to give him 5/11 of his top vote, he actually winds up slightly behind Nixon in the national popular vote total. See Neal R. Peirce and Lawrence D. Longley, *The People's Choice: The Electoral College in American History and the Direct Vote Alternative* (New Haven, CT: Yale, 1981), pp. 65–67; Walter McDougall, "The Slippery Statistics of the Popular Vote," *New York Times*, 16 November 2000, p. A-35.

68. See Theodore C. Sorenson, *Kennedy* (New York: Harper & Row, 1965), p. 688; Hugh Sidey, *John F. Kennedy, President*, 2nd ed. (New York: Atheneum, 1964), p. 354.

Ideological Conflict
in the President's Cabinet

Shirley Anne Warshaw

GETTYSBURG COLLEGE

How the war on terrorism was managed in the White House after the September 11, 2001, terrorist attacks cannot be separated from how the White House managed foreign or domestic policy before the terrorist attacks. The policymaking apparatus of the Bush administration was dominated by conservatives from the moment that the president took office. Policies were developed and implemented within the core principles of a conservative Republican ideology. Both the White House staff and the cabinet were dominated by conservatives, with the exception of moderates Colin Powell and Condoleezza Rice.

The terrorist attacks of September 11 did not change how the administration ran domestic policy. Conservatives continued to manage departmental policy issues and administrative actions moved the conservative agenda forward. The attacks did provide a crisis in which the president had to pick and choose from his foreign policy advisors where there were deep personal and political divisions. Those divisions did not exist in the domestic policy arena. The terrorist attacks forced Bush for the first time to seriously weigh very different viewpoints. How Bush moved from a cohesive decision-structure in domestic policy to a noncohesive and often combative decision-structure in foreign policy is the focus of this chapter. Not surprisingly, given the tightly knit structure he had created for domestic policy, Bush was not comfortable in the tugs of war between the various political factions of the war cabinet and soon sided with the conservatives. Powell, a moderate in an administration of conservatives, quickly was relegated to a secondary role in the war cabinet. This chapter examines how the decision-structure in the White House and the cabinet was dominated by conservatives, leading to predictable winners and losers in the president's war cabinet during the war in Afghanistan.

PRE-SEPTEMBER 11: THE WHITE HOUSE
BASED POLICY-MAKING STRUCTURE

Throughout the 2000 presidential campaign, polls showed that the race between Texas Governor George W. Bush and Vice President Al Gore was at a statistical dead heat. As election day grew closer, pollsters regularly proclaimed the election too close to call.[1] Neither Bush nor Gore was willing to step forward with strong policy initiatives for fear of alienating any segment of the voting public. Consequently, the proposals put forth by Bush during the campaign focused on nondivisive issues designed to gain a broad base of support. These issues included education reform, tax cuts, and rebuilding the national defense. Most other positions by Bush were wrapped around the campaign rhetoric of "compassionate conservatism." Bush proclaimed himself a conservative and routinely offered his support for the pro-life agenda and the right to bear arms, but few other specific domestic positions. His position on foreign policy was even more vague than his position on domestic policy, largely due to his limited experience in the international arena.

The election proved as divisive as the polls had shown, with Gore winning a slim popular majority but not the electoral majority. Florida held the votes to tip the electoral college either way. After a month of lawsuits in Florida, the U.S. Supreme Court finally resolved the issue supporting the claim to victory by Bush. The divisiveness of the election, however, was not lost on the Bush staff who quickly sought to repair the political damage. During the transition period, president-elect Bush designed a cabinet-building strategy to repair the political damage from the 2000 election and to build new electoral coalitions for 2004. Bush emulated the Clinton model for cabinet-building, which had included more women and minorities than any cabinet in history.[2] The president-elect began to build bridges to constituencies he had failed to capture in the 2000 election.

THE CABINET-BUILDING STRATEGY: DIVERSITY IN APPOINTMENTS

In order to build bridges to constituencies lost in the 2000 election, the Bush political team sought to create a cabinet with gender and ethnic diversity, as Bill Clinton had done eight years earlier. The Bush cabinet, once completed, consisted of four women, two African Americans, two Asian Americans, one Hispanic, and one Arab American. The members of the cabinet, while ethnically and gender diverse, were not well known within the national electorate. Only Secretary of State Colin Powell had a national reputation, having served very publicly both as chairman of the joint chiefs of staff during the Persian Gulf War and as head of a private foundation called America's Promise—the Alliance for Youth.[3] Prior to the 1996 election many had hoped to recruit Powell for the Republican presidential nomination. Historian Stephen Ambrose led the drive for Powell to run for president, describing

Powell's personal and wartime leadership as reminiscent of Dwight Eisenhower.[4] In spite of broad-based support for Powell, Powell himself refused to seek the nomination citing family opposition. His wife was particularly opposed to the nomination, fearing for his safety.

Subcabinet appointments in the administration came predominately from the ranks of conservative organizations and business groups and had little diversity. Press Secretary Ari Fleischer noted in February, 2001, on the difference between the cabinet appointees and the subcabinet appointees, "[I]t will be difficult for the subcabinet to reflect the ethnic diversity even of his [Bush's] own cabinet, much less the public at large, given the slim roster of minority Republicans from which to choose."[5] Subcabinet appointments were chosen for their conservative credentials, not their public face or management skills as the cabinet had been. The exception was the Department of State, where Colin Powell chose from the career ranks of the foreign service rather than from the political hiring lists of the White House.

All subcabinet nominees were reviewed and cleared through Clay Johnson, director of the White House personnel office. Johnson or his staff interviewed every candidate for a political appointment in the departments.[6] In addition, Johnson regularly met with staff from the White House office of political affairs, which reviewed the names of all political nominees before they were seen by Johnson's office.[7] Appointments that were cleared had both Republican and conservative credentials, and many had served in the Reagan and Bush I administrations. A survey by the *National Journal* found that 43 percent of political appointees had worked in top positions during the Bush I administration and 31 percent in the Reagan administration.[8] Many of the political appointments had strong business connections and often had represented lobbying groups.[9]

In addition to a pro-business orientation, the political ranks were filled with conservatives with a pro-life, religious orientation. Writing in the *Washington Post* on the conservative orientation of subcabinet appointees, Dana Milbank and Ellen Nakashima noted that "Bush's collection of 'movement' conservatives, those identified with moral, religious, or small movement causes, is wide-ranging."[10] The religious agenda had been openly put forth by President Bush himself.[11] Bush supported, for example, interweaving government and religion in programs that were moved forward by a newly created White House staffing unit called the Office of Faith Based and Community Initiatives.[12] His focus on religion included describing the job of political leaders as "calling upon the love that exists not because of government, that exists because of a gracious and loving God."[13] Vice President Cheney reinforced a strong religious orientation when he said, "Every great and meaningful achievement in this life requires the active involvement of the One who placed us here for a reason."[14]

The effort to dominate the subcabinet appointments with conservatives was moved quickly through the domestic cabinet with little opposition. The process was mirrored at the Defense Department but not at the State Department. At the Department of Defense, a group of conservative defense strategists led by Paul Wolfowitz dominated the subcabinet.[15] Wolfowitz, a conservative Republican, had served as Dean of the Johns Hopkins University School of Advanced International Studies following jobs in the Reagan Department of Defense and Department of State under George H. W. Bush.[16] He and Rumsfeld supported the appointment of a host of conservative Republicans from the Reagan and Bush I administrations, including E. C. Aldridge (Under Secretary of Defense for Acquisition, Technology, and Logistics), Dov Zakheim (Comptroller), David Chu (Under Secretary of Defense for Personnel and Readiness) and Douglas Feith (Under Secretary of Defense for Policy).[17]

In contrast, only Secretary of State Colin Powell objected to recruiting political conservatives to fill subcabinet jobs. Powell preferred to fill his political appointments with seasoned veterans in foreign policy, often from the career ranks, and from a small cadre of long-time associates. As his chief deputy, Powell chose Richard Armitage, who was his closest friend from their days together in the George H. W. Bush administration. Armitage, among his other positions, had been Special Emissary to Jordan during the Gulf War.

Powell quickly became a rebel within the White House inner circle for his refusal to abide by the political hiring rules. Powell chose many of his senior staff from the career ranks within the State Department. For example, he chose Marc Grossman as Under Secretary for Political Affairs. Grossman, a foreign service officer since 1976, had served as Director General of the Foreign Service, Ambassador to Turkey, and Assistant Secretary of State for European Affairs. Powell also chose Alan P. Larson, a career foreign service officer since 1973 as Under Secretary for Economic, Business, and Agricultural Affairs; William A. Eaton, a career foreign service officer since 1979 as Assistant Secretary for the Bureau of Administration; and Maura Harty, a career foreign service officer since 1981 for Assistant Secretary of the Bureau of Consular Affairs. For Under Secretary of Global Affairs, Powell brought in Paula Dobriansky, the vice president and director of the Washington Office of the Council of Foreign Relations. Although not a career foreign service officer, Dobriansky was not part of the political hiring network that was evident in other departments. As one columnist noted in an article on hiring in the State Department, "Powell relies on the professional staff and that has meant a lot of people in State [are promoted]. In his first few months there, he has made Foreign Service professionals the core of his management"[18]

Rumsfeld moved closer into the White House inner circle through his decisions on subcabinet appointees. Rumsfeld had served as director of the Office of Economic Opportunity and the Director of the Economic Stabilization Program under Richard Nixon and as White House staff coordinator and secretary of defense for Gerald Ford.[19] Rumsfeld also had political capital in the White House from his relationship with Vice President Cheney.

Cheney had worked for Rumsfeld first in Congress and then in the Nixon White House. When tapped to be White House staff coordinator for President Ford in 1974, Rumsfeld turned to Cheney again to serve as his deputy. Cheney followed Rumsfeld into the staff coordinator position in 1975 when Rumsfeld was appointed secretary of defense by Ford. Their bond continued throughout the years as Cheney was later appointed secretary of defense by George H. W. Bush and sought Rumsfeld's advice. By the time both joined the administration of George W. Bush, their paths had repeatedly intersected.

Although Powell had worked closely with Cheney and George H. W. Bush during the Persian Gulf War, he had never been part of George W. Bush's inner circle, both due to his political ideology and his independent political base. Powell, whose political ideology was more moderate than that of Bush and most members of the administration, was openly pro-choice and supported affirmative action.[20] During the 2002 presidential campaign, Powell had rarely been sent to lobby for votes for fear that his pro-choice positions would alienate members of the conservative Republican base. Only Powell, of all the members of the cabinet, was a political moderate. While he had never been part of the conservative inner circle of friends that Bush turned to, he failed to anticipate how tightly the network of conservative political activists would control decision-making in the war on terrorism.

MANAGING THE CONSERVATIVE POLICY AGENDA: WHITE HOUSE CONTROL

The management team in the White House was led by a troika consisting of political strategist Karl Rove, communications director Karen Hughes, and chief of staff Andrew Card. Rove and Hughes had been brought to the White House directly from the campaign, where each had played a major role in the successful election. Both had also worked for Bush in Texas, where he was in his second term as governor, and both had Bush's ear. He rarely made major decisions without discussing them with Rove and Hughes first.

Rove had played a pivotal role as Bush's campaign manager and chief political strategist in the 2000 presidential election. Rove subsequently became the political strategist for the new president and subjected all policy issues to the political lens of the 2004 election. Policies that jeopardized political coalitions were questioned if not placed on hold. As the director of the newly created White House Office of Strategic Initiatives, Rove became the power center of the White House.[21]

Card, however, had not played a major role in the 2002 presidential campaign and served only as an occasional advisor. He was chosen for the chief of staff position based on the recommendation of George H. W. Bush, for whom Card had served as deputy chief of staff under John Sununu and as secretary of transportation.[22] After leaving government in 1993, he became the chief executive of the American Automobile Association. His reputation as a Washington insider provided the important Beltway connections that the Texas team lacked.

Although given the top White House position, Card was always part of a troika with Hughes and Rove. Rove and Hughes drove the policy agenda and how that agenda would be communicated to the public. Card was charged with moving that agenda through the administrative or legislative process. The engine of the White House policy process centered on Rove, who endeavored to ensure that policy initiatives were part of a larger strategy to build political coalitions that would reelect Bush in 2004. Rove's title, director of the office of strategic initiatives, was indicative of the policy role he played. Not surprisingly, the key roles that Rove and Hughes played in managing policy and communications was seen in their placement in the White House phone directory. Rove was placed directly under the president, with Hughes below Rove, followed by Card. Their placement in the directory paralleled their influence with the president. The three members of the White House staff with the greatest access to the president also had the most power in the White House.

The troika focused primarily on domestic issues. In essence, Secretary of Defense Donald Rumsfeld had been given free rein by the president to change the way the department of defense looked at warfare. Rumsfeld wanted a stronger orientation toward innovative weaponry, air defense systems, and more mobile units. He was willing to battle the defense establishment to achieve these goals, including a major battle over the $11 billion tank development program, the Crusader, that the army wanted.[23] Rumsfeld killed the tank development program, in spite of active opposition from the army, arguing that tanks were too slow and cumbersome to continue limited funding. Rather, he wanted funding for new weapons systems, such as advanced fighter planes and satellite-based weapons.

Since the primary function of the troika was to move the conservative agenda forward and to protect the president's political base, Rumsfeld had authority to revamp the defense establishment. Bush had publicly supported revitalizing the department of defense and how Rumsfeld chose to do that went largely unchallenged by the White House staff. After all, they reasoned, Rumsfeld had more experience dealing with defense issues, as a former secretary of defense in the Ford administration, than anyone in the White House. It should be pointed out here that Rove and Hughes apparently carefully monitored Powell. Bob Woodward notes in *Bush at War*, "Whenever Powell was too out in front on an issue and became the public face of the administration, the political and communications apparatus at the White House reined him in, kept him out of the limelight."[24]

In addition, Rumsfeld had the support of Vice President Cheney for his initiatives in the Department of Defense. Rumsfeld's personal relationship with Cheney was mirrored by Paul Wolfowitz's relationship with Lewis Libby, the vice president's chief of staff. Wolfowitz had been Libby's professor at Yale University, where they had become friends and in future years would become colleagues.[25] The political views of Rumsfeld, Cheney, Wolfowitz, and Libby were all similar, directed at reshaping the military establishment and building a technologically superior defense system. In addition, all were viewed as neoconservatives, sharing a unilateral perspective of America's international role. Cheney's input into foreign-policy decision-making was further enhanced by thirteen foreign-policy staffers that were added to the vice president's office. Cheney chose not to rely on the eighty foreign-policy staffers in the National Security Council but rather to create his own in-house, foreign-policy think-tank.[26]

In contrast to the nearly unwavering support that Rumsfeld had from the White House and from Vice President Dick Cheney, Secretary of State Colin Powell did not fare as well. Powell lacked the conservative focus, the clear direction, and the alliance with Cheney that Rumsfeld had. In addition, there was always the fear within the White House that if Powell were given too prominent a role in the administration, he might rethink his political future. The result was a more careful handling of Powell, with National Security Advisor Condoleezza Rice working closely with him.

Rice's role working with Powell was a natural outgrowth of her position during the Bush I administration as a staff member of the National Security Council. She knew Powell from his service as chairman of the joint chiefs of staff and from other projects they had worked on together. Commenting at the end of a National Press Club speech in July 2001 on her relationship with Powell, Rice said, "I've actually never had a better working relationship with anyone. First of all, Colin Powell and I know each other from a very, very long time ago and we even know each other through family ties of [Powell's wife] Alma Powell, who is also from Birmingham, Alabama. We are good friends and good colleagues."[27]

Her background as an academic and provost of Stanford University separated her from the more politically oriented White House staff. Although she had served as the foreign-policy advisor for the 2000 presidential campaign for George W. Bush, she had never become part of the Hughes-Rove-Bush inner circle. She also had not become part of the Rumsfeld-Cheney-Wolfowitz-Lewis inner circle. Publicly, she said she wanted to be a neutral player, ensuring that the president had well-developed options from which to make decisions. As one observer noted, "Rice . . . acts more as an honest broker for Bush, a traffic cop for information and news."[28] But Rice's position as an honest broker was most likely created by her concern that only one viewpoint was being heard by the president from the foreign-policy inner circle. She thus became Powell's protector in the White House, ensuring that his voice was heard by the president.

In spite of the dominance of the neoconservative inner circle in foreign-policy decision-making, Rice created a hybrid version of multiple-advocacy for presidential decision-making. She worked to ensure that Bush heard Powell's views, which sought a multilateral approach to decisions, rather than the unilateral approach of Cheney and Rumsfeld. One can assume that her multiple-advocacy approach was both to protect Powell and to follow in the footsteps of Brent Scowcroft, national security advisor for George H. W. Bush. Rice had worked with Scowcroft in the NSC under Bush.

The concept of multiple advocacy had also been heavily used by Roger Porter, director of the domestic policy apparatus in the White House under both Gerald Ford and George H. W. Bush. Scowcroft had served under both Ford and Bush in the same position. Porter, a Harvard professor, created a policy-development structure that ensured various points of view were routinely heard by Bush before decisions were made.[29] The policy agenda in the Ford administration had incorporated broad policy input from within the administration under the multiple-advocacy system. While Rice did not create the broad-based, multiple-advocacy system that Porter encouraged, she did ensure that foreign-policy decisions included the perspectives of Powell in the decision process. In spite of Rice's attempts to include Powell in the foreign-policy decision-making process, the conservatives controlled the agenda. Powell appeared to have little influence within the administration, leading to a cover story in *Time Magazine* the day before the terrorist attacks calling Powell the "odd man out."[30]

The terrorist attacks of September 11 did not change how the administration ran domestic policy. Conservatives continued to manage departmental policy issues and administrative actions moved the conservative agenda forward. The attacks did provide a crisis in which the president had to pick and choose from his foreign-policy advisors where there were deep personal and political divisions. Those divisions did not exist in the domestic policy arena. The terrorist attacks forced Bush to weigh seriously very different viewpoints from his advisors for the first time. How Bush moved from a cohesive decision-structure in domestic policy to a noncohesive and often combative decision-structure in foreign policy is the focus of the next section of this chapter. Not surprisingly, given the tightly knit structure he had created for domestic policy, Bush was not comfortable in the push-and-pull between the various political factions of the war cabinet and soon sided with the conservatives. Powell, a moderate in an administration of conservatives, quickly was relegated to a secondary role in the war cabinet.

The inability of Rice to ensure that Powell was a central part of the decision-structure in the decision to invade Afghanistan and the months that followed imply that the multiple-advocacy structure failed. Rice was unable to ensure that Powell remained a key player in the decision process, since it appears that Bush consistently favored the positions of conservatives. Were Rice to have achieved a successful multiple-advocacy system, Bush would have been receptive to a broad range of Powell's positions.

The next section of this chapter examines how the war cabinet operated. A number of questions are posed, such as did the conservative policymaking staff within the White House become involved in decision-making on the war on terrorism in Afghanistan? If so, how well did the war cabinet collaborate for consensual recommendations to the president? The evidence indicates that the White House domestic policy apparatus *did not* become involved in the war on terrorism but did continue to move the conservative agenda forward. At no point did the events of the war on terrorism in Afghanistan derail the conservative agenda. The evidence also indicates that members of the president's war cabinet were regularly at odds along predictable political lines: Conservatives Dick Cheney and Donald Rumsfeld sought aggressive military actions and moderate Colin Powell sought limited military actions. Condoleezza Rice, the president's national security advisor, played the role of coordinator rather than advocate during the crisis, in spite of her more moderate political leanings.

POST–SEPTEMBER 11: THE WAR CABINET EMERGES

On the morning of September 11, 2001, terrorists flew hijacked commercial airplanes into the Pentagon and the World Trade Center. Passengers on another hijacked plane overcame the hijackers, leading to a fiery crash in the foothills of western Pennsylvania. President Bush had been visiting a school in Florida on the morning of September 11 when Chief of Staff Andrew Card whispered in his ear that the World Trade Center had been struck. The secret service took Bush out of the school and onto Air Force One, which soon was in the air. Using the secure telecommunications system from Air Force One, Bush called National Security Advisor Condoleezza Rice to begin to coordinate a response.

The events of September 11 shifted the president's attention from domestic policy to foreign policy. The "war on terrorism," as the president defined it, became his focus. Bush knew instinctively how he would structure this decision team. The model would be the war cabinet of the Persian Gulf War, which used the principals of the National Security Council. Bush directed Condoleezza Rice to set up meetings with CIA director George Tenet, Rumsfeld, and Powell as soon as possible. Vice President Cheney spoke by phone separately with Bush and also moved into the decision-structure. White House staff, with the exception of Chief of Staff Andrew Card, were excluded. Of note, neither Karl Rove nor Karen Hughes was invited into the deliberations for responding to the terrorist attacks. The war cabinet was in session: Only key players in national security policy had been invited. Perhaps for the first time in any major decision-making process since the Bush administration had taken office had the political machinery of the White House staff been excluded. But the politicization of the decision-making process continued into the war cabinet as conservatives overshadowed the lone moderate.

The decision-making process was controlled not only by conservatives, but by political loyalists Dick Cheney and Donald Rumsfeld. Powell had never been considered a political loyalist or even a friend to George W. Bush. The importance of loyalty was essential to the Bush family. Writing in his memoirs, former secretary of state James Baker said, "Friendship means a lot to George

[H. W.] Bush. Indeed his loyalty to friends is one of his defining personal strengths."[31] This sense of loyalty largely explains how George W. Bush relied totally on Rove and Hughes in the domestic arena and Cheney and Rumsfeld in the war on terrorism. Powell was never viewed by Bush or his senior White House advisors as a loyalist. The administration had been populated with loyalists, both personally and ideologically committed to George W. Bush. Powell never fit the model. Rice seemed to survive because of her close personal relationship to Bush, in spite of differences in ideology.[32]

CREATION OF THE WAR CABINET

"We're at war," Bush said soon after the terrorist attacks.[33] Rice began to coordinate the war cabinet as soon as she received the phone call from Air Force One. Each of the principals needed a clear assignment. Tenet was charged with finding the source of the terrorist attacks, Rumsfeld was charged with raising the military alert to protect against further attacks (which was raised to Def-Con 3), and Powell, who was in Peru to meet with newly elected President Alejandro Toledo, was charged with talking with President Vladimir Putin of Russia. Cheney, in his office when the attacks occurred, was taken by the Secret Service to an underground bunker of rooms in the White House known as the Presidential Emergency Operation Center (PEOC).[34] Cheney remained in constant contact with Bush and the others using video-conferencing and telephones in the PEOC.

By 3:30 P.M. on September 11, only hours after the first attack, Air Force One had landed at Offutt Air Force Base in Nebraska where Bush talked by conference call to the key players. A war cabinet had been created, consisting of Rumsfeld and Powell, Rice, Card, CIA director George Tenet, and Cheney. The relationships that had evolved during the first nine months of the administration would be tested by the terrorist attacks. How would Rumsfeld and Powell work together? Would Bush seek consensual decision-making or rely on certain members of the war cabinet more heavily than others? Would military action be the first response, instantly moving Rumsfeld to center stage? What role would Bush play with the war cabinet?

CIA director George Tenet provided Bush information almost immediately that indicated a terrorist group known as al Qaeda had coordinated the September 11 attacks. For a number of years the CIA had been closely monitoring al Qaeda.[35] Their record for terrorism against the United States was long, including attacks on U.S. embassies in Africa that led President Clinton to order cruise missiles fired at their training grounds in Afghanistan. Speaking on the day after the September 11 attacks, Bush said, "The deliberate and deadly attacks which were carried out against our country were more than acts of terror. They were acts of war."[36] Were we at war? If so, was al Qaeda the enemy? How would the war be conducted if the terrorists were cobbled together from a host of countries?

The war cabinet first met at 9:30 A.M. on September 12 in the White House to begin to analyze these questions. Tenet had become an instant player in the war cabinet as a result of his information linking the attacks to al Qaeda and identifying their training facilities in Afghanistan. Unlike the war cabinet in the 1990–1991 Persian Gulf War, the CIA director in the war on terrorism in 2001 had become a central player. Card, with little experience in foreign policy, took control of developing an executive order that froze assets of any organization suspected of funding al Qaeda.[37] From the White House staff, however, only Card and Rice were part of the decision-structure for the war on terrorism. Karl Rove and Karen Hughes for the first time in the administration had been locked out of the decision-making process.[38] By locking out Rove and Hughes, who had become known as the political arm of the White House, Bush implied to the American public and to the Democrats in Congress that decision-making in the war on terrorism would be free of politics. But would it? Could the political differences between various members of the war cabinet be overcome?

In an astute political move, by keeping Rove and Hughes out of the decision-making process on the war on terrorism, Bush had been able to contain possible Democratic accusations that moving the United States into war had political undercurrents. Rove was known throughout Washington as a political operative, always moving policy in political directions.[39] Bush wanted to ensure that public attention was not drawn to such questions as: Was the war simply being moved forward to gain points in the polls? Was it a "wag the dog" strategy?

In addition, members of the war cabinet were united in their dislike of Rove. Powell was known to refuse to accept calls from Rove.[40] Hughes, however, was directed by Bush to communicate the goals of the war on terrorism to the public. Woodward writes in *Bush at War*, "Bush told Hughes, 'You're in charge of how we communicate this war.'"[41] As Woodward further writes, "The problem was that the communications team was not going to know the details, especially about the covert CIA operations, and the American response was going to be delayed."[42] Hughes would be developing a communications strategy without being part of the decision-making process for the first time in her tenure in the administration.

The response of the president to the terrorist attacks was to some degree preordained by a conversation that he had had with Rumsfeld during the transition process. According to Bob Woodward, Rumsfeld condemned what he believed was too mild a response by the Clinton administration to the terrorist attacks in Africa. Rumsfeld flatly told Bush that if such terrorism were to happen again, a full-scale military response was in order. Bush agreed. The evidence thus pointed to a policymaking process early in the deliberations that would be dominated by Rumsfeld. There was also evidence that Bush would be most comfortable with "individuals whose talents, personalities, and loyalty he counted on," as Carl Cannon from the *National Journal* wrote of the players.[43] This, of course, implied that he would not count on Powell since he would always question Powell's loyalty.

After meeting on September 12, the president directed the members of the war cabinet to prepare response proposals and to convene on Saturday, September 15, at Camp David. By the Camp David meeting, Bush was convinced that al Qaeda had carried out the attacks. Intelligence from the CIA showed that al Qaeda operated primarily from Afghanistan, which left the question for the war cabinet: How to retaliate? Since the United States did not have diplomatic relations with Afghanistan, what options were available? George Tenet made the first proposal, seeking large sums of money for the CIA to fund coalitions of tribal leaders that would root out al Qaeda operatives and destroy their camps.[44] General George Shelton, Chairman of the Joint Chiefs of Staff, made the second proposal, which included three military options. Option one was to send in cruise missiles on known al Qaeda camps. Option two was to combine cruise missiles with manned bombers. Option three was to also send in ground troops.[45] The broader question then arose as to whether those harboring al Qaeda, such as the Taliban, would be subject to retaliation, too. Powell objected, arguing that the governments that he had talked with opposed any actions that did more than rooting out al Qaeda terrorists.

Positions of the war cabinet were first drawn at the September 15 Camp David meeting, with only Powell questioning unilateral military action in Afghanistan. Powell never opposed limited actions to find the al Qaeda network, but was consistently reluctant to support broader military action. He had questioned the worth of losing American soldiers to fight in Kuwait when he served George H. W. Bush and in the Balkans when he served Bill Clinton. For Powell, "war should be the politics of last resort."[46] The president's September 11 statement that the terrorist attacks were "acts of war" seemed to demand a strong military response, with everyone but Powell seemingly moving in that direction. Powell also was reluctant to move forward unilaterally, without international support. Bush had again sought action in his speech to the nation on September 20, telling the international community, "either you are with us or you are with the terrorists."[47]

By September 23, only twelve days after the terrorist attacks, the war cabinet had made no clear decision on what to do with al Qaeda. Tenet had been authorized by Bush to provide massive sums of money to the Northern Alliance and other tribal groups in Afghanistan to find Osama bin Laden and other leaders of al Qaeda. The early logic was that the millions of dollars that the CIA would funnel into Afghanistan would provide enough purchasing power for al Qaeda to be destroyed without military intervention. The ruling party of Afghanistan, the Taliban, proved more resilient than planned, often supporting al Qaeda and routinely fighting off the Northern Alliance. The Northern Alliance, one of the major tribal groups in northern Afghanistan, failed to purchase the necessary weapons with the CIA money and simply took the money for their own use.[48] The CIA found that other tribal groups that had received money in northern Afghanistan similarly failed to purchase the necessary weapons to fight al Qaeda.

Powell realized that the hawks in the war cabinet had won. If the CIA strategy had worked, perhaps a military assault by the United States would not have been necessary. The CIA strategy had failed and Powell understood military action was inevitable. The decision was made for an assault on Afghanistan to destroy al Qaeda using air power and later using ground troops. Bush had been prepared to order the air strikes from the moment he learned of the September 11 terrorist attacks. In an interview with Howard Fineman of *Newsweek* magazine, Bush described the reflex decision he made to use military force:

> I made the decision early. One, that we could win a guerrilla war with conventional means if we were able to use smart intelligence-gathering, and if we're able to get boots on the ground, to make sure our targets are more precise.[49]

On September 26 the conservatives in the war cabinet were pushing not only for a war in Afghanistan, but for a wider war that included Iraq.[50] The drive by the conservatives to include Iraq in the war on terrorism had actually been broached at the September 15 Camp David meeting of the war cabinet. Deputy Secretary of Defense Paul Wolfowitz had been present with Rumsfeld and had opened the discussion urging Bush to widen the war to Iraq. The issue didn't surface seriously again until September 26, after the initial decision had been made to send troops after al Qaeda into Afghanistan. Bush was toying with the idea of moving into Iraq after Afghanistan, but had not made a final decision. As he often did, he tested the idea by going public and gauging public reaction. He appeared in the Rose Garden with members of Congress accusing Saddam Hussein of Iraq of harboring al Qaeda terrorists but never signaled that military action was forthcoming.[51] This was to determine if public support existed for widening the war on terrorism.

Rumsfeld supported Wolfowitz's view that Iraq should be included in any military action against Afghanistan. He, too, began a public relations sortie and issued a statement that Iraq and al Qaeda had discussed safe harbors in Iraq. In order to counter the drums of war against Iraq, Powell himself went to Capitol Hill and announced that there was no visible link between Iraq and the terrorists of September 11. The drums of war for invading Iraq were mounting in the war cabinet and Powell was trying to mute the drums by mounting his own public relations campaign. In an interview on the CBS News *Face the Nation* on September 16, Powell refused to support the drums of war against Iraq. "At the moment," he said, "we see no fingerprints between Iraq and what happened last Tuesday."[52] The following week Rumsfeld was on *Face the Nation* and directly contradicted Powell. Rumsfeld said that Iraq had "harbored and assisted terrorist organizations engaged in terrorist acts in other countries."[53] Rumsfeld left no question that he had more intelligence information than Powell and he clearly had not shared it with Powell.

Powell had lost the battle in the war cabinet for a full-scale military invasion of Afghanistan and was now focusing his efforts to prevent the war from expanding into Iraq. Powell was also losing power in the war cabinet. According to Bob Woodward in *Bush at War,* Rumsfeld began demanding that he be involved in or approve all discussions that Powell had with other countries involving the war on terrorism.[54] Rumsfeld had moved another step toward marginalizing Powell.

Powell would continue to work on the international coalitions, but the military would be sent to Afghanistan, using Shelton's third option. It would be a full-scale military strike, using both airpower and ground troops. "Operation Enduring Freedom" was about to be launched.[55] When President Bush announced on October 7 that "Operation Enduring Freedom" was underway in Afghanistan, he also announced that food, medicine, and supplies were being sent to "starving and suffering men, women, and children" of Afghanistan.[56] This was a small victory for Powell, who had been able to build international support by arguing that the focus of the war was only on al Qaeda terrorists and not on Afghanistan or any other nation. But the war cabinet was now dominated by Donald Rumsfeld. According to Condoleezza Rice, Bush compared the war to a football game and named Rumsfeld as the quarterback.[57] Cheney's role is unclear at this point. He was spending most of his time at an undisclosed secret location for security reasons, maintaining daily contact with the war cabinet through secure telecommunications equipment. He gave no interviews to the press and few seem to have met with him. As a result, there is little information on his role at this point in the war cabinet except to speculate that he was supporting Rumsfeld and broad military action. Cheney did not provide any interviews to Bob Woodward for his series on the war cabinet in the *Washington Post* or for his book, which leaves another vacuum in the material available on Cheney's interaction with the war cabinet.

By October 15, one week after "Operation Enduring Freedom" began, the war cabinet met to determine how the CIA and the military could work cooperatively. Now Tenet was on the spot, since Rumsfeld viewed the CIA as having spent millions of dollars with no result and having lost valuable time. Rumsfeld was quickly gaining the upper hand, having first defeated Powell and now Tenet. Since Cheney had always been Rumsfeld's ally, Rumsfeld had become the dominant player in the war cabinet. Powell, conscious of his ever decreasing role in the war cabinet, had left the country to meet with Pakistan's President Pervez Musharraf.[58] Powell had been concerned throughout the war cabinet deliberations that opposition in Pakistan could topple Musharraf and destroy a critical ally.[59] For most of the week, Powell shuttled between India and Pakistan to bolster support for U.S. military action in Afghanistan.

By now, Powell was less concerned with how and when the United States went to war than how to maintain international support. Powell was consistently opposed to a unilateral approach in Afghanistan using only U.S. forces, which encouraged the philosophy of "America First."[60] For Powell, building international support for any military action in Afghanistan was essential. Rumsfeld had won the debate on what the U.S. response should be, but Powell remained determined to build international support for the war in Afghanistan. On October 19, Rumsfeld announced that the U.S. military would stay in Afghanistan until the country's ruling Taliban government and the al Qaeda network "are gone."[61] On October 31, 2001, the United States began carpet bombing in northern Afghanistan to destroy the Taliban and al Qaeda.[62]

The war cabinet was no longer meeting regularly. Cheney was no longer in an undisclosed location and had returned to making speeches at political dinners, such as he did on October 18 at the annual Al Smith dinner in New York City.[63] Powell and Bush had gone to Shanghai for the Asian-Pacific Economic Cooperation Summit in mid-October. Rumsfeld was at the Pentagon, giving daily press briefings on the war in Afghanistan.[64] Rumsfeld was not only prepared in his knowledge of the military activities, he was prepared in his off-the-cuff remarks. "We are patient, we are determined, we are committed,"[65] said Rumsfeld, in what must have been a well-thought-out remark. While Powell shunned the limelight, Rumsfeld grabbed it.

By November 4, Rumsfeld began to challenge Powell's shuttle diplomacy. Rumsfeld began a five-nation tour (Pakistan, India, Russia, Tajikistan, and Uzbekistan) to build support for the war on terrorism.[66] Could Powell have handled this trip? Did Rumsfeld distrust negotiations that Powell was conducting? While it is difficult to answer these questions, the most obvious answer is that Rumsfeld was exerting his power and trying again to marginalize Powell.

The lack of communication between Powell and Rumsfeld continued to grow. On November 9, Powell said in an interview that the United States did not plan an offensive on Kabul. That offensive took place only weeks later, which must have been in the planning stages by the Defense Department soon after September 11. It appears that the war cabinet had not been fully informed of the plans or Powell would have been less forthcoming with his statement.

By January 3, 2002, the war in Afghanistan was winding down. Rumsfeld announced that the role of the Taliban in Afghanistan had ended and that a new government would be formed. The military would continue to fight al Qaeda and look for Osama bin Laden, he said.[67] The war would have fewer air strikes but more ground troops. By now, the war cabinet had been meeting less and less often, with Rumsfeld managing the war in Afghanistan and Powell keeping the international coalition from dissolving.

POLITICS AND THE WAR ON TERRORISM

The war cabinet met rarely after the first few weeks following the terrorist attacks. In Reaganesque-fashion, the president relied on others to manage the war, giving Rumsfeld authority to determine how the war was conducted in Afghanistan and giving Powell authority to manage the international coalition.

The war cabinet had been created for limited reasons, dealing with the terrorists in Afghanistan, and for a limited span of time. Afghanistan had been taken militarily, a new regime had been put in place, and most al Qaeda members had been killed or captured or had surrendered. Some fled to neighboring countries and remained the target of U.S. special forces operations.

Not surprisingly, other issues surfaced to dominate the president's attention as the war on terrorism progressed. Domestically, the economy continued to fail. The Dow Jones industrial average was moving below 8,500, nearly 25 percent lower than when the administration took office. Throughout the spring and summer of 2002, corporate misconduct and bankruptcies dominated the news, with accusations that the Bush administration was not monitoring big business. In October, 2002, the nation was riveted by a series of sniper attacks over several weeks in Washington, D.C.

International issues heated up again surrounding Iraq and weapons of mass destruction. Iraq again became a central player in the spring of 2002 when Bush threatened military action if Iraq did not adequately ensure that they had no nuclear, biological, or chemical weapons. The hawks of the foreign-policy team, Cheney, Rumsfeld, and Wolfowitz, argued that Iraq was dangerous and must be dealt with. The lone dove of the foreign-policy team, Powell, argued for restraint and for working through the United Nations rather than a unilateral approach. For the first time in the deliberations of the war cabinet, Powell's views prevailed, but largely due to overwhelming international opposition to a unilateral approach. But Powell had not gained equal status in foreign-policy decision-making and remained a second-tier player during most of 2002.

For example, in March 2002, Bush sent the vice president rather than the secretary of state to meet with the heads of state of eleven Middle East countries to build support for widening the war to Iraq. One analyst quoted in *USA Today* described Cheney as "the diplomatic front man on this mission because Bush wanted to show we're serious."[68] To add insult to injury, Bush assigned a retired general, Anthony Zinni, to go to Israel to work on the Israeli-Palestinian conflict that had heated up again. The conservatives in the administration were managing not only the war on terrorism but related diplomatic issues normally handled by the Department of State. There is mounting evidence that Cheney's deputies often sat in on meetings with foreign dignitaries, rather than allowing Powell to be the sole spokesman for the administration.

Tensions continued in the Middle East throughout 2002, with numerous suicide bombings by Palestinians in Israel. When Israel used military force to respond, often with massive tank incursions into Palestinian towns, further bombings occurred. The cycle seemed never-ending. By April 2002, Powell had reemerged as a power player in the administration, becoming the person of the week for *Time Magazine*.[69] Where Cheney and Zinni had failed to resolve issues in Israel, Powell seemed to make progress. His star rose further as he appeared to be the voice of moderation during the fall of 2002 when Cheney and Rumsfeld supported unilateral military action against Iraq.

The question is whether Cheney and Rumsfeld will win the internal debates on using military force in Iraq. The lessons learned from Afghanistan is that they will. Powell will again be marginalized. Will Powell survive in the administration or have the conservatives won?

It appears that Powell is determined to remain in the administration, understanding that he plays a secondary role to Rumsfeld and Cheney. But Powell is a realist and knows that Bush will not fire him given his own strong political base. As the only moderate in the cabinet, Powell maintains an important role in an administration constantly challenging political policy moves.

But the manner in which the administration focused on moving conservatives into key positions was an early indication that Powell could not survive internecine fighting. He had few political allies in the administration and few in the White House. Only National Security Advisor Condoleezza Rice appeared to be an ally, but she viewed her role as the national security policy coordinator not as an ally of any single cabinet officer.

CONCLUSION

Barely three months after the September 11 terrorist attacks, President Bush went to Capitol Hill to deliver his 2002 State of the Union address. By then the war on terrorism had become the focus of U.S. foreign policy. In the State of the Union address, Bush left no question as to where foreign policy had moved. It had moved from a broad international set of policies to a single policy to fight the war on terrorism. In unequivocal language as to his position, he stated in the January address,

> From public diplomacy to a prepared military, National Security is the result of a strong military policy. . . . Our national security depends on success in the war on terrorism.[70]

Six months later, on June 1, 2002, President Bush spoke to the cadets at the U.S. Military Academy at West Point and presented the new national security strategy that he had alluded to in the State of the Union address. He cited new strategic goals for the United States that were directed at preventing "our enemies from threatening us, our allies, and our friends, with weapons of mass destruction." In addition, he promised to strengthen "alliances to defeat global terrorism and work to prevent attacks against our friends."[71]

The conservatives had won the war for managing the nation's foreign policy. Foreign policy was now a more structured policy centered on a military strategy that prevented "our enemies from threatening us." Rumsfeld rather than Powell would be the architect of this strategy, leaving Powell to build the diplomatic bridges and coalitions required by the military posturing. However, Bush had no qualms about preempting Powell from certain diplomatic missions, such as when he sent Vice President Cheney and General Zinni to the Middle East. Powell's role in the war on terrorism and in other national security plans seemed to be secondary to other players in the war cabinet.

There is also the question of whether the president's chief political advisor, Karl Rove, eventually did move into policy discussions on the war on terrorism. In a story in the *National Review,* Karl Rove is discussed as being "kept abreast of" foreign-policy issues and having "a voice on important foreign-policy decisions."[72] The concept of Rove discussing the war on terrorism in meetings with Card and Bush seems plausible, given that the president needed to rally public support for his positions.

Whether Rove was part of the decision-making rather than simply responding to the decision-making in order to send the message is unclear. But one suspects that Rove did have some role in decision-making with the war on terrorism. Given his animosity with Powell, it is again reasonable to assume that he routinely supported Rumsfeld and Cheney and sought to minimize Powell's role. As *BBC News* described Rove soon after the president took office, "Within the White House, George Bush's political advisers hold real power; the undisputed chief is his former campaign manager and strategist Karl Rove."[73] In yet another discussion of Rove's role in decision-making, the *New York Times* noted the following in a story on Rove's lobbying against easing travel restrictions to Cuba: "Mr. Rove has denied a profound role in foreign policy affairs, though White House advisers acknowledge his hand in decisions affecting the Middle East, steel tariffs and Mr. Bush's trip with the President of Poland to Michigan, a heavily Polish state that Mr. Bush lost in 2000."[74] It seems unlikely that Rove would abandon the politics of the war on terrorism given his focus on the 2004 presidential election.

Had politics been the dominant factor in marginalizing Powell? To quote Ari Fleischer, the president's press secretary, "I don't think you would expect the president to appoint people who hold wildly different views than he does."[75] Bush wanted loyalty and wanted symmetry in the views of the people around him. Powell offered neither and thus was not a key player in the White House decision-making in the war on terrorism in Afghanistan. The administration was dominated by conservatives and political loyalists. Powell was always an outsider.

As we examine the decisions made by the war cabinet through this political lens, it becomes apparent that Powell was consistently marginalized by Bush, Rumsfeld, and Cheney. Surprisingly, Rice does not seem to have been a major influence in the decision-making process. Are there any similar cases of a single cabinet member such as Colin Powell being marginalized in the decision-making process? There appear to be several cases, although none fit the Powell scenario. For example, during the Nixon administration, Henry Kissinger dominated foreign-policy decisions and marginalized both Secretary of Defense Melvin Laird and Secretary of State William Rogers. Even when moved to Secretary of State, Kissinger dominated the foreign-policy decision process including issues related to the war in Vietnam, detente with the Soviet Union, and opening diplomatic relations with mainland China. Nixon and Kissinger developed the policies on the Soviet Union and China without consulting the secretaries of state or defense.

Another example can be seen when President Carter made the decision to send a rescue mission to free the hostages in Tehran in 1979 without consulting his Secretary of State, Cyrus Vance. Another example was when President Reagan made the decision to fund the Nicaraguan Contras in 1986 without telling his secretary of state or secretary of defense. Both Carter's national security advisor, Zbigniew Brzezinski, and Reagan's national security advisor, John Poindexter, made decisions with the president with minimal input from cabinet officers.

We can therefore find a number of precedents from presidents acting with minimal input from their broader foreign-policy decision team. Decisions were made in these cases by the president and a small group of advisors, usually centered around the national security advisor. The fact that George W. Bush did not rely heavily on Colin Powell is not unusual for presidential decision-making in foreign policy. Nixon, for example, made statements early in the administration that he would work with Henry Kissinger to develop the administration's foreign-policy strategy.

There are no obvious models for a president and other members of his cabinet marginalizing a single cabinet member for political reasons, as the Bush war cabinet did with Colin Powell. Perhaps the closest model is that of the Carter administration, when Cyrus Vance was marginalized in the later months as he continually opposed military action to rescue the hostages. Vance, who had been chosen for the cabinet due to his ties to the establishment of the Democratic Party, had never been close to Carter and his White House staff. Nor had Vance built a strong rapport with national security advisor Zbigniew Brzezinski. Vance, the only member of the Carter cabinet with a national political reputation, never meshed with Carter's Georgia advisors. While this is not a perfect match to the relationship that Powell had with Bush and his advisors, there are certain parallels.

The conclusion can therefore by drawn that Powell's relationship with the foreign-policy decision-making team was weakened by his own political stature and his political ideology. While there have been fractures in foreign-policy teams in other administrations, this seems to be the first case of a fracture based primarily on a single cabinet member being marginalized for political differences. Even Clinton's secretary of defense, Bill Cohen, who was a Republican, was not marginalized the way Powell was. The reason for Powell's marginalization seems to be that the decision-makers in the Bush administration were all politically conservative and had no diversity of political thought. Only Colin Powell varied from the political monolith created in the hiring process. Multiple advocacy was not part of the decision-structure in this single-minded administration.

NOTES

1. See for example the lead paragraph of an election article calling the race "too close to call." Report by Major Garrett, "Gore Not Tapping Clinton Despite Close Campaign," www.cnn.com (accessed October 19, 2000).
2. Stephen Hess, *Organizing the Presidency,* 3rd ed. (Washington, D.C.: Brookings Institution, 2002), pp. 168–169.
3. See http://www.whitehouse.gov/state for a biography of Colin Powell.
4. Stephen E. Ambrose, "Looking for a Hero," *Newsweek,* 11 September 1995, p. 34. See also, "Why Powell Must Make the Race," *Newsweek,* 4 March 1996, p. 31.
5. Ellen Nakashima and Dana Milbank, "Bush Cabinet Takes Back Seat in Driving Policy," *Washington Post,* 5 September 2001, p. A-1.
6. James A. Barnes, "Bush's Insiders,"*National Journal,* 23 June 2001, p. 1869.
7. Op cit.
8. Op cit.
9. Examples of probusiness subcabinet appointments included Mark Rey, under secretary of agriculture for natural resources and environment. Rey had been a lobbyist for the timber industry and supported expanded logging on public lands. Michael Parker, assistant secretary of the Army for civil works, had been a lobbyist for the barge industry and opposed the Corps of Engineers' shifting focus to environmental protection from navigation issues. Michael Jackson, deputy secretary of transportation, had been vice president of the American Trucking Association and supported expanding the highway system. William Myers, solicitor of the Interior Department, was director of the National Cattleman's Association and supported ranching interests. Bennett Raley, assistant interior secretary for water and science, had been a lobbyist representing mining interests and was a critic of the Clinton administration's environmental policies. Steven Griles, deputy interior secretary, had been a lobbyist for the American Petroleum Institute and supported oil and gas development on public lands. As one commentator noted, "President Bush is quietly building the most conservative administration in modern times, surpassing even Ronald Reagan in the ideological commitment of his appointments." The conservative agenda was similarly moved forward in policy-making units such as the Office of Personnel Management, the Department of Justice, and the Office of Management and Budget. Examples of politically conservative appointments in these units included Kay Coles James, former dean of the Robertson School at Pat Robertson's Regent University as director of the Office of Personnel Management; Theodore Olson, a board member of the conservative *American Spectator* magazine who argued against affirmative action, as U.S. solicitor general; Jay Lefkowitz, a former law partner of Kenneth Starr, as chief counsel in the Office of Management and Budget, and Michael Chertoff, who assisted the Republicans in the Senate during the Whitewater investigation. Even Christine Todd Whitman, director of the Environmental Protection Agency, was widely viewed as pro-business as a result of her enforcement decisions of environmental regulations while governor of New Jersey.
10. Dana Milbank and Ellen Nakashima, "Bush Team Has 'Right Credentials,' Conservative Picks Seen Eclipsing Even Reagan's," *Washington Post,* 21 March 2001, p. A-1.
11. Hess, *Organizing the Presidency,* p. 169.
12. Office of Faith Based and Community Initiatives in the White House created by executive order on January 29, 2001.
13. Peter Beinart, "Bad Faith," *New Republic,* 25 March 2002, p. 6.
14. Op cit. The appointment of conservatives permeated the administration. Dr. Richard Carmona, surgeon general, was quoted by the White House as saying his views on abortion and stem cell research "were similar to the president's." Ari Fleischer, the president's press secretary, was unequivocal in his description of Carmona's conservative credentials. All

appointments, Fleischer said as he described Carmona, "serve [the president's] policies and I don't think you would expect the president to appoint people who hold wildly different views than he does." Dr. Elias Zerhouni was another conservative appointment to a senior position. Dr. Zerhouni, named director of the National Institute of Health, was described by Bush as "someone who shares my views."

15. For an in-depth overview of Wolfowitz and his role in the Bush administration, see Bill Keller, "The Sunshine Warrior," *New York Times Magazine*, 22 September 2002.

16. White House, Office of the Press Secretary, "President Bush Nominates Paul Wolfowitz Deputy Secretary of Defense," February 5, 2001.

17. Biographies can be found for each at http://www.whitehouse.gov/defense.

18. Ben Barber, "The Colin Powell Difference," www.salon.com (accessed May 19, 2001).

19. See http://www.whitehouse.gov/defense for a biography of Donald Rumsfeld.

20. Powell's position on affirmative action gained national attention when he opposed President Bush's position in the Supreme Court case involving the University of Michigan Law School's affirmative action policies. See David Firestone, "From 2 Bush Circles, 2 Positions on Affirmative Action Case," *New York Times*, 19 January 2002, p. A-1.

21. Carl M. Cannon and Alexis Simendinger, "The Evolution of Karl Rove," *National Journal*, 27 April 2002, p. 1214.

22. Michael Duffy, "How Bush Hires," www.Time.com (accessed December 17 2000).

23. Bill Keller, "The Sunshine Warrior," *New York Times Magazine*, 22 September 2002.

24. Bob Woodward, *Bush At War* (New York: Simon & Schuster, 2002), p. 13.

25. Libby graduated from Yale in 1972, graduated from Columbia Law School in 1975, and joined the Reagan administration in 1981 in the State Department. He later served as deputy under secretary of defense in the administration of George H. W. Bush under Wolfowitz.

26. Barbara Slavin and Susan Page, "Cheney Is Power Hitter in White House Lineup," *USA Today*, 29 January 2003, p. A-1.

27. Paul Bedard, "Washington Whispers," *U.S. News and World Report*, 31 July 2001.

28. Slavin and Page, "Cheney Is Power Hitter in White House Lineup," p. A-1.

29. Roger Porter, *Decision-Making in the White House* (Cambridge, England: Cambridge University Press, 1980).

30. Johanna McGeary, "Odd Man Out," *Time Magazine*, 10 September 2001.

31. James A. Baker, *The Politics of Diplomacy: Revolution, War, and Peace, 1989–1992* (New York: G. P. Putnam's Sons, 1995), p. 21.

32. Laura and George Bush had become especially close to Condoleezza Rice during the campaign. Both of Rice's parents were deceased, she had no siblings, and was not married and had no children. Her complete dedication to her job and to her role as Bush's foreign policy advisor created a special bond between the president and Rice that allowed her to remain close to Bush, in spite of being a moderate in the sea of conservatives within the White House staff and cabinet.

33. Bob Woodward, *Bush At War*, p. 17.

34. Howard Fineman and Martha Brant, "This Is Our Life Now," *Newsweek*, 3 December 2001, p. 25.

35. Woodward, *Bush at War*, pp. 75–78.

36. White House, Office of the Press Secretary, "Remarks of the President," September 12, 2001.

37. The principals of the national security team in 1991 consisted of George W. Bush, John Sununu (White House chief of staff), Secretary of State James Baker, National Security Advisor Brent Scowcroft, and Secretary of Defense Dick Cheney. The director of the CIA was not part of the decision-structure of the national security team for the Persian Gulf War. See Bob Woodward, *The Commanders* (New York: Simon & Schuster, 1991), p. 108.

38. Dan Balz, "Bush's Political Guru Finds Himself on Periphery," *Washington Post*, 31 October 2001, p. A-3.

39. James Carney, "General Karl Rove, Reporting for Duty," *Time Magazine*, 26 September 2002.

40. Ibid.

41. Bob Woodward, *Bush at War*, p. 95.

42. Ibid., p. 95.

43. Carl M. Cannon and Alexis Simendinger, "The Evolution of Karl Rove," *National Journal*, 27 April 2002, p. 1214.

44. Bob Woodward, *Bush at War*, pp. 75–79.

45. Bob Woodward, *Bush at War*, p. 80.

46. Steven Mufson, "Reluctant Warrior Is Political Veteran," *Washington Post,* 16 December 2001, p. A-1.
47. White House, Office of the Press Secretary, September 20, 2001.
48. The reliability of the Northern Alliance was always of concern to Powell and the war cabinet. See "Interview of Colin Powell," by Peter Jennings, ABC News, November 9, 2001. Department of State, Bureau of Public Affairs.
49. Howard Fineman and Martha Brant, "We Can Handle It," interview with President Bush, *Newsweek,* 3 December 2001, p. 32.
50. Woodward, *Bush at War,* p. 83.
51. "Making the Case: White House Says It Has Evidence of Iraq–al Qaeda Ties," http://www.abcnews.com (accessed September 26, 2001).
52. CBS News, *Face the Nation,* September 16, 2001.
53. CBS News, *Face the Nation,* September 23, 2001.
54. Woodward, *Bush at War,* p. 173.
55. "Operation Enduring Freedom" was explained to the American public in a televised address from the White House treaty room on the evening of October 7. "On my orders," Bush said, "the U.S. military has begun strikes against al Qaeda terrorist training camps and military installations of the Taliban regime." "We're Ready to Go," http://www.abcnews.com (accessed October 8, 2001).
56. White House, Office of the Press Secretary, Remarks by the President, October 7, 2001.
57. Fineman and Brant, "This Is Our Life Now," p. 27.
58. http://www.abcnews.com (accessed October 15, 2002.)
59. "Bombs and Words, Kabul Pounded by Bombs," http://www.abcnews.com (accessed October 15, 2001).
60. Oren Hararri, *The Leadership Secrets of Colin Powell* (New York: McGraw-Hill, 2002).
61. Vernon Loeb, "Rumsfeld Voices Caution about Success," *Washington Post* 19 October 2001, p. A-1.
62. "U.S. Carpet Bombs Taliban Lines," http://www.cnn.com (accessed October 31, 2001).
63. "Grim Statistic," http://www.abcnews.com (accessed October 19, 2001).
64. "U.S. Ground Forces Square Off with Taliban; Bush Seeks Asian Support," http://www.abcnews.com (accessed October 19, 2001).
65. http://www.abcnews.com. (accessed October 30, 2001).
66. Michael Wines, "Rumsfeld Visits Russia and Central Asia to Bolster Coalition," *New York Times,* 1 November 2001, p. A-1.
67. "Achieving Goals: Rumsfeld Deflects Concern over Bin Laden's Fugitive Status," http://www.abcnews.com (accessed January 3, 2002).
68. Judy Keen, "Cheney Tries to Build Support for Iraq Plan," *USA Today,* 11 May 2002, p. A-7.
69. Tony Karon, "Person of the Week: Colin Powell," *Time Magazine,* 12 April 2002.
70. White House, National Security Council, "National Security Strategy," no date.
71. White House, National Security Council press release, June 1, 2002.
72. Rich Lowry, "Rove for Secretary of State," *National Review* on-line, May 13, 2002.
73. Jonny Dymond, "Who Runs the Bush White House," *BBC News* on-line, April 30, 2001.
74. Christopher Marquis, "It's Republican vs. Republican on Cuba," *New York Times,* 28 July 2002, p. A-14.
75. Robert David and Dan Vergano, "Surgeon General Pick Has SWAT on Resume," *USA Today,* 27 March 2002, p. 1-A.

NATIONAL SECURITY POLICYMAKING
AND THE BUSH WAR CABINET*

JAMES P. PFIFFNER

GEORGE MASON UNIVERSITY

George W. Bush certainly did not expect to be a war president. In his private sector career and as Governor of Texas he had seldom traveled abroad, and he did not demonstrate much interest in international affairs. In his campaign for the presidency he expressed skepticism about foreign entanglements and a disdain for "nation building." Yet events conspired to make war the central concern of his presidency; after the terrorist attack on the United States in September 2001, Bush saw the war on terrorism as the primary mission of his presidency. "I'm here for a reason, and this [the war on terrorism] is going to be how we're to be judged."[1] Soon thereafter he decided that the United States should conduct a campaign for regime change in Iraq, by military means, if necessary.

Within his first two years in office, President Bush was to pursue two quite different wars: One was against terrorism and toppled the Taliban regime in Afghanistan and hunted terrorists throughout the world; the other overthrew the dictatorship of Saddam Hussein in Iraq. This chapter will examine President Bush and his war cabinet during the conduct of the war in Afghanistan. It will then turn to his domestic and international campaign for a war with Iraq, during which he had to overcome domestic skepticism about the wisdom of attacking Iraq as well as international concerns that war in Iraq would dangerously destabilize the Middle East region. The conclusion will analyze the Bush administration's national security policymaking process during its first two years.

---

*The author would like to thank Jason Hartke for many helpful comments on an earlier version of this essay.

THE ADMINISTRATION TRANSFORMED AND THE WAR CABINET

The tragedy of the September 11 attacks transformed the world and the administration in striking ways. The first and most striking political effect of the terrorist bombings of September 11 was a huge jump in public approval of President Bush. In the September 7–10 Gallup poll, public approval of the president stood at 51 percent; the next poll, on September 14–15, registered 86 percent approval—a 35 percent jump virtually overnight.[2] The broad outpouring of grief, anger, and political support for the president provided the backdrop for the administration's war on terrorism.

To plan the administration's response to the terrorist attacks, President Bush assembled his "war cabinet," which included Vice President Richard Cheney, National Security Advisor Condoleezza Rice, Secretary of State Colin Powell, Secretary of Defense Donald Rumsfeld, Chief of Staff Andrew Card, and Director of Central Intelligence, George Tenet. When it was suggested that Cheney might chair the war cabinet for the president, Bush rejected the idea and said that he would chair the meetings and that Rice would act as chair in his absence.[3]

Although Tenet had been appointed to head the CIA by President Clinton, President Bush came to trust him personally and came to rely on his judgment. In the previous administration, President Clinton had approved several intelligence orders and increased funding for human intelligence sources so that the CIA could undertake covert operations against Osama bin Laden and al Qaeda.[4] Thus in the days immediately following September 11, it was Tenet who was most prepared with intelligence about the terrorists, al Qaeda, and their base in Afghanistan. Tenet prepared a Memorandum of Notification that would give the CIA broad new authority and flexibility in dealing with international terrorism that the president approved in the first days after 9/11.[5]

The war cabinet considered several options for the U.S. pursuit of al Qaeda in Afghanistan. A strike with cruise missiles could have been implemented quickly, but the targets might have been abandoned by the terrorists, and that option seemed too much like President Clinton's strike in 1998 that killed no one. Another option was sending cruise missiles along with bomber attacks, and a third was a combination of the first two along with "boots on the ground," that is, U.S. soldiers in Afghanistan.[6] The president decided that it was important to have U.S. soldiers committed to battle in order to demonstrate U.S. resolve and commitment. The problem was that there were no existing military plans, and it would take time to set up staging areas and rescue teams before U.S. personnel could be placed in the country.

The U.S. bombing attack on Taliban targets began on October 7, and the president was impatient to get U.S. troops into Afghanistan, but by September 26, only the CIA had a covert team of about ten men in Afghanistan.[7] Although some hard Taliban targets were hit (e.g., buildings and airfields), the major early challenge was the lack of targets to bomb. The Taliban did not mass their troops, and there were no U.S. personnel on the ground in position to call in air strikes on the enemy.[8]

At one point in early October when Rice informed him that more time for planning and staging was needed by the military, he responded, "That's not acceptable!"[9] Rice was in the position of absorbing the president's frustration and explaining the military's position to him. Often close presidential advisors take the brunt of presidential anger as part of their jobs, for instance H. R. Haldeman for Nixon, George Stephanopolous for Clinton, or many White House staffers for Lyndon Johnson. Bush felt comfortable expressing his frustration to Rice. "I can be totally unscripted or unrehearsed with Condi."[10]

In mid-October, early in the war with still no military personnel in Afghanistan, Rumsfeld became exasperated at the seeming CIA dominance of war planning and operations. "This is the CIA's strategy. They developed the strategy. We're just executing the strategy . . . you guys are in charge. You guys have the contacts. We're just following you in. We're going where you tell us to go." President Bush then told Rice, "Get this mess straightened out." Rice had to go to Rumsfeld later and convince him that he ought to be in charge of military strategy and tactics, "Don, this is now a military operation and you really have to be in charge. . . . One person's got to be in charge of this, and it's you." Rumsfeld replied, "Got it." When Bush asked her, "Am I not the quarterback?" she replied, "No, I think you're the coach."[11] Rice's role as NSC advisor had expanded during the months after 9/11. Beginning the administration as junior to the other principals in age and experience, she demonstrated her skill in her role as neutral broker as well as enforcer of the president's wishes.

Later in October the Army had placed several Special Forces units on the ground, but the lack of targets was still a problem. Bush had made a key decision not to introduce significant numbers of American troops to fight the war. Instead, the United States would depend on the "tribals" in Afghanistan, including the loose "Northern Alliance" to confront the Taliban and do the ground fighting. While not as well equipped or trained as the professional U.S. troops, the local ethnic groups had the advantage of knowing the territory and language as well as having scores to settle with the Taliban, which they had been fighting for years. But the United States, while spending millions of dollars supplying and "renting" the tribals, could not make them engage the enemy before they felt they were ready.

This delay in the U.S. timetable by the Northern Alliance made it seem like the war was stagnating and the specter of a Vietnam quagmire was being raised in the press. On October 25 the situation prompted Rice to tell Bush, ". . . we've bombed everything we can think of to bomb, and still nothing is happening."[12] This situation was the backdrop for a dramatic meeting the next day in which Bush asserted his leadership to quell second thoughts in his war cabinet. With stories in the papers about bogging down in Afghanistan, some of his advisors began to consider the possibility of introducing significant numbers of U.S. ground troops and Americanizing the ground war.

At the NSC meeting in the Situation Room in the White House, Bush told his war cabinet, "I just want to make sure that all of us did agree on this plan, right?" When there were no dissents, he asked, "Anybody have any ideas they want to put on the table?"[13] No one suggested any because it was clear that the president had decided. The president was not asking their advice, but demanding their agreement. This was not the time for exploring options or voicing concerns; the president wanted them to affirm their confidence in the plan.[14]

Bush pointed out that it had been only nineteen days that they had been pursuing the strategy and that it was too soon to abandon it. He wanted them to be patient while they waited for the Northern Alliance to decide to move against the Taliban; then the United States could use its air power to support them and destroy the enemy. Bush later referred to his leadership in this instance, "First of all, a president has got to be the calcium in the backbone. If I weaken, the whole team weakens. If I'm doubtful, I can assure you there will be a lot of doubt."[15] His stiffening of the spine of the war cabinet served to forestall discussion of further commitment of U.S. troops to the war. The irony was that a week later, on November 2, the president himself was considering the possibility of sending in more than 50,000 U.S. troops to do the job that the local tribals did not seem to want to initiate. This possible Americanization of the war was seen as a worst-case scenario by U.S. military planners.[16]

In early November the United States had four CIA paramilitary and three military Special Forces teams in Afghanistan that were assisting the local warlords and preparing to call in airstrikes when the battle was engaged.[17] Despite the doubts and contingency planning by the president and his advisors, by mid-November the whole picture had turned around. The Northern Alliance had begun to attack the Taliban, which had begun to mass its troops. One of the indicators of the type of war being conducted was a cavalry charge of six hundred men on horses attacking Taliban forces at the same time they were being hit by massive and accurate bombing support by U.S. planes using the most sophisticated guidance systems in the world.[18] Once the tribal warriors began to attack in the north and the south, the tide quickly turned against the Taliban, and within several weeks Kabul had been taken in the north (November 12) and Kandahar in the south of Afghanistan (December 7). Even the president expressed his surprise, "It's amazing how fast the situation has changed. It is a stunner, isn't it?"[19]

The total number of U.S. personnel in Afghanistan during the war were 110 CIA paramilitary troops and 316 Special Forces soldiers, and the defeat of the Taliban had taken only 102 days, with very few U.S. casualties (26 dead and 121 wounded as of January 25, 2003).[20] The new president, Hamid Karzai, took his oath of office in Kabul on December 22. The key to the U.S. victory was the desire of the Afghanistan tribal leaders to rid Afghanistan of the Taliban, which had oppressed the country for years. But the key to getting the active support of the tribal leaders was the strategic dispersion by the CIA, in country, of $70 million in cash to the various leaders to gain their support and supply their troops. U.S. airpower was decisive, but victory could not have been achieved without the Afghan warriors on the ground. Indigenous troops were probably more effective than would have been the better-equipped and more professional U.S. soldiers in the mountains and valleys of Afghanistan.

President Bush had molded his cabinet into an effective advisory mechanism for the conduct of the war and exhibited his leadership style. He was willing to be decisive, and was often impatient with the progress of the military in getting assets in place in Afghanistan. Despite understandable disagreements within his cabinet, often between Powell and Cheney or Powell and Rumsfeld, the president with the assistance of Rice contained the disagreements and used them constructively.

Bush later reflected on his role as leader of his war cabinet. "One of my jobs is to be provocative . . . seriously, to provoke people into—to force decisions, and to make sure it's clear in everybody's mind where we're headed."[21] Woodward asked whether he warned his staffers when he was being provocative or overstating his position in order to elicit a reaction. The question was about how to effectively exploit staff advice. Would the president get a better response, for his purposes, if they knew he was playing devil's advocate or if they thought he was serious? Bush's response was to ignore the implications of the question and respond to the question of whether he warned his staffers:

> Of course not. I'm the commander—see, I don't need to explain—I do not need to explain why I say things. That's the interesting thing about being the president. Maybe somebody needs to explain to me why they say something, but I don't feel like I owe anybody an explanation.[22]

While consensus may be useful, Bush clearly did not see building consensus as the key to presidential leadership; making the right decision and holding to the course was more important. Bush commented further on the need for unanimity in his war cabinet,

> . . . one of the things I know that can happen is, if everybody is not on the same page, then you're going to have people peeling off and second-guessing and the process will not, will really not unfold the way it should, there won't be honest discussion.[23]

It seems that his concern for "honest discussion" was expected to take place from the perspective of the "same page" rather than venturing beyond the assumed (or imposed) consensus.

After Afghanistan had been liberated from its Taliban rulers, U.S. forces were introduced in large numbers to ensure the peace and begin rebuilding the country. They engaged Taliban forces with mixed success in the Tora Bora area mountains adjacent to Pakistan. Their mission was to destroy remnants of the Taliban and their supplies and block their escape across the border into Pakistan. During this period Osama bin Laden apparently slipped out of the country while his aide took his cell phone on a different route to mislead U.S. forces.

Although President Bush rejected the idea of U.S. troops as nation builders, there was little choice but to try to establish stability so that the country could rebuild itself. After the Soviets withdrew their forces in defeat, warring factions led to chaos and anarchy and paved the way for takeover by the oppressive Taliban regime. By the fall of 2002 there were 10,000 U.S. troops in Afghanistan, though the new government did not fully control the country outside the capital of Kabul. U.S. troops were training a new Afghan army, but the government had trouble raising the money to pay the new recruits. Although the United States was spending billions of dollars on maintaining the U.S. military in Afghanistan, spending on reconstruction projects was relatively low. According to one account in the fall of 2002, "Abject poverty, malnutrition, and starvation still haunt each section of the country."[24]

Along the Afghanistan border with Pakistan, U.S. forces continued to search for terrorists and Taliban fighters, many of whom sought refuge in tribal areas in Pakistan and intermittently fired rockets and set up small guerrilla operations against American forces. The area was difficult to control because the opposition to U.S. forces did not mass troops or present significant targets, but rather used snipers and set mines and bombs in classic guerrilla fashion.[25] By the summer of 2003 there were a number of international troops and aid workers in Afghanistan along with U.S. troops, but the country was still not stabilized under Afghan governmental authority.

THE CAMPAIGN FOR WAR WITH IRAQ

Although the public campaign for war with Iraq did not begin until 2002, President Bush and part of his administration began considering it immediately after September 11, 2001. At the war cabinet meeting at Camp David on September 15, 2001, the issue of Iraq was raised by Deputy Secretary of Defense Paul Wolfowitz who strongly favored going after Saddam Hussein and argued that war in Iraq might be easier than war in Afghanistan. Powell argued that the coalition backing the United States would not hold if the target was shifted to Iraq. Cheney said, "If we go after Saddam Hussein, we lose our rightful place as good guy." Tenet and Card agreed against attacking Iraq. The president finally decided not to pursue Iraq at that time and recalled, "If we tried to do too many things . . . the lack of focus would have been a huge risk."[26]

On September 17, 2001, President Bush signed a top secret plan for the war in Afghanistan that also contained a direction for the Defense Department to plan for a war with Iraq.[27] Attacking Iraq was the subject of a meeting of the Defense Policy Board, a group chaired by Richard Perle, that advised the secretary of defense on national security issues. In 2003 White House officials said that Bush decided soon after the terrorist attacks that Iraq had to be confronted, but that he did not make his decision public because "[h]e didn't think the country could handle the shock of 9/11 and a lot of talk about dealing with states that had weapons of mass destruction."[28]

President Bush did not make public his decision to pursue Iraq until the State of the Union message on January 29, 2002, though his decision was somewhat obscure and stated at a high level of generality because of his inclusion of Iraq, Iran, and North Korea in what he called an "axis of evil." The phrase, which carried heavy freight for both his partisans and his critics, worked its way into the speech gradually, as his speechwriters labored over drafts in late 2001. One of them was assigned to "provide a justification for war" with Iraq.[29] He came up with the phrase "axis of hatred" in order to evoke the Axis powers in World War II (Germany, Italy, and Japan). As the drafts progressed, Condoleezza Rice decided to include Iran along with Iraq, and near the end of the drafting the phrase was changed to "axis of evil," and North Korea was added to the list of evil states.

In the speech Bush declared that the United States will "prevent regimes that sponsor terror from threatening America or our friends and allies with weapons of mass destruction. . . . States like these and their terrorist allies constitute an axis of evil, arming to threaten the peace of the world." He argued that the United States could not afford to delay, "We'll be deliberate; yet, time is not on our side. I will not wait on events while dangers gather. I will not stand by as peril draws closer and closer. The United States of America will not permit the world's most dangerous regimes to threaten us with the world's most destructive weapons. . . . History has called America and our allies to action. . . ."[30]

Officials at the State Department were not sure what the president meant by designating the "axis of evil" states in his talk. They mistakenly concluded that it did not constitute a shift in policy.[31] They were concerned about the tone of the speech, but Powell instructed them that there would be no criticism of the speech from State.[32] In the spring of 2002, military planning for Iraq began, and in April Bush told a British reporter, "I made up my mind that Saddam needs to go."[33] The administration publicly started talking about "regime change" in Iraq. The next major public pronouncement by the president on national security and Iraq came at the 2002 commencement address he gave at the U.S. Military Academy at West Point. The president said:

> Containment is not possible when unbalanced dictators with weapons of mass destruction can deliver those weapons on missiles or secretly provide them to terrorist allies. . . . We cannot put our faith in the word of tyrants. . . . If we wait for threats to fully materialize, we will have waited too long. . . . Yet, the war on terror will not be won on the defensive. We must take the battle to the enemy, disrupt his plans, and confront the worst threats before they emerge. In the world we have entered, the only path to safety is the path of action, and this nation will act. . . . We are in a conflict between good and evil, and America will call evil by its name."[34]

During the summer of 2002 some of the professional military began to voice reservations about U.S. plans to attack Iraq. It is not unusual for the professional military to not see eye-to-eye with the White House, but it is very unusual for their concerns to be voiced so openly to the press. *Washington Post* articles cited "senior U.S. military officers" and "some top generals and admirals in the military establishment, including members of the Joint Chiefs of Staff," who argued for a cautious approach to Iraq. They were not convinced that Iraq had any connection to the 9/11 terrorist attacks; they felt that containment had worked up until then; they thought a military invasion would be costly; and they thought that a likely U.S. victory would entail a lengthy occupation of Iraq.[35] Echoing another president from Texas, Lyndon Johnson, who similarly minimized the concerns of opponents of the Vietnam War, George Bush dismissed the concerns of the professional military: "There's a lot of nervous nellies at the Pentagon."[36]

In August, members of President Bush's father's administration came out publicly against war with Iraq. Brent Scowcroft, Bush's (41) national security advisor and Rice's mentor, wrote in an op-ed piece entitled "Don't Attack Saddam" that ". . . there is scant evidence to tie Saddam to terrorist organizations, and even less to the Sept. 11 attacks. . . . An attack on Iraq at this time would seriously jeopardize, if not destroy, the global counterterrorist campaign we have undertaken. . . . Worse, there is a virtual consensus in the world against an attack on Iraq at this time."[37] James Baker, Secretary of State for Bush (41), also expressed reservations about an attack on Iraq. "If we are to change the regime in Iraq, we will have to occupy the country militarily. The costs of doing so, politically, economically and in terms of casualties, could be great."[38]

Combat veterans also expressed reservations about the wisdom of war with Iraq.[39] Vietnam veteran Chuck Hagel (R-NE) said, "It is interesting to me that many of those who want to rush this country into war don't know anything about war."[40] Retired General Anthony Zinni, senior advisor to Secretary of State Powell and former chief of the U.S. Central Command (which includes the Middle East), said: "We need to quit making enemies that we don't need to make enemies out of. . . . It's pretty interesting that all the generals see it the same way and all the others who have never fired a shot and are not to go to war see it another way."[41] James Webb, Vietnam veteran and assistant secretary of defense and secretary of the Navy in the Reagan administration argued that war with Iraq was ill-considered. Webb wrote:

> Meanwhile, American military leaders have been trying to bring a wider focus to the band of neoconservatives that began beating the war drums on Iraq before the dust had even settled on the World Trade Center. Despite the efforts of the neocons to shut them up or dismiss them as unqualified to deal in policy issues, these leaders, both active-duty and retired, have been nearly unanimous in their concerns. Is there an absolutely vital national interest that should lead us from containment to unilateral war and a long-term occupation of Iraq?[42]

General Wesley Clark, former NATO Supreme Allied Commander, said, "Had I been [in Washington, D.C.], I would have recommended we not go against Saddam Hussein yet." Clark continued, "We have not gone far enough in the war on terror. . . . No evidence supports the Bush administration's assertion that the United States may need to invade Iraq soon, or else suffer terrorism at the hands of Iraqi dictator Saddam Hussein."[43] General Norman Schwartzkopf, commander of U.S. forces in the 1991 Gulf War, also expressed reservations about an attack on Iraq in early 2003: ". . . I don't know what intelligence the U.S. government has. . . . I guess I would like to have better information. . . . I think it is very important to wait and see what the inspectors come up with, and hopefully they come up with something conclusive."[44]

On August 5, 2002, at Colin Powell's initiative, Rice arranged for him to spend two hours with the president in order to explain his own reservations about war with Iraq. He argued that it would destabilize the Middle East, that an American occupation would be seen as hostile by the Muslim world, and that it could not be done unilaterally. He argued that if the president wanted to pursue a military attack, that the United States had to recruit allies, preferably through the United Nations.[45] Although Bush was not persuaded by Powell's reservations about war with Iraq, by mid-August the administration decided that the president should make Iraq the subject of his previously scheduled speech of September 12 to the UN about Iraq.

The Bush administration felt that opposition to war with Iraq was building and had to be countered, so Vice President Cheney took the occasion of an address to the Veterans of Foreign Wars convention on August 26, 2002, to lay out the administration's case in blunt terms.

> Deliverable weapons of mass destruction in the hands of a terror network or a murderous dictator, or the two working together, constitutes as grave a threat as can be imagined. . . . The risks of inaction are far greater than the risk of action. . . . Armed with an arsenal of these weapons of terror and a seat atop 10 percent of the world's oil reserves, Saddam Hussein could then be expected to seek domination of the entire Middle East, take control of a great portion of the world's energy supplies, directly threaten America's friends throughout the region, and subject the United States or any other nation to nuclear blackmail.[46]

Cheney also dismissed the possibility that UN inspections would be effective. "A return of inspectors would provide no assurance whatsoever of his compliance with UN resolutions. . . . On the contrary, there is a great danger that it would provide false comfort that Saddam was somehow 'back in his box'."[47] Cheney's public argument that a preemptive strike against Iraq was justified and that further UN inspections were useless seemed to undercut Powell's argument to seek UN inspections and approval of U.S. action against Iraq.

President Bush had carefully gone over the speech with Cheney before it was delivered, but that fact was not immediately released to the public. According to a senior advisor to the vice president, "Dick Cheney doesn't freelance. He said what he did because the president wanted him to."[48] Cheney's bellicose statements allowed the president to adopt a seemingly more moderate stance on the war issue. "If you didn't have the Cheney side out there to tell the whole world 'we're studded up here and ready to go,' if you didn't announce that to the whole world, then Bush couldn't move to the other side of all that," said a senior administration aide.[49]

At a meeting on September 7, the president reaffirmed his decision to go to the United Nations, though Cheney and Rumsfeld pressed their argument that the United States should move against Saddam and that there did not have to be a new UN resolution to do it. Whether the president should ask the UN for a resolution during his speech on September 12 was the subject of vigorous debate among the principals, with Powell arguing that Bush ought to ask for a new resolution and Cheney arguing that it would allow Saddam to delay indefinitely. Bush decided to include a call for a new resolution in the speech, but the lines in the speech were mysteriously dropped out of the final, twenty-fifth draft of the speech. When Bush noticed that the sentence was not coming up on his TelePrompTer, he ad-libbed the call for "necessary resolutions."[50]

After the administration convinced Congress to give the president authority to attack Iraq, Colin Powell and U.S. diplomats went to work building a coalition to convince the UN Security Council to pass a new resolution on Iraq. Intense negotiations took place throughout the month of October and early November 2002 to bring around the members of the UN Security Council. The United States backed off its insistence that a new resolution was not needed and agreed to French insistence that if Saddam did not comply with the inspection regime, that the Security Council would meet again to "consider" options. At the last minute France, Russia, China, and Syria went along with the rest of the Council on a strongly worded, unanimous resolution. Resolution 1441 gave Iraq one week to promise to comply with it and until February 21, 2003, at the latest for the UN inspectors to report back on Iraq's compliance.

While the United States did not get everything that it sought in the resolution, it was a major victory for the administration. Saddam was on notice that he had to comply with UN orders to get rid of his weapons of mass destruction, and if he did not, there would be widespread international support for U.S. military action against Iraq.

The UN weapons inspectors searched Iraq with seeming carte blanche and surprise visits to sites of possible weapons manufacture, but by late January had found no "smoking gun." Chief UN inspector, Hans Blix, said that he needed more time to do a thorough job. The United States began to deploy troops to the Middle East in preparation for war with Iraq, and the buildup was expected to exceed 150,000 troops in the region by late February.[51]

As the initial reporting date for the UN inspectors (January 27, 2003) approached, the Bush administration became increasingly impatient with the inability of the UN inspection team to locate evidence of Iraq's weapons of mass destruction. Rice called the Iraqi declaration accounting for its weapons a "12,200 page lie." She argued that the declaration was "intended to cloud and confuse the true picture of Iraq's arsenal . . . and constitutes a material breach of the United Nations Security Council Resolution 1441. . . ."[52] Donald Rumsfeld said in response to a statement of Hans Blix, "The fact that the inspectors have not yet come up with new evidence of Iraq's WMD [weapons of mass destruction] program could be evidence, in and of itself, of Iraq's noncooperation."[53] President Bush said, "This business about, you know, more time—you know, how much time do we need to see clearly that he's not disarming?. . . . This looks like a rerun of a bad movie and I'm not interested in watching it."[54]

Secretary of State Colin Powell also expressed impatience with U.S. allies who wanted to give the UN inspectors more time in Iraq before deciding whether a military attack was justified. "The question isn't how much longer do you need for inspections to work. Inspections will not work."[55] Powell's statement came after France declared at a UN Security Council meeting on January 20, 2003, that it would not vote for a resolution authorizing a military attack on Iraq.[56] Two days later at a NATO meeting in Brussels, France and Germany blocked the alliance from supporting the United States in an attack on Iraq.[57] The preemptive moves by France and Germany undercut Powell's position within the administration. He had convinced Bush that achieving UN support was necessary for an effective war against Iraq and that it was possible. Hard-liners in the administration had argued that going to the UN would allow Saddam to delay indefinitely any decisive UN action by pretending to cooperate with inspectors but in fact continuing to hide his weapons of mass destruction.[58]

In his State of the Union address on January 28, 2003, President Bush said that the UN had given Saddam Hussein his "final chance to disarm," but "he has shown instead utter contempt for the United Nations and for the opinion of the world." Bush declared that ". . . the course of [the United States] does not depend on the decisions of others. . . . Whatever action is required, whenever action is necessary, I will defend the freedom and security of the American people." He said, "The British government has learned that Saddam Hussein recently sought significant quantities of uranium from Africa. . . . With nuclear arms or a full arsenal of chemical and biological weapons, Saddam Hussein could resume his ambitions of conquest in the Middle East and create deadly havoc in that region."[59] On March 19, the United States began the war in Iraq with the bombing of Baghdad followed by a ground invasion. Saddam's forces were defeated within several weeks, and on May 1, President Bush declared that the direct combat portion of the war was over. During the summer of 2003 resistance to the occupation was sporadic, and the United States had not yet found weapons of mass destruction.

THE NATIONAL SECURITY POLICYMAKING PROCESS

Over the first two years of the Bush administration, the president's national security advisory team underwent significant changes as a consequence of the war on terrorism and planning for the war on Iraq. Condoleezza Rice had risen from a low-key advisor and tutor to an influential actor within a very senior and more experienced national security team. Donald Rumsfeld had been transformed from a resented Pentagon reformer to a very visible spokesman for the war on terrorism, though he managed to retain the resentment from the professional military, Congress, veterans groups, and the "old Europe" of France and Germany.[60] Colin Powell was resurrected from being "odd man out" in the administration to playing a major role in the lead up to both wars. Richard Cheney continued to play a key role as advisor to the president and driver of policy, with his public visibility waxing and waning but his policy clout steady and significant.

Rice's role as national security advisor resembled most closely that of her mentor, Brent Scowcroft, who served both Gerald Ford and George Bush (41) in that capacity. Scowcroft was the classic "neutral broker" among the other principals; he did not have strong policy preferences in opposition to other actors, and he faithfully presented their views to the president. He gave his personal advice to the president but did not load the process to favor his own views. And he, like Rice, had a close personal relationship to the president. Rice saw her job as

> . . . first, to coordinate what Defense, State, the CIA and other departments or agencies were doing by making sure the president's orders were carried out; and second, to act as counselor—to give her private assessment to the president, certainly when he asked, perhaps if he didn't. In other words, she was to be the president's troubleshooter.[61]

According to President Bush:

> She is an honest broker. She does not share with me her private opinions on issues (nor should she). I imagine she gives the President her unvarnished opinions, but she also is sure the President receives without distortion or prejudice the views of his key foreign policy leaders such as Secretaries Powell and Rumsfeld.[62]

Rice's approach to her job was certainly in contrast to some previous national security advisors, such as Henry Kissinger or Zbigniew Brzezinski who played much more visible and confrontational roles for their presidents.

President George W. Bush felt uncomfortable with process, and he depended on people, rather than structures or processes, for his advisory system. "If I have any genius or smarts, it's the ability to recognize talent, ask them to serve and work with them as a team."[63] The Bush administration did not resemble the Eisenhower White House with its formalistic system of NSC meetings and processes. Eisenhower had a full career working in large organizations before he got to the White House, and he used them effectively. According to Burke and Greenstein, Eisenhower's policy deliberation meetings were "spirited, no-holds-barred debate" in which "[t]he participants did not appear to hold back out of deference to the president or to tailor their advice to him."[64] Eisenhower said:

> I know of only one way in which you can be sure you've done your best to make a wise decision. That is to get all of the people who have partial and definable responsibility in this particular field, whatever it may be. Get them with their different viewpoints in front of you, and listen to them debate. I do not believe in bringing them in one at a time, and therefore being more impressed by the most recent one you hear than the earlier ones.[65]

President Bush conducted NSC meetings in the wake of the terrorist attacks to deliberate about the U.S. response and strategy. Contrasting views would be presented, but Bush did not encourage spirited debate over important issues. For instance, recalling one meeting when Rumsfeld became upset about the CIA seeming to dominate war planning, Bush said, "That's the kind of discussion that frustrates me, because I like clarity." He did not pursue the disagreement and settle it; he told Rice, "Get this mess straightened out." Some of the most spirited debates among the principals took place when the president was not there. Like John Kennedy who occasionally left Executive Committee meetings during the Cuban Missile Crisis in order to let his team speak more freely, Bush observed, "It's hard for a deputy to go against a principal in a debate at an NSC meeting."[66]

Bush was impatient with formal structures and processes, but that did not mean that he did not hear alternative perspectives on major issues. But the presentation of these alternatives was dependent upon the people he chose, not a formal process of deliberation. In her role of neutral broker, Rice was able to tell the president bad news and explain the concerns of others, as when she told him that the military was not yet ready to move in Afghanistan. She was also able to arrange meetings between the president and Colin Powell when he wanted to present his perspective to the president.

Powell's role was particularly important for President Bush. Powell was the only person in the administration with sufficient stature and clout to be able to present an alternative perspective to the hard-line point of view of Cheney, Rumsfeld, and Wolfowitz. Rice could arrange for Powell to see the president, but she did not see it as her role to make a strong case in opposition to the other principals. It was Powell who put together the coalition in support of U.S. military action in Afghanistan in the fall of 2001. In 2002 it was Powell who persuaded the president to go to the UN for a resolution in support of U.S. demands on Iraq. And it was Powell who led the diplomacy to get Security Council approval of UN Resolution 1441. Whether these presidential decisions were wise or not, it was only Powell who could have made the case credibly to the president.

Thus, in his first three years in office, President Bush was oriented toward the personal rather than the procedural or structural aspects of his advisory system, and he used his national security team effectively for his purposes. Even though he often did not feel comfortable with the policy advice of Colin Powell, he did take that advice at key points, most importantly the decision to go to the United Nations for a resolution on Iraq. But Powell's advice was most often rejected, particularly with respect to the fundamental decision to go to war with Iraq, in favor of the judgments of Dick Cheney, Donald Rumsfeld, and Paul Wolfowitz. Bush also chose to minimize the concerns of many in the Army officer corps regarding the size of troop commitment that would be necessary to prevail in Iraq over the longer term. As the 2004 election approached, one of the main issues of the campaign was the wisdom of President Bush's key decisions about going to war with Iraq and how the occupation was handled.

NOTES

1. Quoted in Bob Woodward, *Bush at War* (New York: Simon & Schuster, 2002), p. 205. Bush told Karl Rove, "Just like my father's generation was called in World War II, now our generation is being called." George H. W. Bush's generation, however, had been involved in fighting World War II. George W. Bush's generation (he graduated from college in 1968) did the fighting in Vietnam, while the president had been in the National Guard and the vice president had a deferment for school and later because of his family. It was the generation after Bush that would have to do the fighting in the wars of his administration. For an analysis of the first year of the Bush administration and the president's cabinet, see James P. Pfiffner, "The Transformation of the Bush Presidency," in James P. Pfiffner and Roger H. Davidson, *Understanding the Presidency*, 3rd ed. (New York: Longman, 2003), pp. 453–471.
2. Gallup Organization, *2001 Poll Trend, Presidential Ratings–Job Approval*, http://www.gallup.com (accessed December 12, 2001).
3. Woodward, *Bush at War*, pp. 37–38. Important portions of this paper are based on the reporting in Woodward's book, which calls for a note on his credibility. Woodward has published a number of books on the internal working of politics at the top of the U.S. government. There is no doubt that he has had privileged access and that many government officials over the past thirty years have wanted to tell their side of the story to him. For this book, the president himself spent several hours with Woodward and gave his tacit permission for other members of the administration to talk with him. None has publicly said that Woodward misrepresented what they said to him. According to Paul Bedard ("Washington Whispers," *U.S. News and World Report*, 2 December 2002, p. 4), White House officials said the book was "85 to 90 percent accurate," and "made us look as good as we are." It must also be kept in mind that as he was writing this book, Woodward was also working on his presumed next book on U.S. war with Iraq. He could not be too tough on the Bush administration without jeopardizing his access for his next book. Thus, Woodward's reporting is valuable, but must be read carefully.
4. Woodward, *Bush at War*, pp. 34–35, 156, 316, 318.
5. Woodward, *Bush at War*, pp. 77–78, 97.
6. Woodward, *Bush at War*, pp. 79–80.
7. Woodward, *Bush at War*, p. 147.

8. Woodward, *Bush at War*, p. 312.
9. Woodward, *Bush at War*, p. 157.
10. Woodward, *Bush at War*, p. 158.
11. Woodward, *Bush at War*, pp. 243–246.
12. Woodward, *Bush at War*, p. 257.
13. Woodward, *Bush at War*, p. 261.
14. Chester Cooper, an aide on Lyndon Johnson's NSC staff, recalled his response to presidential questions at NSC meetings: "During the process I would frequently fall into a Walter Mitty-like fantasy: When my turn came I would rise to my feet slowly, look around the room and then directly look at the President and say, very quietly and emphatically, 'Mr. President, gentlemen, I most definitely do *not* agree.' But I was removed from my trance when I heard the President's voice saying, 'Mr. Cooper, do you agree?' And out would come a 'Yes, Mr. President, I agree.'" Quoted in Larry Berman, *Planning a Tragedy* (New York: Norton, 1982), p. 3.
15. Woodward, *Bush at War*, p. 259.
16. Woodward, *Bush at War*, pp. 265, 291–292.
17. Woodward, *Bush at War*, pp. 293–294.
18. Woodward, *Bush at War*, p. 301.
19. Woodward, *Bush at War*, p. 306.
20. Woodward, *Bush at War*, pp. 212–213. Casualty figures from Marc Kaufman, "On Afghan Border, War Drags On," *Washington Post*, 25 January 2003, p. 1, A-14.
21. Woodward, *Bush at War*, p. 144.
22. Woodward, *Bush at War*, pp. 145–146.
23. Woodward, *Bush at War*, p. 73.
24. Peter Tomsen, "A Rebuilding Plan That Already Needs Repair," *Washington Post*, 27 October 2002, p. B-3. See also Margaret Coker, "Afghan War Over, but Nation-Building Battle Continues," Cox News Service, 6 October 2002 [no page number]; Carlotta Gall, "Half a Million Are Left Homeless in Afghan Cities as Winter Bites," *New York Times*, 2 January 2003, p. 1, A-8. For an upbeat analysis that calls for more U.S. aid to Afghanistan, see Robert Oakley, "The New Afghanistan: Year 2," *Washington Post*, 3 January 2003, p. A-19.
25. Marc Kaufman, "On Afghan Border, War Drags On," *Washington Post*, 25 January 2003, p. 1, A-14.
26. Woodward, *Bush at War*, pp. 84–91.
27. Glenn Kessler, "U.S. Decision on Iraq Has Puzzling Past," *Washington Post*, 12 January 2003, p. 1, A-20.
28. Kessler, "U.S. Decision on Iraq," p. A-20.
29. This is based on the account of the speech by Bush speechwriter David Frum in Chapter 12 of his book. Frum notes condescendingly that "Bush read the speech closely. He edited it in his own bold hand. He understood all its implications." Frum added, "Once he uttered it, 'axis of evil' ceased to be a speechwriter's phrase and became his own. . . ." David Frum, *The Right Man* (New York: Random House 2003), pp. 224, 238–240.
30. Weekly Compilation of Presidential Documents, *Administration of George W. Bush, 2002*, 29 January 2002, pp. 133–139.
31. Kessler, "U.S. Decision on Iraq," p. 1, A-20.
32. Frum, *The Right Man*, p. 240.
33. Kessler, "U.S. Decision on Iraq," p. A-20.
34. Weekly Compilation of Presidential Documents, *Administration of George W. Bush, 2002*, "Commencement Address at the U.S. Military Academy in West Point, New York," 1 June 2002, pp. 944–948.
35. Thomas E. Ricks, "Some Top Military Brass Favor Status Quo in Iraq," *Washington Post*, 28 July 2002, p. 1, A-23. Also, Thomas E. Ricks, "Generals, Officials Are Split over Iraq," *Washington Post*, 1 August 2002, p. 1, A-24, in which he says, "Much of the senior uniformed military, with the notable exception of some top Air Force and marine generals, opposes going to war anytime soon, a stance that is provoking frustration among civilian officials in the Pentagon and in the White House."
36. Steven R. Weisman. "History Lessons for Wartime Presidents and Their Generals," *New York Times*, 15 September 2002, p. wk14.
37. Brent Scowcroft, "Don't Attack Saddam," *Wall Street Journal*, 15 August 2002, p. A-12.
38. James A. Baker III, "The Right Way to Change a Regime," *New York Times*, 25 August 2002, p. wk9.

39. Those who argued strongly for war with Iraq who did not have combat experience included: President Bush, Vice President Cheney, National Security Advisor Condoleezza Rice, Secretary of Defense Rumsfeld (who flew Navy jets in 1953–1954), Deputy Secretary of Defense Paul Wolfowitz, House Whip Tom DeLay, Chair of Defense Policy Board Richard Perle, and commentator William Kristol. Combat veterans who were skeptical of the wisdom of war with Iraq included: Secretary of State Colin Powell, Deputy Secretary of State Richard Armitage, some members of the Joint Chiefs of Staff (in the summer of 2002), many career military officers (in the summer of 2002), Senator Chuck Hagel (voted for the Resolution on Iraq on 10/12/02), Senator John Kerry (voted for the resolution), Retired General Anthony Zinni (former Chief of U.S. Central Command), Retired General and former national Security Advisor Brent Scowcroft, James Webb (Vietnam veteran and former Secretary of the Navy), General Wesley Clark, former NATO Supreme Allied Commander, Norman Schwartzkopf, commander of U.S. forces in the 1991 Gulf War.

40. *Newsweek*, September 2002, p. 28. See also Associated Press story in the *New York Times*, 26 August 2002, p. 1.

41. *Washington Post*, "Powell Aide Disputes Views on Iraq," 28 August 2002, p. A-16.

42. James Webb, "Heading for Trouble," *Washington Post*, 4 September 2002, p. A-21.

43. Tara Tuckwiller, "Don't Invade Yet, Ex-NATO Chief Says," *Charleston Gazette*, 15 October 2002, p. A-1.

44. Thomas E. Ricks, "Desert Caution," *Washington Post*, 28 January 2003, p. C-1. Schwartzkopf prefaced the above remarks with, "The thought of Saddam Hussein with a sophisticated nuclear capability is a frightening thought, okay?"

45. Woodward, *Bush at War*, pp. 333–334.

46. Dana Milbank, "Cheney Says Iraqi Strike Is Justified," *Washington Post*, 27 August 2002, p. 1, A-8.

47. Woodward, *Bush at War*, p. 334.

48. Nancy Gibbs, "Double-Edged Sword," *Time*, 30 December 2002 and 6 January 2003, p. 91.

49. Nancy Gibbs, "Double-Edged Sword," *Time*, 30 December 2002 and 6 January 2003, p. 91.

50. Woodward, *Bush at War*, pp. 346–348.

51. Erick Schmitt, "U.S. Force in Gulf Is Said to Be Rising to 150,000 Troops," *New York Times*, 12 January 2003, p. 1.

52. Condoleezza Rice, "Why We Know Iraq Is Lying," *New York Times*, 23 January 2003, p. A-27.

53. Quoted in *Newsweek*, 27 January 2003, p. 25.

54. Karen DeYoung, "U.S. Escalates Iraq Rhetoric," *Washington Post*, 22 January 2003, p. 1.

55. Glenn Kessler, "Moderate Powell Turns Hawkish on War with Iraq," *Washington Post*, 24 January 2003, p. 1, A-20. Earlier in January 2003 Powell had shown support for the inspection regime, saying, "The inspectors are really now starting to gain momentum," and that the first report of the inspectors was only "the first formal official report."

56. Glenn Kessler and Colum Lynch, "France Vows to Block Resolution on Iraq War," *Washington Post*, 21 January 2003, p. 1.

57. Keith B. Richburg, "NATO Blocked on Iraq Decision," *Washington Post*, 23 January 2003, p. 1.

58. Perhaps the reason that U.S. officials were so certain that Saddam had chemical and biological weapons was that in the 1980s the U.S. Department of Commerce authorized the sale to Iraq of biological agents such as anthrax and bubonic plague. According to a memo to Secretary of State George Shultz in 1983 the Iraqis were using chemical weapons against the Iranians on an "almost daily basis." The Commerce Department also approved the sale by Dow Chemical of insecticides that were thought to be used for chemical weapons. Reported by Michael Dobbs, "U.S. Had Key Role in Iraq Buildup," *Washington Post*, 30 December 2002, p. 1, A-12.

59. It was later disclosed that the claim that Saddam had sought nuclear materials from Niger was based on forged documents.

60. Many in the military in 2003 continued to regard Rumsfeld as arrogant, brusque, and demanding. From Rumsfeld's perspective, the military establishment was protecting its turf and resources in its resistance to modernizing. In a memo he said about the many reports the Joint Chiefs of Staff prepared, "It is just a lot of people spinning their wheels, doing things we probably have to edit and improve." (Rowan Scarborough, "Defense Secretary Criticizes Top Staff," *Washington Times*, 24 January 2003, p. 1.) Military professionals also thought Rumsfeld was unnecessarily micromanaging the logistical, tactical, and strategic elements of military planning for war with Iraq. While head of Central Command, General Franks projected

a need for 250,000 troops, Rumsfeld thought it could be done with 100,000; planning in late January 2003 called for 150,000. Franks thought that air bombardment should last for up to two weeks before ground attack, and Rumsfeld decided that one week was sufficient. According to retired General Merrill McPeak, Air Force Chief of Staff during the 1991 Gulf War, "Rumsfeld is running this on a very short string. . . . This is a Rumsfeld show. He's really running this buildup, hands on the throttle and steering wheel." (Mark Thompson and Michael Duffy, "Pentagon Warlord," *Time*, 27 January 2003, pp. 22–29.) Norman Schwartzkopf contrasted Rumsfeld with Cheney's approach in 1991, "He [Cheney] didn't put himself in the position of being the decisionmaker as far as tactics were concerned, as far as troop deployments, as far as missions were concerned." (Thomas E. Ricks, "Desert Caution," *Washington Post*, 28 January 2003, p. C-1.) Rumsfeld alienated veterans groups when he said in response to a question about reestablishing the draft, that draftees during the Vietnam War added ". . . no value, no advantage, really, to the U.S. armed services over any sustained period of time. . . ." (Vernon Loeb, "Rumsfeld Apologizes for Remarks on Draftees," *Washington Post*, 22 January 2003, p. 1, A-4.) Rumsfeld irritated the French and Germans when he referred to them as part of the "old Europe."

61. Woodward, *Bush at War*, p. 254.
62. Nicholas LeMann, "Without a Doubt," *New Yorker*, 14 and 21 October 2002, p. 167.
63. Woodward, *Bush at War*, p. 74.
64. See John P. Burke and Fred I. Greenstein, *How Presidents Test Reality* (New York: Russell Sage, 1991), p. 54.
65. Quoted in John P. Burke and Fred I. Greenstein, *How Presidents Test Reality* (New York: Russell Sage, 1991), p. 54.
66. Woodward, *Bush at War*, p. 244.

CHALLENGES TO CIVIL LIBERTIES
IN A TIME OF WAR

LOUIS FISHER

CONGRESSIONAL RESEARCH SERVICE

The terrorist attacks of 9/11 cast a shadow over civil liberties in the Unit-ed States, both for citizens and noncitizens. Erosions of civil liberties during war are not new. They appear whenever emergency power is exer-cised. Rep. John Conyers (D-MI) reviewed the record of the twentieth cen-tury: "In the wake of World War I, we experienced the [Palmer] raids when thousands of immigrants were wrongfully detained, beaten and deported. World War II brought about the shameful internship of Japanese American citizens. The Korean War led to the era of McCarthyism, guilt by associa-tion, and the Vietnamese War resulted in the FBI digging into the personal lives of those opposed to the Administration policy."[1]

What is new about 9/11 is that it ushered in a state of war with no like-ly termination date, a condition aptly referred to as "permanent war." For that reason, the restoration of civil liberties that typically comes with the cessation of hostilities may not occur this time. No one knows when the cur-rent war will end because there is no state enemy to surrender, unless it is the loose organization known as al Qaeda. In these circumstances, how much will executive power expand permanently at the cost of civil liberties?

President George W. Bush came to Congress after September 11 to seek legislative authority to respond to the terrorist attacks. According to the Constitution, Congress has the option of either declaring or authorizing war. When he requested congressional authority, Bush broke ranks with Presidents Harry S. Truman, George H. W. Bush, and Bill Clinton, all of whom claimed that they could order large-scale military operations in Korea, Iraq, and Yugoslavia without seeking statutory authority from Con-gress. After this promising start, Bush and his administration began to fol-low a different theory of government, one that relies on unilateral actions based on perceived inherent powers of the president. The executive branch often claimed that it did not need to obtain authority from Congress or even consult members of Congress.

Senator Patrick Leahy (D-VT) laid down an early marker after the tragedy of 9/11. He cautioned against tipping the scales to the extent of endangering and jeopardizing civil liberties. "The worse thing that could happen is we damage our Constitution," he said. "If the Constitution is shredded, the terrorists win."[2] Similarly, Senator Russ Feingold (D-WI) warned: "Preserving our freedom is the reason we are now engaged in this new war on terrorism. We will lose that war without a shot being fired if we sacrifice the liberties of the American people in the belief that by doing so we will stop the terrorists."[3] But for many citizens and noncitizens in the country, the Constitution seemed to disappear, and it is too early to tell whether lawmakers or the courts will intervene to restore and protect civil liberties.

WITHHOLDING AND LEAKING INFORMATION

In time of war, administrations typically overclassify documents and withhold information from Congress and the public. One of the first initiatives, quickly reversed, was a Bush memo of October 5, 2001, to limit the disclosure of classified and sensitive law enforcement information. Such briefings were to be restricted to eight members of Congress: House Speaker, House Minority Leader, the Senate Majority and Minority Leaders, and the chairs and ranking members of the Intelligence Committees.[4] Anyone familiar with executive–legislative relations should have recognized the memo's absurdity. It read like something drafted late at night without enough alert, experienced people to stop it before it went out.

Someone from Bush's own party, Senator Chuck Hagel of Nebraska, remarked: "To put out a public document telling the world he doesn't trust the Congress and we leak everything, I'm not sure that helps develop unanimity and comradeship." Added Senate Armed Services Committee Chairman Carl Levin (D-MI): "We have to have classified briefings if we're going to do our oversight role."[5] Other lawmakers pointed out that members of the Foreign Relations, Armed Services, Judiciary, and Appropriations Committees could not function without access to classified materials.[6]

What prompted this overblown, misguided memo? Bush was clearly upset by what he considered an inappropriate statement by a member of Congress who received a classified briefing from an executive official. Exactly who the lawmaker was, and what sensitive information was released to the public, is unclear. Apparently an intelligence official said that there was a "100 percent" chance of an attack on America if U.S. troops conducted military operations against Afghanistan, and a lawmaker might have repeated something of that nature.[7] No one could argue that the information was at all sensitive or did any injury to national security. In the face of a bipartisan congressional revolt, Bush beat a quick and predictable retreat.[8]

In mid-2002, the administration charged that Congress had leaked classified intelligence information. Amazingly, the two Intelligence Committees allowed the FBI to conduct a probe to determine the source of the leak on Capitol Hill. Eventually, seventeen Senators on the Intelligence Committee were asked to turn over their phone records, appointment books, and schedules to reveal possible contacts with reporters.[9] Congress should never have authorized an executive agency to investigate the legislative branch. Congress creates the agencies, not the other way around. If concern is expressed about possible leaks on Capitol Hill, the investigative body should be Congress, not the executive branch.

In the midst of these interbranch battles, the Bush administration regularly dumped massive amounts of classified and sensitive data into the public arena whenever it seemed politically opportune to do so. During debate in 2002 over going to war against Iraq, newspapers were filled with detailed battle plans, supposedly the most secret of all executive documents. Nevertheless, perhaps as a way of intimidating Iraq or displaying the administration's toughness, battle plans made front page news week after week.[10] When President Bush wanted to buttress his case for going to war against Iraq, he declassified satellite photos and released them to the press.[11]

Consider a story that appeared in the *Washington Post* on October 29, 2002, describing efforts to interrogate detainees at Guantanamo Bay. It gave the name of Omar al Farouq, a suspected al Qaeda operative captured in Indonesia, "who is now revealing many al Qaeda secrets." Giving his name to the press amounts to a virtual death sentence for al Farouq if he is ever released and sent back to the Middle East. Also named is Omar Khadr, a "particularly talkative prisoner." The story quotes a U.S. official: "He's singing like a bird."[12] Information of that nature should never be released to the public.

Some of these leaks from the executive branch may have been unauthorized: the kinds that would offend any president. But the outpouring of military information and battle plans strongly implies that the Bush administration was willing to transmit highly sensitive data to journalists on a routine basis as part of its strategy of saber-rattling and well-orchestrated threats. Defense Secretary Don Rumsfeld issued a memo objecting to the leaking of classified information: "It is wrong. It is against the law. It costs the lives of Americans. It diminished our country's chance for success."[13] It may be all that, but administrations will release whatever information promotes their policy.

Another step in withholding information was the position of the Bush administration in interpreting and administering the Freedom of Information Act (FOIA). On October 12, 2001, Attorney General John Ashcroft issued a guideline to agency heads, instructing them of the need to consider sensitive business data and personal privacy as well as national security and law enforcement before releasing documents to the public. He promised them that the Justice Department "will defend your decisions [to withhold records] unless they lack a sound legal basis or present an unwarranted risk of adverse impact on the ability of other agencies to protect other important records."[14]

In other words, he extended an invitation to agencies to limit public access. The House Government Reform Committee, which has jurisdiction over FOIA, included this line in the new edition of its "Citizen's Guide," which describes how to best use FOIA and the Privacy Act in requesting government records: "Contrary to the instructions issued by the Department of Justice on October 12, 2001, the standard should not be to allow the withholding of information whenever there is merely a 'sound legal basis' for doing so."[15]

Finally, what should we make of the refusal of Tom Ridge, head of the Office of Homeland Security, to testify before Congress? Senators Robert C. Byrd and Ted Stevens, chairman and ranking member of the Appropriations Committee, wrote to Ridge on March 4, 2002, inviting him to testify before the Committee on the $38 billion budget for homeland security. Ridge declined to testify on the ground that he was a presidential advisor and not a Senate-confirmed head of an agency.[16] Later he agreed to take questions from lawmakers "informally" but in public, explaining that this compromise would meet the needs of Congress "and avoid the setting of a precedent that could undermine the constitutional separation of powers and the long-standing traditions and practices of both Congress and the executive branch."[17] He followed through on this promise by meeting informally with a subcommittee of House Appropriations and the House Government Reform Committee.[18]

What does any of this have to do with constitutional principles and separation of powers? First, there are no "long-standing traditions and practices" that prohibit presidential advisors from testifying before congressional committees. White House aides, national security advisors, White House counsels, and other White House staff have come to Congress to testify.[19] There is no magic immunity for presidential advisors. Second, was it at all persuasive for Ridge to agree to meet informally and take questions, but draw the line at appearing formally to take questions? That type of artificial legalism merely added fuel to congressional efforts to create, by statute, an agency headed by someone who must be confirmed by the Senate.

LIMITS ON FREE SPEECH

The intent of the Bush administration to act unilaterally, without constitutional checks and balances, was evident in the December 6, 2001, testimony of Attorney General Ashcroft before the Senate Judiciary Committee. He bluntly warned that criticism of the administration helps the terrorists. His language was somewhat qualified, but not much: "We need honest, reasoned debate, not fear-mongering. To those who pit Americans against immigrants and citizens against non-citizens, to those who scare peace-loving people with phantoms of lost liberty, my message is this: Your tactics only aid terrorists, for they erode our national unity and diminish our resolve. They give ammunition to America's enemies, and pause to America's friends. They encourage people of good will to remain silent in the face of evil."[20]

Who decides what is "honest" and "reasoned"? Shall there be a Truth Unit created within the Justice Department, always on the alert for wayward comments? How much does the quest for "national unity" discourage public debate and the individual voice? The executive branch can claim no monopoly on wisdom.

A day after the hearing, the Justice Department announced that Ashcroft did not intend to discourage public debate. What he found unhelpful to the country are "misstatements and the spread of misinformation about the actions of the Justice Department."[21] Yet the administration itself—as with any administration—has made its share of "misstatements." At the Senate Judiciary hearings, Ashcroft claimed that the president's authority to establish military tribunals "arises out of his power as Commander-in-Chief. For centuries, Congress has recognized this authority and the Supreme Court has never held that any Congress may limit it." Ashcroft appeared to claim that tribunals are created under the exclusive authority of the president and that, according to judicial precedents, Congress may not limit that authority. The legal and historical record of military tribunals presents quite a different picture: The creation of tribunals is typically done jointly by Congress and the president, Congress has not recognized a unilateral presidential authority to create these tribunals, and the Supreme Court has repeatedly held that Congress has the constitutional authority to create tribunals, decide their authorities and jurisdiction, and limit the president were he to act unilaterally by military order or proclamation to create these tribunals.[22] In the face of this record, does it make any sense to suggest that Ashcroft's "misstatements and the spread of misinformation" give aid to terrorists?

The war against terrorism does not justify any weakening of the constitutional rights of free speech and free press. It is particularly during war, and not just during time of peace, that free speech and public debate must be respected. During World War I, Zechariah Chafee, Jr., convinced Justice Oliver Wendell Holmes, Jr., that the war clauses of the Constitution cannot break down the freedom of speech. It is in time of war that the government must be "vigorously and constantly cross-examined, so that the fundamental issues of the struggle may be clearly defined, and the war may not be diverted to improper ends, or conducted with an undue sacrifice of life and liberty, or prolonged after its just purposes are accomplished."[23]

On May 30, 2002, Attorney General Ashcroft released new guidelines that will permit FBI agents to conduct domestic surveillance of public events, such as political rallies and religious gatherings. The changes he ordered loosen the guidelines adopted in 1976 to prevent the FBI from spying on domestic groups.[24] Reporters asked President Bush whether there was "a risk of going too far in the battle against terrorism and actually losing some freedoms that are very important to the nation." He replied: "We intend to honor our Constitution and respect the freedoms that we hold so dear."[25]

It could be argued that the FBI has the right, along with any citizen, to attend public events and listen for information that might be helpful in the fight against terrorism. However, citizens do not have the capacity, or the incentive, to maintain files and dossiers on various groups and organizations, the kind of conduct that the FBI pursued from the 1950s to the 1970s. Moreover, having hundreds of FBI agents attend public events and record remarks does not seem a wise use of strained government resources.

MILITARY TRIBUNALS

The executive branch claimed exclusive authority for President Bush to issue his military order of November 13, 2001, creating a military tribunal to try terrorists. The administration did not touch base with anyone on Capitol Hill (even the Judiciary Committees), nor did it consult with experts in the Judge Advocate General's office in the Pentagon. To justify the Bush order, the administration cited *Ex parte Quirin* (1942) as a solid legal precedent. In that case, a unanimous Supreme Court upheld the use of a military tribunal for eight Nazi saboteurs. Bush clearly modeled his order on a 1942 proclamation by President Franklin D. Roosevelt creating a tribunal to try the Germans.[26] However, the FDR proclamation targeted a subgroup of eight people, while Bush's order covered a much larger population: "any individual who is not a U.S. citizen" (about eighteen million inside U.S. borders) who gave assistance to the September 11 terrorists. Any noncitizen, including resident aliens, is at risk of being detained and tried by a military tribunal, perhaps because they donated to what they thought was a legitimate charitable organization, but one that turned out to be a front for al Qaeda.

Why did Bush focus only on noncitizens? His legal advisors may have convinced him, because of *Ex parte Milligan* (1866), that U.S. citizens have a right to be tried in civil courts when they are open and operating.[27] But imagine how different the public reaction would have been if the military tribunal had jurisdiction over everyone—citizen or noncitizen—who gave assistance to the terrorists.

At closer look, *Ex parte Quirin* turns out to be an unattractive precedent. The trial was held in secret on the fifth floor of the Justice Department, Washington, D.C., to keep from the public the fact that one of the Germans turned himself in and fingered his colleagues. The administration wanted the public to think that the FBI had the capacity to ferret out any saboteurs who attempted to enter the United States. Instead of letting the War Department handle the military trial, subject to procedures spelled out in the statutory Articles of War and the published *Manual for Courts-Martial*, procedures were made up as the trial went along and prosecution was handled by Attorney General Francis Biddle and Judge Advocate General Myron Cramer.

The Supreme Court was poorly prepared to hear the case. The briefs are dated the same day that oral argument began. There was only a cursory district court decision, issued the evening before oral argument, and no action yet by the D.C. Circuit.[28] The Court handed down a brief per curiam on July 31, but without any legal reasoning.[29] It would take another three months to produce a full opinion, but by that time six of the eight Germans had been executed. Chief Justice Stone had his hands full trying to write the opinion for the Court without judicial unity being marred by dissents or concurrences.[30] Constitutional scholar Edward S. Corwin dismissed the final opinion as "little more than a ceremonious detour to a predetermined end."[31] Justice Frankfurter later said that "the Quirin experience was not a happy precedent."[32] In an interview on June 9, 1962, Justice Douglas made a similar comment: "The experience with *Ex parte Quirin* indicated, I think, to all of us that it is extremely undesirable to announce a decision on the merits without an opinion accompanying it. Because once the search for the grounds, the examination of the grounds that it has been advanced is made, sometimes those grounds crumble."[33]

The conduct of the military trial in 1942 so angered Secretary of War Henry L. Stimson that he intervened forcefully three years later, when another tribunal was established to try two more saboteurs who had arrived from Germany. Unlike the military order of July 2, 1942, President Roosevelt did not name the members of the tribunal or the counsel for the prosecution and defense. Instead, he empowered the commanding generals, under the supervision of the Secretary of War, "to appoint military commissions for the trial of such persons." Moreover, the trial record would not go directly to the president, as it did in 1942. The review would be processed within the Judge Advocate General's office.[34] This time, Attorney General Biddle had no role as prosecutor, and Judge Advocate General Cramer would be limited to his review function within the JAG office. The trial took place not in Washington, D.C., but at Governors Island, New York City.[35]

Bush's military order of November 13, 2001, covers any individual "not a U.S. citizen" that the president determines there is "reason to believe" (i) "is or was a member of the organization known as al Qaeda," (ii) "has engaged in, aided or abetted, or conspired to commit, acts of international terrorism, or acts in preparation therefore, that have caused, threaten to cause, or have as their aim to cause, injury to or adverse effects on the United States, its citizens, national security, foreign policy, or economy," or (iii) has "knowingly harbored one or more individuals described in subparagraphs (i) and (ii)."

What process will be used to "determine" a terrorist or a terrorist organization? Does the president merely announce the result and force the target to mount a defense? In 2002, a district court in California ruled that the process used by the Secretary of State in designating foreign terrorist organizations—

without notice to the organization and on the basis of classified information that remains secret upon judicial review—violates on its face the Fifth Amendment's due process clause.[36]

USA PATRIOT ACT

The USA Patriot Act, enacted on October 26, 2001, strengthens the power of the administration to deter and punish terrorists. Yet the statute goes far beyond the threat of terrorism, because it gives the government broad new powers to conduct any criminal investigation. An increase in the power of the executive branch—especially over law enforcement—inevitably places at risk some constitutional rights and liberties. Especially is that so for legislation, such as the USA Patriot Act, that shoots through Congress at great speed without the regular care and deliberation of legislative hearings, committee mark-ups, and floor debate.[37] How much individual rights and liberties are eroded will depend on the manner in which the administration implements the statute and the willingness of Congress, the courts, and the public to monitor the executive branch and supply necessary checks.

The House Judiciary Committee held one hearing on September 24, conducted a mark-up with amendments offered and agreed to, and issued a lengthy committee report on H.R. 2975.[38] This bill, reflecting bipartisan support, passed the committee by a vote of 36 to 0 and rejected some of the extreme measures advocated by the administration. However, on the floor, the House acted under a closed rule to prohibit amendments, except an amendment in the nature of a substitute consisting of the text of a new bill, H.R. 3108, that few members had seen. Among other changes, the House deleted a two-year sunset provision for foreign intelligence surveillance and replaced it with a five-year termination date. Many of the sections in the bill had no sunset provision at all. The House rejected a motion to recommit the bill to House Judiciary and have it report back clearer definitions of surveillance procedures.

On the Senate side, Senator Feingold objected that there was not "a single moment of markup or vote in the Judiciary Committee."[39] He offered three amendments during floor action, but each was tabled rather than put to a vote on the merits. Senate Majority Leader Tom Daschle (D-SD) objected to all amendments, urging his colleagues to join him in tabling the first Feingold amendment and "every other amendment that is offered."[40] When the House acted on the bill that became the USA Patriot Act (H.R. 3162), it did so under suspension of the rules, a procedure that prohibits amendments. The final bill adopted a four-year sunset for some of the surveillance procedures.

Many of the provisions of the USA Patriot Act had been considered in previous years and rejected. For example, Section 219 authorizes nationwide service of search warrants in terrorism investigations. A single judge, having authorized the first warrant, may grant future warrants in other jurisdictions.

The warrant is not limited to a particular locality. It will apply to any district "in which activities related to the terrorism may have occurred." The purpose is to build expertise and accountability in a single judge rather than having to bring judges up-to-speed in other jurisdictions. While this is convenient for law enforcement, it means that many defendants will lack the funds to hire attorneys in distant states.

Section 206 provides for roving wiretaps under the Foreign Intelligence Surveillance Act (FISA). This provision allows surveillance to follow a person, thus avoiding the need for a separate court order that identifies each telephone company every time the target of investigation changes phones. Section 213, referred to as "sneak and peek," authorizes surreptitious search warrants and seizures without the previous requirement to immediately notify a person of the entry and seized items. Law enforcement officers may therefore enter someone's home without giving immediate notice, which may be delayed for "a reasonable period." Section 216 updates existing statutory authority relating to the use of pen registers, which allow government officers to determine the telephone number being dialed from a phone. Federal judges may grant pen register authority to the FBI to cover not just telephones but also such communications as e-mail. Like roving wiretaps, once authority is obtained to install a pen register, it will now apply anywhere in the United States.

In Section 411, Congress added language to help soften a provision that would have enabled the administration to deport someone who had innocently contributed to a charitable organization that the administration determined to have ties to terrorism. Congress limited the retroactive effect of this provision, but it still places the burden on an alien to demonstrate that "he did not know, and should not reasonably have known," that his actions would further terrorist activity.[41]

One of the most controversial provisions appears in Section 218, which changed the FISA requirement that had allowed surveillance only if "the purpose" is to obtain foreign intelligence information. Originally, Congress wanted to maintain separation between wiretaps conducted by the intelligence community and criminal investigations pursued by law enforcement officers. For criminal investigations, a wiretap requires both probable cause that a crime has been committed and an authorizing order from a federal judge. Wiretaps for intelligence are conducted with a lower standard, and the information obtained was to be used only for foreign intelligence.

FISA was enacted in 1978 after congressional investigations revealed that intelligence agencies had violated the rights of U.S. citizens. For years, the federal government had been conducting warrantless surveillance over domestic organizations and the private lives of citizens. FISA created a special court—the Foreign Intelligence Surveillance Court (FISC)—to authorize surveillance over foreign activities, not domestic affairs. The Bush administration wanted to relax a requirement in the 1978 statute by allowing FISA surveillance if "a purpose" is to obtain foreign intelligence information. The two branches compromised by adopting the words "a significant purpose." Section 504 added language to clarify when federal officers who conduct FISA wiretaps may consult with federal law enforcement officers to investigate or protect against actual or potential attacks of international terrorism.

From the operation of FISA in May 1979 to 2002, the FISA court approved all of the government's applications for a search order. That pattern changed on May 17, 2002, when the court released its first published opinion. It challenged the government's argument that FISA can be used "primarily for a law enforcement purpose, so long as a significant foreign intelligence purpose remains." The court was troubled by an inadequate "wall" between FISA information-gathering and the criminal investigations conducted by the Justice Department. It charged that procedures adopted by the administration in March 2002 "appear to be designed to amend the law." The court objected not to information-sharing but to the capacity of law enforcement investigators to give advice to FISA searches. To the court, *coordination* between intelligence and criminal investigators had been replaced by the *subordination* of both investigations to law enforcement objectives.[42]

The Justice Department appealed this ruling to a three-judge FISA appeals court, the first time that this court found it necessary to meet. On November 18, 2002, the appeals court reversed the May 17 ruling and upheld the authority of criminal prosecutors to be actively involved in foreign intelligence wiretaps. The court did not find in the 1978 statute, or in any litigation since that time, a requirement that a "wall" be maintained between the acquisition of intelligence and the needs of criminal law enforcement. Moreover, Congress was aware in passing the USA Patriot Act that it was relaxing a requirement that the government demonstrate that the primary purpose of surveillance be the collection of intelligence rather than criminal prosecution.[43] As a result of this appellate decision and the USA Patriot Act, it is possible to conduct a criminal investigation without the probable cause standard of the Fourth Amendment.

THE RIGHTS OF DETAINEES

In terms of damage done to civil liberties, the USA Patriot Act has thus far been far overshadowed by other techniques of law enforcement: holding individuals under the material witness statute, detaining suspects without charging them or giving them access to attorneys, holding closed immigration hearings, and relying on secret evidence.[44] Beginning in December 2002, the Justice Department required men from certain countries (predominantly Muslim) to register with the INS, be fingerprinted and photographed, and respond to questions. Exceptions were made for certain categories, such as permanent residents and men with "green cards." Failure to register risked deportation.

When the men showed up, hundreds were handcuffed and detained for days because their student or work visas had expired. Some of the men lacked proper papers because their application for permanent residency had been delayed for years in INS proceedings.[45] Beyond the harassment of the Arab-American and Muslim communities, the policy of registration and detention seems to have little bearing to the war on terrorism. Undocumented terrorists are unlikely to show up at an INS office to be registered.

After 9/11, much of the harshness, arbitrariness, and abuse of law enforcement fell on Arab Americans and Muslims. Dr. Al Bader al Hamzi, a thirty-four-year-old radiologist from Saudi Arabia, was arrested at his townhouse in San Antonio the day after the September 11 terrorist attacks. He was held for twelve days before he was permitted to answer questions put to him by authorities. On September 24 he was finally released. The government brought no charges against him.[46] Supposedly these men are held to obtain information about terrorism, but many of them have been detained for weeks and months without ever being interrogated by the FBI or the INS.

Ali al Maqtari, born in Yemen, came to the United States with the hope of becoming a French teacher. Four days after the September 11 attacks, he arrived at Fort Campbell, Kentucky, to drop off his American wife, who was reporting for active duty with the U.S. Army. He was ordered out of his car and later detained for two months by the INS in Mason, Tennessee. He appeared before a Senate subcommittee to explain what had happened to him.[47]

On September 12, 2001, Hady Hassan Omar was placed in jail because the FBI was convinced he had some connection to al Qaeda. Born in Egypt, he lived in Fort Smith, Arkansas, with his American wife and baby daughter. A deputy from the local sheriff's office asked him to come to the station for a few questions. He was then held in captivity for seventy-three days, some of it in solitary confinement, until he became suicidal. He was released, but legal expenses left the couple broke and he was fired from his job. The government never presented charges against him.[48]

One more example. Tony Oulai, a Catholic from the Ivory Coast, was arrested as a suspect in the 9/11 attacks. After a deportation order was issued on November 15, 2001, the government designated him a material witness. Three months later, federal prosecutors filed a court document acknowledging that they had no evidence he was involved in any terrorist activity. Still, he was held on a new charge: making a false statement to federal officials (telling them he was living in the United States legally, when in fact his visa had expired). All told, he was held for 422 days before being sent back to the Ivory Coast.[49]

The Justice Department has not adopted consistent or even understandable principles in its prosecution of suspects. John Walker Lindh, born in California but captured in Afghanistan among Taliban forces, was tried in civil court. Yasser Esam Hamdi, born in Louisiana and captured in the same Afghan prison rebellion as Lindh, was held initially at Guantanamo Bay but was moved to a brig at the Norfolk Naval Station. He has not been charged. Zacarias Moussaoui, a French citizen of Moroccan descent, was arrested in Minnesota as the "twentieth hijacker." He has been charged and is being tried in civil court. Richard E. Reid, the British "shoe bomber," is also being tried in civil court. Jose Padilla, born in New York, was held by the military as a suspect in a plot to detonate a radiological dispersal device—or "dirty bomb"—in the United States. Although arrested by the FBI on May 8, 2002, and incarcerated since that time, he has yet to be charged with a crime.

After 9/11, the Immigration and Naturalization Service began to close deportation proceedings to the press and the public. The government used this period to question a number of noncitizens, primarily young men of Arab or Muslim background. Rabih Haddad, cofounder of a Muslim charity in Illinois, was held for nine months because the government suspected that he had supplied money to terrorist organizations. He was finally able to testify at an open hearing after a federal judge ordered the Justice Department to either give him an open hearing or release him.[50] Several court decisions found that the government's interest in closing these proceedings was not compelling.[51]

The Sixth Circuit held that there is a First Amendment right of access by the press and the public to deportation proceedings. In his ruling, Judge Damon J. Keith explained why the press had to watch executive branch decisions: "Democracies die behind closed doors."[52] After this decision was issued, Associate Attorney General Jay Stephens admitted that the release of past transcripts on the Haddad immigration proceedings "will not cause irreparable harm to the national security or to the safety of the American people."[53]

In the one case that reached the Supreme Court—a district court decision in New Jersey that supported open deportation hearings—the Court stayed the decision pending appeal.[54] The Third Circuit later overturned the district court decision, finding that the tradition of open hearings for criminal and civil trials did not apply to the same extent to administrative hearings. Writing for a 2-1 majority, Chief Judge Edward R. Becker agreed that, procedurally, "deportation hearings and civil trials are practically indistinguishable,"[55] and that openness in deportation hearings offers all the salutary functions recognized in civil and criminal trials: educating the public; promoting public perception of fairness; providing an outlet for community concern, hostility, and emotion; serving to check corrupt practices in court; enhancing the performance of all involved; and discouraging perjury. However, he accepted the Justice Department's argument that open deportation hearings could threaten national security by revealing sources and methods, giving terrorists organizations an opportunity to see what patterns of entry work and which ones fail, and providing other facts that might assist terrorist attacks. Although closed deportation hearings would shield that type of information, nothing prevents the detainees or their attorneys from making that information public.

Chief Judge Becker, agreeing with the newspapers that the government's representations were "to some degree speculative," declined to "lightly second-guess" the concerns of Attorney General Ashcroft about national security. In reversing the district court, Becker said that he was "keenly aware of the dangers presented by deference to the executive branch when constitutional liberties are at stake, especially in times of national crisis, when those liberties are likely in greatest jeopardy."[56]

In his dissent, Judge Anthony J. Scirica noted that deportation hearings have "a consistent history of openness," and that Congress left deportation hearings presumptively open while expressly closing exclusion proceedings. He agreed with the majority that judicial deference to the executive branch is appropriate, but not to the extent of "abdicating our responsibilities under the First Amendment."[57] Instead of accepting the INS policy of a blanket closure rule on deportation hearings, Judge Scirica preferred a case-by-case approach to allow immigration judges to weigh the conflicting values between the First Amendment and the government's national security responsibilities.

Another dispute is the government's decision to conceal the identities of hundreds of people arrested after the 9/11 attacks. On August 2, 2002, Judge Gladys Kessler ordered that most of the names be released within fifteen days.[58] Secret arrests, she said, are "a concept odious to a democratic society."[59] Judge Kessler suspended her order two weeks later to allow the government to appeal her decision to the D.C. Circuit.[60] The Justice Department argues that disclosing the names of hundreds of people arrested on immigration charges would help terrorists of al Qaeda determine how the government was conducting its antiterrorist campaign.[61] Why? What persuasive reasons (rather than conclusory statements) can be advanced?

Some of these individuals were held as "material witnesses," a category that Congress authorized in 1984 to assure the testimony of a person that is "material in a criminal proceeding." If it is shown that it "may become impracticable to secure the presence of the person by subpoena," a judicial officer may arrest the person. Release of a material witness "may be delayed for a reasonable period of time."[62] Thus, Congress did not establish a time limit for detention. Although these people are held to provide information for a criminal proceeding, many of them have never been called to testify before a grand jury or even give depositions. Nabil Almarabh, a former Boston cab driver from Kuwait, was arrested one week after the 9/11 attacks. As of November 23, 2002, he had been held in custody for 432 days without appearing before a grand jury.[63]

Two federal district judges from New York's Southern District have split on the government's authority under the material witness statute.[64] Judge Shira A. Scheindlin ruled that federal authorities cannot use the statute to detain witnesses for grand jury proceedings, concluding that Congress has never granted authority to the government "to imprison an innocent person in order to guarantee that he will testify before a grand jury conducting a criminal investigation."[65] On the other hand, Judge Michael B. Mukasey held that the material witness statute does apply to grand jury witnesses.[66] His ruling would allow the government to hold someone as a material witness for the length of a grand jury (up to eighteen months).

As to the six hundred suspected terrorists held at Guantanamo Bay, a federal judge held that they had no right to bring a case in U.S. courts. Judge Colleen Kollar-Kotelly rejected their lawsuit, which stated that they were being held without charges and without access to attorneys or trial dates. Their geographical location, she said, denied them the right to press their interests in U.S. courts. Because writs of habeas corpus are not available to "aliens held outside the sovereign territory of the United States, this court does not have jurisdiction" to hear the case.[67]

ENEMY COMBATANTS

What emerged from the Hamdi and Padilla cases is the concept of "enemy combatant." Whoever fits that category is held but not charged, has no right to an attorney, and (according to Justice) federal judges have no right to interfere with executive judgments. A Justice Department brief for the Fourth Circuit argued: "The court may not second-guess the military's enemy combatant determination. Going beyond that determination would require the courts to enter an area in which they have no competence, intrude upon the Constitutional prerogative of the Commander in Chief . . . and possibly create 'a conflict between judicial and military opinion highly comforting to enemies of the United States.'"[68]

"Enemy combatant" is another term for unlawful combatants. Lawful combatants are held as prisoners of war and may not be prosecuted for criminal violations for belligerent acts that do not constitute war crimes. Lawful combatants wear uniforms with a fixed distinctive emblem and conduct their operations in accordance with the laws and customs of war.[69] On November 26, 2002, the General Counsel of the Defense Department defined "enemy combatant" as "an individual who, under the laws and customs of war, may be detained for the duration of an armed conflict. In the current conflict with al Qaeda and the Taliban, for example, the term includes a member, agent, or associate of al Qaeda or the Taliban. In applying this definition, we note our consistency with the observation of the Supreme Court of the United States in *Ex parte Quirin*, 317 U.S. 1(1942): 'Citizens who associate themselves with the military arm of the enemy government, and with its aid, guidance and direction enter this country bent on hostile acts are enemy belligerents within the meaning of the Hague Convention and the law of war.'"[70] However, Hamdi did not enter the United States. He was apprehended in Afghanistan.

Both Hamdi and Padilla, as American citizens, are supposedly covered by this provision in the U.S. Code: "No citizen shall be imprisoned or otherwise detained by the United States except pursuant to an Act of Congress."[71] The Bush administration, however, argues that it is not limited by this statute because "Article II alone gives the president the power to detain enemies during wartime, regardless of congressional action."[72]

In the Hamdi case, a federal district judge several times rejected the broad arguments put forth by the Justice Department, insisting that Hamdi had a right of access to the public defender and without the presence of military personnel. However, he was repeatedly reversed by the Fourth Circuit.[73] In its most recent ruling of January 8, 2003, again overturning the district court, the Fourth Circuit juggled two values—the judiciary's duty to protect constitutional rights versus the judiciary's need to defer to military decisions by the president—and came down squarely in favor of presidential power.

The Fourth Circuit arrived at that conclusion through a strange reading of separation of powers. It cites an opinion by the Supreme Court in 1991 that the "ultimate purpose of this separation of powers is to protect the liberty and security of the governed."[74] Instead of reading this language as an affirmation of the checks and balances that prevent an accumulation of power in a single branch, the Fourth Circuit interprets the Court's sentence as a warning to the federal judiciary not to interfere with powers vested in another branch: "For the judicial branch to trespass upon the exercise of the war-making powers would be an infringement of the right to self-determination and self-governance at a time when the care of the common defense is most critical." The reading is bizarre because whereas the Fourth Circuit acquiesces wholly to the judgment of the president, the Supreme Court in 1991 expressly intervened to strike down a statutory procedure adopted by Congress. No philosophy of deference appears in the 1991 decision.

Although the Fourth Circuit pays lip service to independent judicial scrutiny ("The detention of U.S. citizens must be subject to judicial review"[75]), the review here scarcely exists. The Fourth Circuit left little doubt about its willingness to defer to the president. "The judiciary is not at liberty to eviscerate detention interests directly derived from the war powers of Articles I and II."[76] With such a frame of reference, judicial review is emptied of meaning.

Compare the Hamdi case with the treatment of Padilla. The FBI arrested Padilla in Chicago on May 8, 2002, on a material witness warrant to secure his testimony before a grand jury in New York City. After President Bush designated him an enemy combatant, the material witness warrant was withdrawn and the government moved Padilla to a Navy brig in Charleston, South Carolina. He had access to an attorney, Donna Newman, in New York City, but not after his removal to Charleston. In a ruling on December 4, 2002, a district judge in New York City ruled that Padilla had a right to consult with counsel under conditions that would minimize the likelihood that he could use his lawyers as "unwilling intermediaries for the transmission of information to others."[77] The court held that Padilla had a right to present facts and the most convenient way to do that was to present them through counsel.[78] Moreover, on the issue of Padilla's status, the court insisted on evidence to support Bush's finding that Padilla is an enemy combatant.

The court did not grant to Padilla the right of counsel because of the Sixth Amendment, which applies only to "all criminal prosecutions." With no charges filed against him, there was no criminal proceeding. Instead, the court looked to congressional policy on habeas corpus petitions, entitling an applicant to "deny any of the facts set in the return or allege any other material facts" (28 U.S.C. § 2243). As to the government's concern that Padilla might somehow use his attorney to communicate to the enemy, the court noted that such an argument would even prohibit an indicted member of al Qaeda from consulting with counsel in an Article III proceeding.[79]

CONCLUSIONS

Although there have been many deprivations of civil liberties since the 9/11 attacks, some public officials have made efforts to limit the damage to Arab Americans and Muslims. President Bush went out of his way to emphasize that the war in Afghanistan was not a war against Islam or against the Arab world.[80] Two days after the terrorist attacks, standing in the company of New York City Mayor Rudy Giuliani and New York Governor George Pataki, he cautioned that "our Nation must be mindful that there are thousands of Arab Americans who live in New York City who love their flag just as much as the three of us do."[81] In a visit to the Islamic Center of Washington, D.C., Bush stated that Muslims in America "make an incredibly valuable contribution to our country. Muslims are doctors, lawyers, law professors, members of the military, entrepreneurs, shopkeepers, moms and dads. And they need to be treated with respect. In our anger and emotion, our fellow Americans must treat each other with respect."[82]

Three days after the terrorist attacks on New York City and Washington, D.C., the House passed a concurrent resolution condemning bigotry and violence against Arab Americans, American Muslims, and Americans from South Asia. Rep. George Gekas (R-PA) said that part of the purpose of the resolution was to avoid repeating "the insidious events that took place after Pearl Harbor with respect to the treatment of Japanese-American citizens."[83] Rep. Dave Bonior (D-MI) spoke out in defense of diversity "and for the rights of every American of every heritage and faith to live and worship with safety and confidence and pride."[84] The resolution passed with overwhelming support in the House and in the Senate.[85]

The USA Patriot Act includes Section 102, which condemns discrimination against Arab and Muslim Americans, stating that these groups "play a vital role in our Nation and are entitled to nothing less than the full rights of every American." The statutory language condemns acts of violence against Arab and Muslim Americans and states that anyone who commits acts of violence against these communities "should be punished to the full extent of the law."

The tragedy of 9/11 has helped educate Americans on Arabs and Muslims. Most Arabs in the United States are probably not Muslim. They are likely to be Christians from such countries as Lebanon. Moreover, most Muslims are not Arabs. They come from South Asia or are African Americans. People from the Middle East need not be Arabs. They can be Turks, Iranians, or Kurds. Each step of education helps puncture erroneous and dangerous stereotypes.

With some unfortunate incidents of vandalism, the Muslim and Arabic communities in the United States have been largely spared the kinds of violence that can be directed toward minorities. Elected officials and community leaders have helped keep violence in check. There have been major demonstrations throughout the country on the Middle East, often pitting pro-Palestinians against pro-Israelis. These protests have been emotional, tense, and angry, but thus far not violent.[86]

Facing opportunities and difficulties like other immigrant groups, Arabs are finding acceptance politically, economically, and socially. Americans are learning more about the history of Islam and the extent to which it builds upon Judaism and Christianity. They understand that neither Islam nor "Arabs" are monoliths, that they are complex social entities with many subsets within. Many Muslims in America, after September 11, have been rediscovering their religious faith.[87] The Fourth Circuit rejected an attempt by a conservative Christian group to prevent the University of North Carolina from using a text on the Koran to teach incoming students.[88] With patience and understanding, America can hold true to a motto that has, over the centuries, made possible a community: "E Pluribus Unum."

NOTES

1. H. Rept. No. 107-236 (Part 1), 107th Cong., 1st Sess. 291 (2001).
2. Adriel Bettelheim and Elizabeth A. Palmer, "Balancing Liberty and Security," *Congressional Quarterly Weekly Report*, 22 September 2001, p. 2210.
3. 147 Cong. Rec. S10570 (daily ed. October 11, 2001).
4. White House Memorandum of October 5, 2001, "Disclosures to the Congress," from President Bush to the Secretary of State, the Secretary of the Treasury, the Secretary of Defense, the Attorney General, the Director of Central Intelligence, and the Director of Federal Bureau of Investigation. See "Bush Orders Limits on Disclosure of Classified Data to Congress," *Washington Times*, 9 October 2001, p. A-15.
5. "Bush Edict on Briefings Irks Hill," *Washington Post*, 10 October 2001, p. A-1.
6. "Bush, Angered by Leaks, Duels with Congress," *New York Times*, 10 October 2001, p. B-11.
7. Susan Schmitt and Bob Woodward, "FBI, CIA Warn Congress of More Attacks as Blair Details Case against Bin Laden: Retaliation Feared if U.S. Strikes Afghanistan," *Washington Post*, 5 October 2001, p. A-1
8. "TV Networks to Limit Use of Tapes from Bin Laden: White House to Reinstate Some Congressional Briefings," *Washington Post*, 11 October 2001, p. A-8; "Bush Lifts Some Restrictions on Classified Information," *New York Times*, 11 October 2001, p. B-11; "Congress Maintains Its Right to Remain in the Loop," *Congressional Quarterly Weekly Report*, 13 October 2001, p. 2395.
9. Dana Priest, "Probe of Hill Leaks on 9/11 Is Intensified," *Washington Post*, 24 August 2002, p. A-1.
10. For example, David E. Sanger and Eric Schmitt, "U.S. Has a Plan to Occupy Iraq, Officials Report," *New York Times*, 11 October 2002, p. A-1; Thom Shanker and Eric Schmitt, "Rumsfeld

Orders War Plans Redone for Faster Action," *New York Times*, 13 October 2002, p. 1; David E. Sanger, Eric Schmitt, and Thom Shanker, "War Plan for Iraq Calls for Big Force and Quick Strikes," *New York Times*, 10 October 2002, p. 1.

11. *Weekly Compilation of Presidential Documents*, vol. 39, p. 1718; Dana Milbank, "With Congress Aboard, Bush Targets a Doubtful Public," *Washington Post*, October 8, 2002, p. A-21.

12. John Mintz, "Detainees at Base in Cuba Yield Little Valuable Information," *Washington Post*, 29 October 2002, p. A-15.

13. Memorandum of July 12, 2002, "The Impact of Leaking Classified Information," from Secretary Rumsfeld to top officials in the Defense Department and the Joint Chiefs of Staff.

14. Memorandum of October 12, 2001, "The Freedom of Information Act," from Attorney General John Ashcroft to the heads of all federal departments and agencies.

15. H. Rept. No. 107-371, 107th Cong., 2nd Sess. (2002), p. 3.

16. "Letter to Ridge Is Latest Jab in Fight over Balance of Powers," *New York Times*, 5 March 2002, p. A-8; "Ridge Declines to Testify for Panel," *Washington Post*, 5 March 2002, p. A-8.

17. "Ridge Offers Compromise on Testimony before Congress," *New York Times*, 26 March 2002, p. A-13.

18. "From Bush Officials, a Hill Overturn and a Snub: Ridge Meets House Panel in a Closed, Informal Session, but Criticism Persists," *Washington Post*, 11 April 2002, p. A-27; "Ridge Briefs House Panel, but Discord Is Not Resolved," *New York Times*, 11 April 2002, p. A-17.

19. Louis Fisher, "White House Aides Testifying before Congress," 27 *Presidential Studies Quarterly* 139 (1997).

20. Senate, "Department of Justice Oversight: Preserving Our Freedoms While Defending against Terrorism," *Hearings before the Senate Committee on the Judiciary*, 107th Cong., 1st sess., 2001, p. 313.; *New York Times*, 7 December 2001, p. B-6, col. 1.

21. "Ashcroft Aide Says Criticism Wasn't Aimed at Policy Foes," *Washington Post*, 8 December 2001, p. A-11.

22. For example, 1 Ops. Att'y Gen. 233 (1818); 11 Ops. Att'y Gen. 297 (1865); William Winthrop, Military Law and Precedents 831 (2000 ed.); *Ex parte Milligan*, 71 U.S. 2, 121–122 (1866); *Coleman v. Tennessee*, 97 U.S. 509, 514 (1878); *Ex parte Quirin*, 317 U.S. 1, 28–29 (1942); *In re Yamashita*, 327 U.S. 1, 10–11, 16, 23 (1946); *Duncan v. Kahanamoku*, 327 U.S. 304 (1946); *Madsen v. Kinsella*, 343 U.S. 342, 348–349 (1952).

23. Zechariah Chafee, Jr., "Freedom of Speech in War Time," 32 Harv. L. Rev. 932, 958 (1919); Louis Fisher, *American Constitutional Law*, 4th ed. (Durham: Carolina Academic Press, 2001), pp. 486–487.

24. Bill Miller, "Ashcroft: Old Rules Aided Terrorists," *Washington Post*, 31 May 2002, p. A-13; Don Van Natta, Jr., "Government Will Ease Limits on Domestic Spying by the F.B.I.," *New York Times*, 30 May 2002, p. A-1.

25. *Weekly Compilation of Presidential Documents*, vol. 38, pp. 934–935 (May 30, 2002).

26. Louis Fisher, "Bush Can't Rely on the FDR Precedent," *Los Angeles Times*, 2 December 2001, p. M-3.

27. *Ex parte Milligan*, 4 Wall. (71 U.S.) 2 (1866).

28. *Ex parte Quirin*, 47 F.Supp. 431 (D.D.C. 1942).

29. *Ex parte Quirin*, 63 S. Ct. 1–2 (1942). The per curiam is also reproduced in a footnote in *Ex parte Quirin*, 317 U.S. 1, 18–19 (1942).

30. *Ex parte Quirin*, 317 U.S. 1 (1942); Alpheus Thomas Mason, "Inter Arma Silent Leges: Chief Justice Stone's Views," 69 Harv. L. Rev. 806 (1956).

31. Edward S. Corwin, *Total War and the Constitution* (New York: Knopf, 1947), p. 118.

32. "Memorandum Re: *Rosenberg v. United States*, Nos. 111 and 687, October Term 1952," June 4, 1953, p. 8; Papers of Felix Frankfurter, Manuscript Room, Library of Congress, Part I, Reel 70.

33. Conversation between Justice William O. Douglas and Professor Walter F. Murphy, June 9, 1962, pp. 204–205; Seeley G. Mudd Manuscript Library, Princeton University.

34. Military Order, 10 Fed. Reg. 548 (1945).

35. For further details, see Louis Fisher, *Nazi Saboteurs on Trial: A Military Tribunal and American Law* (Lawrence, KS: University Press of Kansas, 2003).

36. *United States v. Rahmani*, 209 F.Supp.2d 1045 (C.D. Cal. 2002).

37. "Terrorism Bill's Sparse Paper Trail May Cause Legal Vulnerability," *Congressional Quarterly Weekly Report*, 27 October 2001, pp. 2533–2535.

38. H. Rept. No. 107-236 (Part 1), 107th Cong., 1st Sess. (2001).

39. 147 Cong. Rec. S10575 (daily ed. October 11, 2001).
40. Ibid. at S10574.
41. See remarks of Senator Leahy at 147 Cong. Rec. S10558 (daily ed. Oct. 11, 2001).
42. *In re All Matters to Foreign Intelligence Surveil.*, 218 F.Supp.2d 611 (Foreign Intel. Surv. Ct. 2002).
43. *In re Sealed Case*, 310 F.3d 717 (Foreign Intel. Surv. Ct. of Rev. 2002).
44. "U.S. Use of Secret Evidence Affirmed," *Washington Post*, 1 January 2003, p. A-9; "U.S. Defends Secret Evidence in Charity Case," *New York Times*, 30 October 2002, p. A-13; "U.S. Defends Secrecy in Terror Case," *Washington Post*, 30 October 2002, p. A-2.
45. John M. Broder and Susan Sachs, "Facing Registry Deadline, Men from Muslim Nations Swamp Immigration Office," *New York Times*, 17 December 2002, p. A-16; Dan Eggen, "2nd Chance to Register Given," *Washington Post*, 16 January 2003, p. A-2; Michael Powell, "Pakistanis Flee to Canada and Uncertainty," *Washington Post*, 18 January 2003, p. A-1; Nurith C. Aizenman, "A Register of Immigrants' Fears," *Washington Post*, 20 January 2003, p. A-1.
46. Elizabeth A. Palmer and Adriel Bettelheim, "War and Civil Liberties: Congress Gropes for a Role," *Congressional Quarterly Weekly Report*, 1 December 2001, p. 2820.
47. Senate, "Department of Justice Oversight: Preserving Our Freedoms While Defending against Terrorism," *Hearings before the Senate Committee on the Judiciary*, 107th Cong., 1st sess., 2001, pp. 211–217.
48. Matthew Brzezinski, "Hady Hassan Omar's Detention," *New York Times Magazine*, 27 October 2002, pp. 50–55.
49. Amy Goldstein, "A Sept. 11 Detainee's Long Path to Release," *Washington Post*, 12 November 2002, p. A-3.
50. Dan Eggen, "Judge Orders Release or Open Hearings," *Washington Post*, 18 September 2002, p. A-14; "Sept. 11 Detainee Testifies at Public Hearing," *Washington Post*, 2 October 2002, p. A-6.
51. *Detroit Free Press v. Ashcroft*, 195 F.Supp.2d 937 (E.D. Mich. 2002); *Detroit Free Press v. Ashcroft*, 195 F.Supp.2d 948 (E.D. Mich. 2002).
52. *Detroit Free Press v. Ashcroft*, 303 F.3d 681, 683 (6th Cir. 2002).
53. http://www.usdoj.gov/opa/pr/2002/April/02_ag_238.htm.
54. *Ashcroft v. North Jersey Media Group, Inc.*, 122 S. Ct. 2655 (2002); *North Jersey Media Group, Inc. v. Ashcroft*, 205 F.Supp.2d 288 (D. N.J. 2002).
55. *North Jersey Media Group, Inc. v. Ashcroft*, 308 F.3d 198, 215 (3rd Cir. 2002).
56. Ibid. at 220.
57. Ibid. at 226.
58. Neil A. Lewis, "Judge Orders U.S. to Release Names of 9/11 Detainees," *New York Times*, 3 August 2002, p. A-1.
59. *Center for Nat. Security v. U.S. Dept. of Justice*, 215 F.Supp.2d 94, 96 (D.D.C. 2002) (quoting *Morrow v. District of Columbia*, 417 F.2d 728, 741–742 (D.C. Cir. 1969)).
60. *Center for Nat. Security v. U.S. Dept. of Justice*, 217 F.Supp.2d 58 (D.D.C. 2002).
61. Neil A. Lewis, "U.S. Says Revealing Names Would Aid al Qaeda," *Washington Post*, 19 November 2002, p. A-18.
62. 98 Stat. 1982, § 3144 (1984); 18 U.S.C. § 3144 (2000).
63. Steve Fainaru and Margot Williams, "Material Witness Law Has Many In Limbo," *Washington Post*, 24 November 2002, p. A-1, A-12.
64. Steve Fainaru, "Judge: U.S. May Jail Material Witnesses," *Washington Post*, 12 July 2002, p. A-12.
65. *United States v. Awadallah*, 202 F.Supp.2d 55, 82 (S.D.N.Y. 2002).
66. In re: *Applic. of U.S. for Material Witness Warrant*, 213 F.Supp.2d 287 (S.D.N.Y. 2002).
67. Neely Tucker, "Judge Denies Detainees in Cuba Access to U.S. Courts," *Washington Post*, 1 August 2002, p. A-10.
68. Tom Jackman and Dan Eggen, "'Combatants Lack Rights,' U.S. Argues," *Washington Post*, 20 June 2002, p. A-10.
69. Hague Convention of October 18, 1907, 36 Stat. 2296.
70. Letter of November 26, 2002, from William J. Haynes II, General Counsel, Department of Defense, to Senator Carl Levin, p. 102.
71. 18 U.S.C. § 4001(a) (2000).
72. Letter of September 23, 2002, from William J. Haynes II, General Counsel, Department of Defense, to Alfred P. Carlton, Jr., President, American Bar Association, p. 2.

73. *Hamdi v. Rumsfeld*, 294 F.3d 598 (4th Cir. 2002); *Hamdi v. Rumsfeld*, 296 F.3d 278 (4th Cir. 2002).
74. *Hamdi v. Rumsfeld*, No. 02-7338 (4th Cir. 2003) (memo op.), at 20, citing *Metro. Wash. Airports Auth. v. Citizens for the Abatement of Aircraft Noise, Inc.*, 501 U.S. 252, 272 (1991).
75. Ibid. p. 23.
76. Ibid. p. 26.
77. *Padilla v. Bush*, 02 Civ. 445 (MBM) (D. N.Y. 2002) (memo op.), p. 3.
78. Ibid. p. 75.
79. Ibid. p. 86.
80. *Weekly Compilation of Presidential Documents*, vol. 37, p. 1429 (Oct. 6, 2001).
81. Ibid. p. 1306 (September 13, 2001).
82. Ibid. p. 1327 (September 17, 2001).
83. 147 Cong. Rec. H5691 (daily ed. September 14, 2001).
84. Ibid. H5692.
85. Ibid. H5698 and S9859 (daily ed. September 26, 2001).
86. "On Campus, a Reflection of Middle East Anger," *Washington Post*, 10 May 2002, p. A-3.
87. "The Fabric of Their Faith," *Washington Post*, 19 May 2002, p. C-1.
88. Stephen Braun, "Appeals Court Rejects Bid to Bar Readings on Islam," *Washington Post*, 20 August 2002, p. A-2.

PATRIOTISM, PARTISANSHIP, AND INSTITUTIONAL PROTECTION

THE CONGRESSIONAL RESPONSE TO 9/11

BARBARA SINCLAIR

UNIVERSITY OF CALIFORNIA, LOS ANGELES

In the latter part of the twentieth century, Congress polarized along partisan and ideological lines. Observers and members alike complained about the bitter partisan warfare that pervaded Washington. Presidents could expect less and less support from members of the opposition party and, given the frequency of divided partisan control of Congress and the White House, encountered increasing difficulty in enacting their programs.[1]

In addition, according to some commentators, high partisanship when combined with frequent divided control and the end of the Cold War had led to a shift in power from president to Congress. Congress, according to this argument, had encroached more and more on executive prerogatives.

Then, on September 11, 2001, three hijacked commercial airliners smashed into the twin towers of the World Trade Center and the Pentagon, and another went down in western Pennsylvania, probably on its way to a target in the nation's capital. These terrorist attacks, as they proved to be, constituted the quintessential "rally" event—an event that by evoking intense patriotism causes Americans to pull together and "rally around the flag" and around their president as the embodiment of the nation.[2]

How did Congress react? Did 9/11 change the character of politics in a fundamental way or was the result more on the surface than deep-seated, temporary rather than long lasting? An examination of Congress's response to 9/11 should shed light on how members' behavior and congressional decisions are shaped by specific major events and by longer-run forces.

This chapter begins with a discussion of the development of partisan polarization in Congress and of the consequences of such polarization for presidential success in the legislative process. Then I examine how Congress reacted to 9/11—first through a brief narrative and then through an analysis of members' voting decisions. Finally I consider whether, in its response to 9/11, Congress surrendered congressional powers to the president or protected its institutional prerogatives.

PARTISAN POLARIZATION IN CONGRESS: DEVELOPMENT AND CONSEQUENCES

In the early 1970s (the 91st Congress), majorities of Democrats and Republicans voted against each other on less than 30 percent of House recorded votes and on 36 percent of Senate votes. And, even on those votes that pitted the parties against each other, members voted with their party colleagues only about 70 percent of the time. Contrast that with the mid-1990s (the 104th Congress) when two-thirds of the recorded votes in the House and Senate were party votes and the average Republican voted with his party colleagues over 90 percent of the time while the average Democrat did so about 85 percent of the time.

More comprehensive figures confirm the increase in partisan voting and the polarization in the voting behavior of the partisan contingents in both houses of Congress. In the 1960s and 1970s (1961–1980), Republican and Democratic majorities on average opposed each other on 40 percent of the recorded votes in the House and 42 percent in the Senate. In the 1980s (1981–1990), the percentage of party votes rose to 51 percent in the House and 45 percent in the Senate.[3] In the 1990s (1991–2000), 58 percent of the roll call votes in the House and 57 percent in the Senate were party votes. Furthermore, on party votes, members were increasingly likely to vote with their party colleagues and against their partisan opponents. As Figure 7.1 (on page 123) shows, the difference between how Democrats and how Republicans voted on recorded floor votes was considerably greater at the end of the twentieth century than at any time in the previous half century. The Poole and Rosenthal DW-nominate scores, which can be interpreted as locating members of Congress on a left-right dimension, show that increasingly there is almost no overlap between the parties, that the most conservative Democrat is to the left of almost all Republicans and conversely the most liberal Republican is to the right of almost all Democrats.[4]

This partisan polarization can be traced to an alteration in the constituency bases of the parties. The change in southern politics that the Civil Rights movement and the Voting Rights Act set off resulted in the conservative southern Democrats so common in the 1960s and before being replaced either by even more conservative Republicans or by more mainstream Democrats. As African Americans became able to vote and as more conservative whites increasingly voted Republican, the supportive electoral coalitions of southern Democrats began to look similar to those of their northern party colleagues. As a result, the legislative preferences of northern and southern congressional Democrats became less disparate.[5]

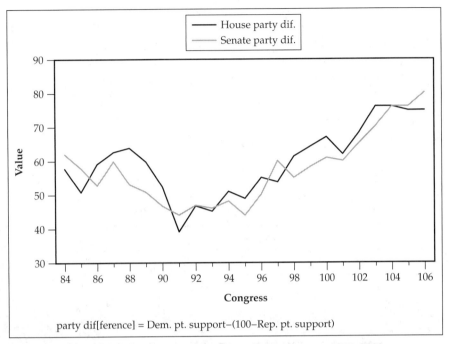

FIGURE 7.1   CONGRESSIONAL PARTY POLARIZATION, 1955–2000

The increasing proportion of House Republicans elected from the South made the Republican party more conservative but accounted for far from all of the change in the party's ideological cast. A resurgence of conservatism at the activist and primary voter level resulted in fewer moderates being nominated; increasingly the Republicans who won nominations and election, especially to the House, were hard-edged, ideological conservatives. Perhaps in response to the polarization of the parties' elected officials and party activists, party identifiers also became more polarized on policy issues.[6] Thus constituency sentiment at both the activist and voter level underlies congressional partisan polarization, especially in the House with its smaller and more homogeneous districts.

Intense partisan polarization has made legislative success more elusive for presidents. Throughout the last century, presidents counted on greater support from their congressional party colleagues than from the opposition and so presidents were more successful when their party controlled Congress.[7] But, so long as the congressional parties were quite ideologically heterogeneous, the president could also expect some support from the members of the other party. As the parties became highly polarized in the late twentieth century, such support has dwindled and a president confronting a Congress controlled by the opposition faces a much harder task. Presidents do considerably less well both on their own agenda (see Table 7.1 on page 124)

TABLE 7.1 THE PRESIDENT'S SUCCESS ON HIS AGENDA UNDER UNIFIED
VERSUS DIVIDED CONTROL AND IN PERIODS OF LESS AND MORE
PARTISAN POLARIZATION (SELECTED CONGRESSES, 1961–1998)

	UNIFIED CONTROL	DIVIDED CONTROL		
		ALL	PRE-100TH	100TH & LATER
President won	63	39	54	33
President lost	31	43	30	49

TABLE 7.2 PRESIDENTIAL SUCCESS ON MAJOR LEGISLATION UNDER UNIFIED
VERSUS DIVIDED CONTROL AND IN PERIODS OF LESS AND MORE
PARTISAN POLARIZATION (SELECTED CONGRESSES, 1961–1998)

	UNIFIED CONTROL	DIVIDED CONTROL		
		ALL	PRE-100TH	100TH & LATER
President supported final bill*	83	40	51	38
President opposed final bill	4	31	25	32

Note: *Final congressional bill is bill as it went to the president.

and on major legislation generally (see Table 7.2) when control is divided.[8]
Moreover divided control is a much greater problem for presidents during
the recent period of high partisan polarization than it was earlier.

DID 9/11 "CHANGE EVERYTHING"?

Private citizens and public officials alike responded to the horrendous attacks
on U.S. soil by rallying around the president and vowing solidarity. Democratic congressional leaders quickly pledged their support. "We are shoulder
to shoulder. We are in complete agreement and we will act together as one.
There is no division between the parties, between the Congress and the president," House Minority Leader Dick Gephardt said. "The world should know
that the members of both parties in both houses stand united," reiterated Majority Leader Tom Daschle.[9] Although George W. Bush ran for president
promising to restore civility and bipartisanship to policymaking and political
debate, the first months of his term looked a lot like the 1990s in their often bitter partisan battles. In fact, by the August recess of 2001, Bush appeared to be
in trouble. Republicans had succeeded in enacting Bush's big tax cut, his number one priority, but had lost control of the Senate when Jim Jeffords (R-VT)
left the party. On issue after issue, the parties were stalemated; neither could

enact its priorities and, given the ideological distance between them, compromise seemed out of reach.[10]

The sense of crisis that 9/11 engendered prompted Congress to act with speed and unity. On September 14 both the House and the Senate approved a resolution authorizing the president to "use all necessary and appropriate force against those nations, organizations, or persons he determines planned, authorized, committed, or aided the terrorist attacks on September 11, 2001, or harbored such organizations or persons."[11] The same day both houses passed an emergency supplemental appropriations bill providing $40 billion for recovery and antiterrorist efforts. One vote was cast against the use of force resolution, none against the money bill. The Senate by voice vote approved the previously controversial nomination of John Negroponte as U.S. ambassador to the U.N. The many Democrats who had questioned Negroponte's fitness dropped their opposition. House Republicans, who had opposed paying dues the United States owed to the UN, backed down so as to facilitate Bush's efforts to build an antiterrorism coalition. On October 25, only six weeks after the attack, Congress sent Bush a far-reaching antiterrorism bill that made it easier for law enforcement to track Internet communications, detain suspected terrorists, and obtain nationwide warrants for searches and eavesdropping.[12]

Even as the Bush administration waged war in Afghanistan, partisan differences began to reemerge. September 11 created a consensus that airline security had to be strengthened significantly and quickly. House Republicans, however, were ideologically opposed to making airline screeners federal employees. The Senate had quickly and unanimously passed legislation that did just that, but House conservatives adamantly refused to go along. House Republican leaders pressured Bush to support their version, which gave the president the choice of whether to federalize screeners and, with both a statement and lobbying help from Bush, they narrowly passed their version in the House. Yet the administration had already signaled that the president was unlikely to veto a bill that federalized screeners. With public opinion strongly backing their position, Democrats hung tough and House Republicans were forced to give in. Few were willing to go into the Thanksgiving weekend without having enacted such legislation. In this case, Republicans and even Bush seemed to be putting ideology ahead of Americans' safety, a politically untenable position, they soon realized.

The year 2002 was characterized by partisan battles on domestic issues but much more bipartisanship on issues related to the terrorism threat. In the fall, Congress passed a resolution approving Bush's Iraq policy, including, if Bush deemed it necessary, a preemptive attack, but Democrats were much less supportive than they had been on the resolution passed right after 9/11.

So what can we conclude about the impact of 9/11 on members' behavior and congressional decisions? Did the catastrophe affect member behavior and presidential success and, if so, how far-ranging and how long-lasting was the effect? Answering those questions requires a systematic analysis, a task the next section undertakes.

TABLE 7.3   PARTISANSHIP AND CONFLICT OVER THE COURSE OF THE 107TH CONGRESS

	PARTY VOTES (%)		NO CONFLICT VOTES* (%)	
PERIOD	HOUSE	SENATE	HOUSE	SENATE
Senate Republican	67	71	16	19
Senate Democratic	56	52	18	34
Immediate post-9/11	42	33	33	50
2002 Pre-election	57	44	20	38
Post-election	79	43	21	29
Total	56	51	21	34

Notes: Votes on suspensions excluded for the House.
*No conflict votes are those on which 90 percent or more of those voting voted on the winning side.

PARTISANSHIP AND PRESIDENTIAL SUCCESS PRE- AND POST-9/11

In terms of its overall level of partisan voting, the 107th Congress (2001–2002) does not differ radically from its immediate predecessors. In the Senate, 51 percent of recorded votes pitted a majority of Democrats against a majority of Republicans. In the House, 42 percent of recorded votes were such party votes; if one excludes bills brought up under the suspension procedure that is used for noncontroversial matters, then 56 percent were party votes.[13] Furthermore, both party contingents in both chambers were highly cohesive on party votes; the average House Republican voted with his party colleagues on 93 percent of party votes; the average House Democrat on 88 percent; the average Senate Republican on 89 percent and the average Senate Democrat on 88 percent.

To ascertain if the events of 9/11 depressed partisanship as has been hypothesized and to determine the duration of any such effect we must examine voting behavior over time within the 107th Congress. I have divided the 107th into five time periods: the early months during which the Republicans controlled both chambers—January through May 26; the period from Jeffords's defection to 9/11; 9/11 through the end of 2001; 2002 through the election and the postelection session. The first division is necessary so that the effect of the switch in Senate control does not get confounded with the effects of 9/11. Just where one should posit the diminution if any of the impact of 9/11 is less clear and several alternatives were examined. For the overall level of party voting, the break seems to come at the end of 2001.

In fact, party voting does vary across these time periods. In both chambers, partisan voting was most frequent during the brief period of unified government and then dropped when Democrats took control of the Senate (see Table 7.3). More to the point here, it dropped further and to its lowest point in the immediate aftermath of 9/11. In 2002, however, the frequency of partisan voting increased again, in the House to about the levels of the period immediately preceding 9/11. In the House but not the Senate, the postelection session is

TABLE 7.4   THE VARIATION OF PARTISANSHIP
ACROSS ISSUES IN THE 107TH CONGRESS (% PARTY VOTES)

ISSUE	HOUSE	SENATE
Domestic	57	63
Defense	49	27
Foreign affairs	51	55
Terrorism-related	58	32

Note: For the House, suspension votes are excluded; for the Senate confirmation votes are excluded.

HOUSE TERRORISM-RELATED ROLL CALLS	% PARTY VOTES
9/11 to mid-2002	47
mid-2002 to end of 107th	70

SENATE TERRORISM-RELATED ROLL CALLS	% PARTY VOTES
9/11 to August 2002	14
September 2002 to end of 107th	50

marked by an extremely high rate of partisan voting. As Table 7.3 shows as well, the immediate post-9/11 period also saw the highest rate of roll calls on which there was essentially no conflict (90 percent or more on the winning side.) Again, however, the frequency of such nonconflictual votes decreased in 2002.

In the wake of 9/11 partisanship in Congress did decrease and unity or near unity increased, though the impact seemed to fade with the new year. Was this change the result of a change in the congressional agenda or did it extend beyond the issues brought to the fore by 9/11?

The vast majority of the issues on which Congress takes recorded votes are domestic: in the 107th, 74 percent in the House (excluding suspensions) and 78 percent in the Senate (excluding confirmations). The events of 9/11 did alter the agenda; in the immediate post-9/11 period, ordinary domestic issues shrank to just under 60 percent of the agenda in both houses. In the House but not the Senate domestic issues then increased again but only to about 70 percent in 2002. Terrorism-related votes became a part of the voting agenda with 9/11; there were none before in both chambers. In the immediate post-9/11 period, terrorism-related votes made up 23 percent of the voting agenda in the House and 17 percent in the Senate. They continued to make up a significant part of the agenda in 2002; 11 percent of House roll calls and 21 percent of Senate roll calls were terrorism-related, when Iraq votes are included. Defense and foreign affairs votes not directly related to 9/11 or the war against terrorism also became a more prominent part of the voting agenda.

The extent of partisanship does vary across issues, especially in the Senate (see Table 7.4). Terrorism-related and defense issues were much less likely to

TABLE 7.5   PRESIDENTIAL SUPPORT BY PARTY AND PERIOD: MEAN SUPPORT
SCORES ON VOTES PRESIDENT TOOK A POSITION ON ACCORDING TO CQ

	HOUSE		SENATE	
PERIOD	*REPUBLICANS*	*DEMOCRATS*	*REPUBLICANS*	*DEMOCRATS*
Senate Republican	92	20	92	17
Senate Democratic	81	28	80	32
Immediate post-9/11	91	50	95	52
2002	85	34	81	39
Total	86	33	86	37

Note: Senate confirmation votes are excluded.

split the Senate along party lines than either foreign policy or domestic issues. In the House, the variation across issues is considerably less than in the Senate, but surprisingly terrorism-related issues were as likely as domestic issues and more so than either foreign-policy or defense issues to provoke partisan splits. However, further examination reveals that the rate of party voting on terrorism-related issues is not uniform in the entire post-9/11 period in either chamber. In the House, terrorism-related issues elicited party votes 47 percent of the time up until about the middle of 2002; thereafter, until the close of the 107th Congress, such votes provoked partisan splits 70 percent of the time. In the Senate, partisanship remained muted on terrorism-related issues until after the August recess; before that point, only 14 percent of terrorism-related roll calls elicited party splits; after, 50 percent did.

Logistic regression allows us to disentangle the effects of issue and time. Predicting the likelihood of a party vote from the vote's issue type and the period in which it was taken, I find that for the House only the period makes a significant difference; party votes were less likely in the immediate post-9/11 period and more likely in the first months of 2001 before the Jeffords switch and in the postelection session, regardless of issue area. In the Senate, party votes are also less likely in the immediate post-9/11 period and more likely in the period before the Jeffords switch but, having taken these time effects into account, terrorism-related issues are still considerably less likely than other issues to elicit party votes. Thus, the events of 9/11 did depress partisanship even beyond specific issues concerning terrorism that it brought to the fore. However the effect seems largely to have worn off by 2002.

Was the decrease in partisanship accompanied by an increase in support for President Bush? As one would expect, in both chambers Republicans supported Bush at a much higher level than Democrats did (see Table 7.5).[14] The high level of Republican support means that variation over time can at most be modest and that is, in fact, the case. Democratic support, in contrast, does shoot up in the immediate post-9/11 period though it drops again in 2002. OLS regression analysis reveals that the higher support from Democrats in

TABLE 7.6   PREDICTING DEMOCRATS' PRESIDENTIAL
SUPPORT FROM ISSUE AREA AND TIME PERIOD

INDEPENDENT VARIABLES	HOUSE	SENATE
Terrorism-related vote		61.1 (13.4)
Terrorism-related vote*		
Immediate post-9/11 period	33.8 (13.1)	
Constant	31.0 (3.8)	29.3 (4.6)
Adjusted R^2	.065	.259

Note: For the Senate, confirmation votes are excluded.

the post-9/11 period is a function of the change in agenda.[15] The support scores of Democrats in both chambers are significantly higher on terrorism-related votes, all of which occurred after 9/11, than on other votes. Once issue area is taken into account, time no longer makes a significant difference for Senate Democrats' support. House Democrats' support for the president are significantly higher specifically on terrorism-related votes in the immediate post-9/11 period (see Table 7.6).

Finally did these changes in voting patterns translate into greater presidential success in the post-9/11 period? President Bush fared well overall on those roll calls on which he took positions. In the House, he won 84 percent of such votes; in the Senate, he won 71 percent if confirmations are excluded. Bush's success rate in the House does not vary much with either issue or time period. In the Senate, Bush's success rate, which dropped with the switch in party control, goes up again post-9/11 and remains high in 2002. In terms of issue area, Bush is considerably less successful on domestic issues than on others—winning 61 percent of the domestic votes on which he took a position and 86 percent of the other votes.

INSTITUTIONAL PROTECTION OR ABDICATION IN A TIME OF CRISIS

"It is for the president to set the course, as in all times of national crisis, and it is for Congress to close ranks behind him."[16] So wrote careful, sensible *Congressional Quarterly*, the antithesis of sensationalist journalism, in the wake of 9/11. Clearly members of Congress were under intense pressure to support the president and give him whatever he claimed he needed to protect Americans and punish the attackers.

Members genuinely believed it essential for the United States to show unity and resolve. They also were acutely aware that the public expected them to support the president and might well punish them at the ballot box if they did not do so. Democrats in particular feared opening themselves to charges of lack of patriotism from the administration and future opponents.

Yet a number of members of Congress were also concerned about protecting the powers and prerogatives of their institution from undue executive encroachment. The Bush administration had argued that Congress had over a course of years encroached on the powers of the executive branch; well before 9/11, it had made reasserting the president's prerogatives a priority. The crisis would give the administration ample opportunity to act aggressively in that effort. In addition to feeling a responsibility to protect the institution, some members also worried that too free a hand for the president in foreign affairs could easily lead to bad policy. The memory of Vietnam when Congress had acquiesced, often without questioning, to presidential policy decisions still cast a shadow.

Caught between these conflicting imperatives, members of Congress trod a careful path. As indicated by the decisions it made, Congress was not willing to hand the president a blank check; yet no majority was willing to carry the challenge to Bush to a high-visibility public showdown.

The use of force resolution was the first instance after 9/11 in which institutional prerogatives were at stake. The administration originally wanted language in the resolution giving the president the authority to use "all necessary and appropriate force" to "deter and preempt any future acts of terrorism or aggression against the United States."[17] The expansiveness of the language worried many members, who recalled the similarly open-ended Gulf of Tonkin resolution of 1964; Presidents Johnson and Nixon repeatedly cited that resolution as authorization for waging war in Vietnam without further congressional approval. Negotiations between the White House and key members of Congress led to a reformulation; the president was authorized "to use all necessary and appropriate force against those nations, organizations or persons he determines planned, authorized, committed or aided the terrorist attacks that occurred on September 11, 2001, or harbored such organizations or persons."[18] Senator Joseph Biden, chair of the Foreign Relations Committee and a drafter of the resolution, said, "We gave the president all the authority he needed, without giving up our constitutional right to decide whether force should be used."[19]

Bush's request for emergency spending would have given him unprecedented power to spend the money as he chose without direction or oversight from Congress. Initially congressional Republicans seemed amenable, but Democrats balked at abdicating the core congressional power over the purse. Democratic members of the Appropriations Committee, which determines spending, took the lead at arguing for a congressional role. "We still have a Constitution," Senator Robert Byrd, chair of the Appropriations Committee, reminded his colleagues.[20] Key Republicans—Appropriations Committee members and party leaders—quickly came to agree. After some tense but private sparring, the bipartisan congressional leadership and senior administration officials struck a deal. Congress gave the president the money but insisted on maintaining significant control over how it was to be spent.

When, on September 19, Attorney General John Ashcroft sent Congress a draft of the antiterrorism legislation, he asked Congress to pass it in a week. With the House taking the lead, Congress insisted on giving the far-reaching proposals more scrutiny. A number of the most conservative House Republicans believed Ashcroft's proposals went too far in empowering the government to snoop on Americans and joined civil liberties groups and many Democrats in working to water down the proposal. In the end, the USA Patriot Act included much of what the administration wanted, but the most controversial provisions were dropped or softened and many of the provisions were "sunsetted" to expire in 2005. Civil libertarians were still unhappy with a number of provisions and some members believed Congress had still acted too quickly and not established a sufficient legislative record; yet Congress had made significant mitigating changes and had not simply given the administration the enormous new powers it requested.

The Congress's response to Bush's Iraq policy in 2002 shows much the same tendencies: Insist on a role, modify the administration's proposals by placing some restrictions on administration discretion, but still give the president much of what he wants. However, unlike the immediate post-9/11 terrorism-related bills, the Iraq policy controversy in the end had a considerable overt partisan component and a showdown on the floors of the chambers did take place.

After the Taliban was driven from power in Afghanistan and the hunt for al Qaeda and bin Laden stalled, the Bush administration began to focus on Iraq, threatening to use force to bring about regime change. During the late summer of 2002, many in Congress and the foreign policy establishment became increasingly concerned that the administration actually intended to proceed against Iraq but had not thought through and justified its policy sufficiently. Members were disturbed by the administration's argument that it required no authorization from Congress to launch an attack on Iraq; officials cited the president's inherent power as commander in chief and the 1991 Persian Gulf War resolution as legal justification for unilateral action. Republicans as well as Democrats responded to this assertion of executive authority by calling on Bush to go to Congress for a formal expression of support. Even House International Relations Chair Henry Hyde, a conservative and usually reliable administration-supporter, warned, "The White House should be mindful of the important distinction between what the president can do and what he ought to do. Any policy undertaken by the president without a popular mandate from Congress risks long term success."[21]

On September 4, Bush, reversing course, announced he would seek congressional backing but demanded that Congress vote quickly and give him carte blanche. Then, on September 12, in a speech to the UN, Bush at least bowed in the direction of seeking UN sanction of and participation in any move against Iraq. On September 19, Bush sent his proposed resolution to Congress; it would give the president wide latitude to "use all means he determines to be appropriate, including force, to . . . defend the national security interests of the United States against the threat posed by Iraq and restore international peace and security to the region."[22]

The decision on the Iraq resolution presented many members of Congress with a complex calculus. Many believed that the resolution was too open-ended, that the United States should not go it alone but should work through the UN or at least with a significant coalition of allies, that the administration had not shown itself to be truly committed to doing so, and that the Bush administration had not yet presented a persuasive case for preemptive action against Iraq either to Congress or to the American people. Yet they also worried that too much hesitancy would undercut U.S. foreign policy and would make support from the UN less likely. Democrats, in addition, had political concerns. Many believe a vote against the president on this issue right before the elections was political suicide. In addition, Democrats were desperate to change the agenda to issues more beneficial to their party and that required disposing of the resolution.

In the face of broad bipartisan opposition, the administration abandoned the language that seemed to authorize Bush to wage war to impose a peace thorough out the Middle East. The president also offered to include explicit language about reporting to Congress.

As negotiations refined and constrained the resolution's language, even the most doubtful Republicans fell into line. In August, Richard Armey, House Republican Majority Leader, had said that attacking Iraq "without proper provocation . . . would not be consistent with what we have been as a nation or what we should be as a nation."[23] Now he expressed support for the president. Republicans were extremely uncomfortable about offering anything less than strong public support.

On October 2, President Bush and House Minority Leader Richard Gephardt announced they had agreed to a compromise resolution. The resolution gave the president broad authority to wage war against Iraq; it also called for ongoing consultations with Congress and required the president to issue a declaration that diplomatic alternatives had been exhausted before he went to war.[24] It did not require Bush to get UN approval or build an international coalition before attacking Iraq, as many Democrats had wanted.

With Gephardt signing on, Senate Democrats were in an untenable position to force more concessions. When the resolution came to a House vote on October 10, it passed by 296-133; Republicans voted in favor 215 to 6; but Democrats opposed it 126 to 81. Thus, despite their Leader's support, a substantial majority of House Democrats voted against the resolution; most believed the president should be required to either get UN approval or come back for further congressional approval before attacking Iraq.[25] The Senate passed the resolution in the early hours of October 11 by 77 to 23; all but one Republican supported the resolution, Democrats split 29 to 21. Richard Lugar, the ranking Republican member of the Foreign Relations Committee and a respected foreign-policy leader, who had intended, with Chairman Joe Biden, to offer an amendment restricting the president's discretion further, backed down and supported the president's language instead. Of Democratic senators in close races, only Paul Wellstone of Minnesota voted against the resolution.

CONCLUSION: THE LESSONS OF CONGRESS'S REACTION TO 9/11

The horrific events of 9/11 did have an impact on Congress; Congress is, after all a representative institution, and any event that strongly affects the American people should also affect member behavior and congressional decisions. The events did not permanently replace bitter partisanship with harmonious bipartisanship nor did they lead to total presidential supremacy, even on terrorism-related policy.

Clearly 9/11 immediately changed the agenda and also the behavior of the members of Congress; it depressed partisanship and increased opposition party support for the president's positions, especially on issues directly related to terrorism. However, on issues beyond terrorism, the effect on the level of partisanship was relatively short-lived. By 2002, domestic issues again split members of Congress along partisan lines.

Members' voting behavior on domestic issues, which make up the lion's share of the congressional voting agenda, even in the post-9/11 era, was not permanently altered because the views of their constituents on such issues were not altered. Public opinion polls and members' myriad contacts with their constituents showed that Democratic voters and Republican voters continued to differ substantially in their domestic policy preferences. Members who desire reelection will generally reflect their constituents' views in their votes.

Given members' sensitivity to their constituents' preferences, explaining the Congress's unwillingness to give Bush all the power he wanted to combat terrorism is perhaps the more difficult task. Both preserving their institution's prerogatives and serious concerns about the substance of policy motivated enough members to enable Congress to impose some restraints on its grants of power to the executive, I contend. To be sure, few members seriously endangered their reelection by their behavior; those who voted against the Iraq resolution, for example, mostly represented districts or states where such a vote would at least be tolerated; in some cases, the activist core of the members' constituency strongly opposed the Bush position. Yet, on many of the bills in question and for many of the members who insisted on changes in what Bush wanted, simply going along would have been the easier course. Members do have goals beyond reelection[26]; and taking that into account is also necessary to understanding how Congress reacted to 9/11.

NOTES

1. See George C. Edwards III and Andrew Barnett, "Presidential Agenda Setting in Congress," Richard Fleisher and Jon R. Bond, "Partisanship and the Quest for Votes on the Floor of Congress," and Barbara Sinclair, "Hostile Partners: The President, Congress, and Lawmaking in

the Partisan 1990s," all in *Polarized Politics: Congress and the President in a Partisan Era*, ed. Jon Bond and Richard Fleisher (Washington, D.C.: CQ Press, 2000).

2. See John Mueller, *War, Presidents, and Public Opinion* (New York: John Wiley, 1973); Richard A. Brody, *Assessing the President* (Stanford, CA: Stanford University Press, 1991).

3. Data are from *Congressional Quarterly Almanacs*, various dates.

4. Keith Poole's Web Site address is http://voteview.uh.edu. See also Keith T. Poole and Howard Rosenthal, *Congress: A Political-Economic History of Roll Call Voting* (New York: Oxford University Press, 1997).

5. David Rohde, *Parties and Leaders in the Post-Reform House* (Chicago: University of Chicago Press, 1991); Jeffery Stonecash, Mark Mariani, and Mark Brewer, *Diverging Parties: Social Change, Realignment, and Party Polarization* (Boulder, CO: Westview Press, 2002).

6. Gary C. Jacobson, "Party Polarization in National Politics: The Electoral Connection," in Bond and Fleisher, *Polarized Politics*.

7. Jon Bond and Richard Fleisher, *The President in the Legislative Arena* (Chicago: University of Chicago Press, 1990).

8. The Congresses are 87th (1961–1962), 89th (1965–1966), 91st (1969–1970), 94th (1975–1976), 97th (1981–1982), 100th (1987–1988), 101st (1989–1990), 103rd (1993–1994), 104th (1995–1996), and 105th (1997–1998). Major legislation is that identified as such by *Congressional Quarterly* and is augmented by legislation on which key votes occurred, again as identified by *Congressional Quarterly*. Legislation is identified as part of the president's agenda if it is mentioned in the State of the Union address or its equivalent or in special messages of some prominence. Using *Congressional Quarterly* accounts, I coded presidential support/agreement or opposition/disagreement (or an intermediate, mixed position) for every major measure at each stage of the process. *Congressional Quarterly's* account is also used to assess the success of the president on each major measure on the chamber floor and on final disposition along a five-point scale ranging from clear win to clear loss. For more detail, see Sinclair, *Legislators, Leaders, and Lawmaking* (Baltimore, MD: Johns Hopkins University Press, 1995), and Barbara Sinclair, *Unorthodox Lawmaking*, 2nd ed. (Washington, D.C.: CQ Press, 2000).

9. *Congressional Quarterly Weekly Report*, 15 September 2002, p. 2116.

10. Barbara Sinclair, "Context, Strategy, and Chance: George W. Bush and the 107th Congress," in *The George W. Bush Presidency: An Early Appraisal*, ed. Colin Campbell and Bert Rockman (Chatham, NJ: Chatham House Publishers, 2003).

11. *Congressional Quarterly Weekly Report*, 15 September 2001, p. 2158.

12. *Congressional Quarterly Weekly Report*, 27 October 2001, p. 2533.

13. Ninety-three percent of suspensions passed with 90 percent or more of the total votes cast.

14. Confirmation votes are excluded; only 8 of 84 Senate confirmation recorded votes were decided by majorities of less than 90 percent. Since Bush took positions on relatively few roll calls—83 in the House and 58 in the Senate excluding confirmation votes—if confirmation votes are included among the presidential support votes, the mean Senate Democratic score would be much higher.

15. Similar regression analyses on Republican support scores finds no significant predictors.

16. *Congressional Quarterly Weekly Report*, 15 September 2001, p. 2115.

17. *Congressional Quarterly Weekly Report*, 15 September 2001, p. 2119.

18. *Congressional Quarterly Weekly Report*, 15 September 2001, p. 2118.

19. *Congressional Quarterly Weekly Report*, 15 September 2001, p. 2119.

20. *Congressional Quarterly Weekly Report*, 15 September 2001, p. 2130.

21. *Congressional Quarterly Weekly Report*, 15 September 2001, p. 2252.

22. *Congressional Quarterly Weekly Report*, 15 September 2001, pp. 2464–2465.

23. Quoted in *Sydney Morning Herald*, 10 August 2002.

24. *Congressional Quarterly Weekly Report*, 15 September 2001, p. 2607.

25. The Spratt amendment that provided for that won the support of 147 of the 207 Democrats voting. *Congressional Quarterly Weekly Report*, 12 October 2002, p. 2696.

26. Richard Fenno, *Congressmen in Committees* (Boston: Little Brown, 1973); Barbara Sinclair, *Legislators, Leaders, and Lawmaking* (Baltimore, MD: Johns Hopkins University Press, 1995).

PRESIDENTIAL AND CONGRESSIONAL STRUGGLES
OVER THE FORMATION
OF THE DEPARTMENT OF HOMELAND SECURITY

RICHARD S. CONLEY

UNIVERSITY OF FLORIDA

O n January 24, 2003, the Department of Homeland Security (DHS)—the fifteenth cabinet-level department created by Congress—officially opened for business. The mammoth new department, which will become the third largest with over 170,000 employees and an initial budget of more than $38 million, has the broad charge of securing the United States from future terrorist attacks and coordinating the domestic response to an attack if one occurs. Former Pennsylvania Governor Tom Ridge, confirmed unanimously by the Senate as the Secretary of the DHS, exchanged his headquarters in the White House as Director of the Office of Homeland Security for a secure naval facility on Nebraska Avenue. The latter site, which had served as a telecommunications command operations center after 9/11, will temporarily house employees of the twenty-two agencies that are to be transferred to the DHS until a permanent location can be found.[1]

In retrospect, the creation of the DHS and the swift consolidation of existing agencies under the umbrella of the new department were anything but assured. Legislative efforts stalled in the summer and fall of 2002 as the White House and the Democratic-controlled Senate reached an impasse over labor issues that would govern the operation of the new department. Senate passage of the bill, which ultimately gave extensive latitude to President Bush in structuring the DHS, came in a lame-duck session of the 107th Congress after Republicans narrowly regained control of the upper chamber in the 2002 midterm elections.

Prospects for the department's success remain decidedly mixed. The massive reorganization of federal responsibilities—the largest of its kind in fifty years—touches not only the presidency and the executive branch but also Capitol Hill. As agencies coalesce into the DHS new structures that will lead to interagency cooperation and organizational competence will take time to develop. Moreover, the reshuffling of agencies under the DHS necessitates the reorganization of congressional committee structures and appropriations processes if Congress is to fund DHS operations adequately *and* exercise meaningful oversight. Civil libertarians are particularly concerned about an erosion of fundamental freedoms in the absence of substantive congressional oversight of, and budgetary control over, the intelligence-gathering activities of the new department.

This chapter focuses on the "dual" politics of reorganization, from Bush's efforts to win legislation on his terms to congressional attempts to refashion internal committee structures to oversee the DHS. The analysis begins with a brief legislative history that offers a critical assessment of interbranch negotiation of the bill, including Bush's preemption of congressional proposals and the interplay of veto threats, "strategic disagreement," and electoral politics in shaping the eventual outcome. The analysis then turns attention to provisions in the legislation concerning civil liberties, with specific reference to domestic intelligence-gathering by the department and unresolved issues. The final section bridges the discussion of civil liberties with the congressional imperative to reorganize internal processes on Capitol Hill, and how House and Senate leaders have responded to the challenge of oversight.

HOMELAND SECURITY, BUSH'S POLITICS OF PREEMPTION, AND THE MIDTERM ELECTIONS OF 2002

Modern presidents typically choose to centralize policymaking functions in the White House as a means of gaining control and influence over the bureaucracy. Their reasons are numerous. Congress poses a major constraint on presidents' ability to use reorganization as a tool of influence, since departmental and agency reorganization requires legislative approval. And executive proposals for reorganization have often been met by skepticism on Capitol Hill: The process is lengthy, and many proposals have failed.[2] "The problems associated with large-scale reorganization," James P. Pfiffner notes, "exact a high cost in terms of presidential energy, political capital, and good-will. They take up valuable time and must be traded off against other policy priorities."[3]

It is little wonder, then, that following the terrorist attacks of 9/11 George W. Bush established the Office of Homeland Security (OHS) in the Executive Office of the President through an executive order. Executive directives do not require legislative approval and enable the president to take swift action. Yet no sooner did Bush's choice to head the OHS, Tom Ridge, take up his position in October 2002 than a cacophony of voices on both sides of the aisle on Capitol Hill emerged to call for a reorganization of governmental agencies to meet the challenges of defending the home front. Critics of Ridge's executive coordinator status, including then Senate Governmental Affairs Committee chair Joseph Lieberman (D-CT), contended that he lacked the requisite budgetary authority and human resources to effectively carry out his coordinative responsibilities. As a presidential advisor without a legislative mandate, Ridge was also allegedly beyond congressional accountability.[4]

Bush was initially insistent that Ridge had all the authority he needed to meet his responsibilities but ultimately gravitated toward the idea of a massive governmental reorganization as proposals sprung forth in Congress in spring 2002. Recognizing that an irreversible momentum had built on Capitol Hill to create a new Cabinet-level department, the White House sought to preempt Congress with its own proposal, which the president detailed in early June.[5] Bush's strategy was straightforward: He sought to maximize leverage over any legislation that would affect a reorganization of federal agencies with responsibilities for carrying out the war on terrorism domestically. In the process, the president and Congress moved from one end of the spectrum to the other in organizational terms—from a statutory coordinator to a full-fledged reorganization of government functions, "leapfrogging" over several other viable organizational choices such as a "czar" position that had short- and medium-term advantages.[6]

Presidential–congressional relations on the legislation to create the DHS were marred by significant conflicts between the White House and Senate Democrats, primarily over labor regulations and collective bargaining arrangements in the new entity. A basic model of presidential strategy is nevertheless visible in the institutional dynamics that ultimately produced a bill granting the president most of his preferences in the lame-duck session of the 107th Congress (2001–2002).

The model may be conceived of as a two-stage process that reflected the unique configuration of divided government, with the House under Republican control and the Senate narrowly in Democratic hands. In the first stage, Bush used the House's swift passage of his proposal as leverage over the Senate. The president wielded the threat of a veto if the Democratic Senate failed to remove objectionable provisions that conflicted with the House bill. The White House used much public rhetoric to clarify and solidify the president's commitment to winning legislation on his terms.

At this stage the president's strategy followed rather well the tenets of the "commitment model" of veto threats, which suggests that the effectiveness of his strategy turns on public engagement. "Going public"[7] with a commitment to veto a bill if select provisions are included or excluded can give the president important leverage to propose and shape the contours of legislation.[8] "The effect of political rhetoric," Charles Cameron asserts, "is to constrain the speaker so he can't retreat from his position without paying a steep price."[9] Reneging on a veto threat might entail electoral retaliation or cost the president in the court of public opinion. These factors enhance the credibility and sincerity of the veto threat from the standpoint of the congressional majority. Presidents can therefore bluff and threaten to veto bills they might otherwise accept.[10]

In the second stage, Bush and the Senate chose "blame-game" politics—faulting one another publicly for the failure to act—in lieu of reaching compromise. By "strategically disagreeing" the White House and the Senate preferred to forestall passage of the bill to retain the support of constituency interests and gain political advantage.[11] Bush used the legislative stalemate as a platform from which to campaign for his copartisans in the 2002 midterm elections. The results of the elections were widely hailed as a referendum on Bush's stance and broke the impasse in the lame-duck session of the 107th Congress. The Republicans' capture of the Senate, and Bush's willingness to lay his reputation and political capital on the line in the fall campaign, convinced Democrats to cede on the provisions opposed by the president.

VETO THREATS, COMMITMENT, AND STRATEGIC DISAGREEMENT

Bush's strategy vis-à-vis Congress reflected the peculiar configuration of divided government in the 107th Congress. With a cohesive Republican majority in the House of Representatives, the president's proposal sailed through that chamber largely intact. The House adopted HR 5005 on July 26, 2002, by a vote of 295-132, with eighty-eight Democrats supporting the legislation. House Republicans fended off a series of Democratic amendments on subjects ranging from Freedom of Information Act (FOIA) requirements for the new department to airport screening timetables.

The air of bipartisan commitment to creating the homeland security department eroded considerably by the time the matter was taken up by the Senate. The Democratic leadership substituted a bill proposed by Joe Lieberman, chair of the Senate Governmental Affairs Committee, in lieu of the president's proposal.[12] Lieberman's bill differed from the House legislation primarily on matters concerning personnel and collective bargaining rights in the new DHS. Bush remained firm about the need for broad latitude to exempt some employees from union membership for reasons of national security. The Lieberman bill gave the president a temporary waiver that Bush felt was inadequate. The president also demanded far greater flexibility than Congress had traditionally been willing to grant chief executives in terms of hiring, firing, and transferring employees in the civil service, as well as the ability to reorganize the department independently.[13] Bush contended provisions in the Senate Democratic bill that retained traditional federal work rules would stymie efforts to streamline the new DHS to meet domestic terror threats. Proposals to limit Bush's decertification of employees' union membership for reasons of national security had been dropped in the House bill, cited as a "deal-killer" by the White House.[14]

In early September the White House signaled Bush's intention to veto the bill if the Senate provisions remained intact. Incredulous Democrats were taken aback that the president might veto his own proposal for the new Cabinet-level department, but Press Secretary Ari Fleischer reiterated the president's commitment to reject any bill that failed to meet his criteria on flexible personnel rules. Key Republicans in the Senate, including Fred Thompson (R-TN), reaffirmed Bush's serious commitment.[15] Moreover, in mid-September Bush twice publicly made known his determination to veto the Senate version of the bill—once while on the campaign trail for Senate candidate Lamar Alexander in Tennessee, and again at a meeting with Sears employees in Iowa.[16]

Veto threats operated in tandem with the strategy of the GOP minority in the Senate, which was emboldened to stall the Lieberman bill through parliamentary tactics. Two key moderate Senators held the balance over passage in the narrowly divided upper chamber. Zell Miller (D-GA) broke ranks with his Democratic colleagues and supported the White House's position, while Lincoln Chafee (R-RI) eventually supported Democrats, tipping the balance against the White House.[17] Republicans then filibustered the bill to prevent a floor vote. Democratic leaders were unable to find the sixty votes necessary to invoke cloture and end unlimited debate. Senate Majority Leader Tom Daschle (D-SD), frustrated by the Republicans' tactics, affirmed that "[w]e're going to stay on the bill . . . they can drag this out as long as they want to, and they can tell us when they've finished dragging it out. But at some point, whenever that is, we'll have a vote on final passage."[18] Daschle nevertheless faced problems within Democratic ranks. While Republicans backed the president's opposition to the bill's provisions concerning collective bargaining, the "Dean of the Senate," Robert Byrd (D-WV), engaged in a "virtual filibuster" of the legislation for entirely different reasons. Byrd lamented the speed with which the White House was moving to reorganize for homeland security and cautioned that Congress was ceding institutional prerogatives in the process.[19]

Blame-game politics between the White House and the Senate came into full-swing between late August and mid-October, at which time members of Congress prepared to return home to campaign for the fall midterm elections. It became clear that the lingering impasse between the White House and the Senate would preclude legislative action by Congress's October 11 adjournment date. The White House remained intransigent and refused to bargain, despite Democratic and Republican moderates' efforts to broker a compromise. Democrats dug their heels in, worried that Bush was trying to set a precedent by first weakening collective bargaining rules in the new DHS and then moving to revamp the entire federal civil service in a similar fashion.[20]

To some, the debate over labor laws was misplaced. Congress and the president conveniently circumvented questions about the financial and human costs of the massive reorganization and the new department's ability to function effectively after consolidation.[21] Instead, as the *Washington Post* aptly summarized: "Both parties appear to be gambling that they can blame the other side for failing to act on a proposal they believe is both necessary and popular. Bush and Republicans have cast Democrats as captives of their union allies, while Democrats complain that the president has shown no willingness to compromise."[22]

To others, the White House's inflexibility on workplace rules for the DHS was motivated by a shrewd political calculus that became evident at the outset of the midterm elections campaign. On the one hand, media attention consistently focused on the congressional backlog on homeland security and a resolution authorizing the use of force against Iraq. The net effect was to preclude Democrats from emphasizing their favored domestic issues, such as Social Security and unemployment—issues of greatest concern to their core constituents.[23] On the other hand, lack of legislative action on the DHS gave Bush and congressional Republicans a campaign issue—national security and defense—on which voters tended to trust the GOP more.[24]

Beginning in August and continuing through the election season, the president repeatedly criticized the Senate for not following the House's lead in passing legislation on his terms.[25] He caused a firestorm of controversy in September when he suggested during remarks in Trenton, New Jersey, that Senate Democrats were less than patriotic by refusing to cede to his demands in the bill. Bush argued that "[t]he House responded, but the Senate is more interested in special interests in Washington and not interested in the security of the American people," reiterating that he would "not accept a Department of Homeland Security that does not allow this president and future presidents to better keep the American people secure."[26] Furious at the comments, Senate Majority Leader Tom Daschle and the Democrats demanded an apology from the president, but none was forthcoming. The White House toned down some of the rhetoric, but it was clear that Bush and the Republicans intended to use the continuing impasse to blame the Senate for adjourning without passing the bill. In early October, White House Press Secretary Ari Fleischer lamented on several occasions that "it would just be unimaginable for the Senate to leave town without having taken action to protect the homeland."[27] But that is exactly what occurred in the absence of any willingness to compromise at either end of Pennsylvania Avenue.

Bush made over three dozen public statements between August and the November 5 election in which he specifically criticized the Senate or blamed "special interests" connected to Democrats for the delay in the homeland security bill.[28] Bush's comments while on the campaign trail or through weekly radio addresses nationalized the issue in the midterm elections, giving Republican candidates a basis from which to attack Democratic incumbents in much the same way that the *Contract with America* enabled Republicans to campaign on common themes in 1994. Moreover, because Republicans were one vote short of being able to pass the president's favored bill in the Senate, each and every recalcitrant Senate Democrat could be blamed individually for holding up the legislation. The cases of Max Cleland (D-GA) and Jean Carnahan (D-MO) are instructive on this account.

Republican Representative Saxby Chambliss of Georgia challenged incumbent Senator Max Cleland for Georgia's senior spot in the upper chamber. Chambliss had chaired the House Subcommittee on Terrorism and Homeland Security in the 107th Congress. In several campaign appearances with Chambliss in the final three weeks prior to the midterm elections, Bush lauded the congressman's efforts in marshaling the legislation on homeland security through the House and reproached the Senate for not doing the same. Chambliss used the issue wittingly against an otherwise formidable incumbent on defense issues—Cleland is a triple-amputee and Vietnam War veteran who also headed the Veterans Administration under President Carter. Chambliss launched a veritable wave of negative television ads that relentlessly attacked Cleland as one of the chief "obstructionist" Democrats blocking the creation of the DHS.[29] Ironically, Cleland had been one of the sponsors of the idea of creating a Cabinet-level department in the spring of 2002 before Bush and the Republicans signed on to the idea.[30]

Chambliss won the race by a seven-point margin. He admitted that his endorsement by the state Veterans of Foreign Wars chapter "inoculated" him against his own lack of military service.[31] Whether the race actually tipped in favor of Chambliss due to the homeland security issue was irrelevant at some level—Bush and the Republicans believed it was the main factor not only in Cleland's defeat but GOP gains generally in the state, which included the ouster of Democratic Governor Roy Barnes. "If any state had a referendum on what the president fought for on homeland security, it was Georgia," argued Terry Nelson, deputy chief of staff at the Republican National Committee.[32]

The close race between House Republican Jim Talent and incumbent Democratic Senator Jean Carnahan for Missouri's Senate election mirrored dynamics in Georgia. Carnahan accused Talent of questioning her patriotism after campaign ads portrayed her with images of terrorists and criticized her for failing to support Bush's preferred legislation on the DHS and a host of other issues.[33] She was held responsible as one of the key votes hamstringing the president's agenda. As Vice President Dick Cheney contended while stumping for Talent, "That one Senate seat could make all the difference in the world."[34] For his part, President Bush visited Missouri several times in October and November to lend support to Talent's senatorial bid, arguing at one campaign stop that "Jim Talent understands what I'm talking about. You put him in the Senate; we'll get us a good homeland security bill, which will make it easier for presidents to protect America."[35] Talent narrowly defeated Carnahan by just under 24,000 votes, and homeland security figured prominently into interpretations of his victory. One local observer noted that "[t]alk of Iraq and 9/11 changed the agenda from the usual off-year concentration upon the economy. The patriotic slant went to the right, and some of the Reagan Democrats might have gone for Talent to rally around the flag."[36]

Coupled with Republicans' Senate victories in Minnesota and North Carolina, as well as additional seat gains in the House, the election results were

broadly interpreted as a national judgment on Bush's stands on homeland security. Bush's success in reversing the typical midterm loss for the president's
party in Congress was bolstered by his willingness to put his own political capital on the line for GOP candidates.[37] Although the results did not suggest a
"realignment" of the electorate—many of the races were extremely narrow—
the White House focus on national security issues seemingly tipped the balance in Republicans' favor.[38]

The net effect of the 2002 midterm elections was to dislodge the stalled
DHS legislation in the Senate almost immediately, along with other elements
of Bush's agenda that had reached an impasse.[39] When the lame-duck session of the 107th Congress convened shortly after the elections, the Senate
quickly passed the bill by a 90-9 margin—and largely on the president's
terms. Several key moderate Democrats and Republicans noted that Bush
and his GOP supporters were "in a better negotiating position following the
election. . . ."[40] The inevitability that Republicans would pass the bill at the
beginning of the 108th Congress even prompted Senator Byrd to drop his filibuster, though not without a final word on the "mon-stros-ity" of a bill he
thought had been put together with haste and at the expense of congressional prerogatives.[41]

CIVIL LIBERTIES AND THE SECOND "AXIS OF REORGANIZATION": CONGRESS

The DHS reorganization bill was long on latitude for the president and short
on details. The first set of agencies to be transferred to the new department—
including the Secret Service, Coast Guard, Customs, the Immigration and
Naturalization Service, Transportation Safety Administration, and federal
protective services—took place March 1, 2003. The president must submit a
reorganization plan, but experts suggest it will take a year to two years before the consolidation of agencies will be complete.[42] In the meantime, many
uncertainties remain. Bush won the ability to reassign personnel in the new
agency with greater ease, unions contend the entire civil service system is in
jeopardy, and much of Secretary Ridge's immediate task has been to calm
the nerves of anxious workers set to be transferred in coming months.[43]

Equally if not more troubling questions about the DHS that received far less
media attention concern the domestic intelligence-gathering capacities of the
new department. Ironically, the most vocal critics have come from the right, not
the left—including GOP stalwarts such as former House majority leader Dick
Armey who, among other things, insisted on sunset provisions in the USA Patriot Act.[44] Civil libertarians are careful to point out that the legislation creating the DHS provided for an intelligence unit that potentially places privacy
rights and civil liberties in question by obscuring the lines between intelligence
gathering, law enforcement, and the military.[45] The relationship between the

Federal Bureau of Investigation (FBI), Central Intelligence Agency (CIA), and the DHS in terms of intelligence-gathering and sharing is of paramount concern. Four of the agencies to be transferred—the Secret Service, Customs, the Border Patrol, and the Coast Guard—have independent intelligence operations that will be merged under the DHS. An independent commission sponsored by the Markle Foundation in conjunction with the Brookings Institution and the Miller Center for Public Affairs at the University of Virginia had recommended a decentralized information-sharing unit in the DHS that bridges the private, federal, and state and local sectors.[46]

How the new intelligence unit evolves in the DHS will be central to the protection of civil liberties. For the moment, the DHS will receive intelligence reports only in the form of summaries. But already there are suggestions that "analysts occasionally will need—and receive—access to a wider range of intelligence, including undigested classified information, to fulfill their primary mission of protecting the nation's infrastructure."[47]

Congress and the courts have moved to address some civil liberties concerns connected to the DHS and the war on terrorism. In late January 2003, the Senate adopted by unanimous consent an amendment sponsored by Ron Wyden (D-OR) that placed limits on the "Total Information Awareness" (TIA) data-mining program being developed by the Defense Advanced Research Projects Agency in the Department of Defense. The pilot project, which is aimed at recovering vast amounts of personal information on individuals, may not be used on citizens in the United States and the developers must consult with Congress.[48] At the time of this writing, legislation is also pending in the Senate that would similarly place a moratorium on data mining in the DHS.[49] In addition, when the Senate approved the DHS, the legislation specifically prohibited the Justice Department's "TIPS" program. The program was called "Orwellian" by its critics and would have encouraged citizens to engage in surveillance and report suspicious activities to authorities.[50] Finally, in early January 2003, a U.S. District Court judge refused to dismiss a case filed by the Electronic Privacy Information Center against the Office of Homeland Security to force the disclosure of public records and discussions about a national identification system.[51] However the case is decided may have spillover effects for the public disclosure of documents in the new DHS.

Privacy concerns, nonetheless, remain at the forefront of the operations of the DHS. The legislation exempts the DHS from elements of the Freedom of Information Act (FOIA). In particular, the legislation creating the DHS places restrictions on the disclosure of information associated with private companies "not customarily in the public domain."[52] To William Raspberry, a conservative columnist, "[t]he way the law is written seems to put someone who blows the whistle on illegal activity in the company in danger of criminal prosecution."[53] Moreover, it is unclear how the "privacy office" created in the DHS will be able to prevent abuse of privacy protections.[54]

REFORMING CONGRESS: THE CENTRALITY
OF STREAMLINING COMMITTEE STRUCTURES

These and other concerns demand that Congress reform internal structures to meet the challenge of oversight for the DHS. Congress must define its oversight role and protect its institutional prerogatives.[55] This was the same conclusion drawn in the Hart-Rudman Commission Report (U.S. Commission on National Security in the Twenty-First Century) prior to the establishment of the DHS.[56] With responsibility for components of the DHS spread out across thirteen committees, Congress must rationalize the authorization and appropriations process or the department's operations may be hindered. Streamlining the committee structure is also necessary to ensure that Congress maintain oversight of the department, lest the balance of control shift to the White House.

In the House of Representatives, several options are possible. One is to retain and/or reconstitute the select committee on homeland security formed to create the DHS. Another option is to constitute a permanent, fourteenth committee for homeland security. A final option is to create separate subcommittees for homeland security, which would exacerbate the diffusion of responsibility.[57] The penultimate problem for Congress is that all of these options require established committees to cede authority. Leaders have not attempted a wholesale rationalization of the committee system since the mid-1970s,[58] and calls for reform threaten turf wars among key power brokers in both chambers.[59] Few lawmakers support the idea of a fourteenth subcommittee given typical delays in completing work on the thirteen annual appropriations measures.[60]

As of spring 2003, Republican leaders in the House and Senate sought a "middle way" to deal with the imperative of oversight of the DHS. In the Senate, oversight responsibility for the new department remained with the Senate Governmental Affairs Committee, chaired by Susan Collins (R-ME), just as it had in the 107th Congress. Collins's committee will have "lead responsibility" vis-à-vis other committees with current responsibilities for homeland security programs.[61] In the House, a Select Committee on Homeland Security was organized. Speaker Hastert appointed the chairmen and ranking members of at least eight other standing committees, including Judiciary, Government Reform, and Transportation.[62] Representative Christopher Cox (R-CA) agreed to chair the committee, with Jim Turner (D-TX) as ranking member. According to Cox's office, Speaker Hastert had no plans to establish a standing committee in the 108th Congress.[63] In sum, these interim steps are pragmatic given that reorganization of the DHS will take time and much is to be determined from the president's plan. Speaker Hastert may be attempting to acclimatize lawmakers to the new committee and then make it permanent. Nonetheless, these steps do not solve the longer-term need to sort out the overlap of jurisdictions. that will undoubtedly prove difficult to untangle in coming months.

CONCLUSION

This chapter began with two objectives. The first was to trace presidential–congressional relations on the passage of legislation creating the DHS. The second was to connect several key issues concerning civil liberties in the new department to congressional oversight and reform of committee structures on Capitol Hill.

The analysis emphasizes a multifaceted perspective on the dynamics surrounding presidential–congressional negotiation of the DHS legislation. In the first stage of negotiations Bush preempted congressional proposals with his own, used rapid approval of his plan by the House to pressure the Democratic Senate to follow suit, and threatened to veto the entire bill if Democrats inserted objectionable language. When the Senate failed to act, the White House and Democratic leaders blamed one another for the legislative impasse, strategically disagreeing in order to posture for political gain in the 2002 midterm elections. Bush's steadfast campaign for Republican candidates tipped the balance of several narrow races in the GOP's favor. Interpretations that the election results were a referendum on Bush's stance on homeland security, and the inevitability of passage of the president's favored provisions in the 108th Congress, prompted Democrats to cede to the White House in the lame-duck session of the 107th Congress.

With passage of the bill on the president's terms and the reorganization of federal agencies underway, privacy rights hang in the balance. The potential domestic intelligence-gathering capacity of the new DHS troubles civil libertarians and necessitates meaningful congressional oversight of the department. For the moment, congressional leaders have taken interim steps to address the question of oversight without provoking internecine jurisdictional wars. These steps, however, are insufficient in the long-term. At stake not only are privacy rights but congressional prerogatives more generally, especially if the organization of the DHS serves as a template for consolidating other governmental functions as recommended by the Volcker Commission.[64]

Few believe that the new DHS will prove a panacea to defending the home front in the war on terrorism. Whether the department can surmount the many obstacles that lay ahead—from the creation of a culture of cooperation between transferred agencies where none has existed before to liaison with state and local governments—is an open question. Critics point to the complexity of the undertaking, carefully underscoring the panoply of unintended consequences and bureaucratic dysfunctions that grew out of Truman-era reforms of the Department of Defense.[65]

Regardless, the success or failure of the DHS—from balancing civil liberties with law enforcement to preventing future terrorist attacks—will be a central criterion in any historical evaluation of the legacy of George W. Bush. The growth of the national security state under his watch would seem to define Bush's conservative vision in the post-9/11 era. Bush has been willing to expand government significantly in the defense and national security arena while seeking to keep domestic programmatic growth to a minimum.[66] Such a stance is consistent with the legacy of his father and of Ronald Reagan, but it threatens to place Bush at odds with the libertarian wing of the GOP. Bush's stance also seems to solidify contemporary Republicans' break with conservatives of yesteryear, including Eisenhower, who warned of the dangers of the military-industrial complex and sought to limit the growth of the federal establishment in the domestic *and* defense/national security domains.

NOTES

1. John Mintz, "Homeland Security Gets First Chief: Ridge Sworn In as Democrats Criticize Bush Policies, Funding," *Washington Post,* 25 January 2003, p. A-2.
2. See Peri E. Arnold, *Making the Managerial Presidency: Comprehensive Reorganization Planning, 1905–1996* (Lawrence, KS: University of Kansas Press, 1998).
3. James P. Pfiffner, *The Strategic Presidency: Hitting the Ground Running,* 2nd ed., revised (Lawrence, KS: University of Kansas Press, 1996), p. 91.
4. Elizabeth Becker, "A Nation Challenged: Domestic Security; Bush Is Said to Consider a New Security Department," *New York Times,* 12 April 2002, p. A-16.
5. Mike Allen, "Bush Campaigns for Creating Homeland Security Department," *Washington Post,* 25 June 2002, p. A-3.
6. See Richard S. Conley, "The War on Terrorism and Homeland Security: Presidential and Congressional Challenges," forthcoming in *George W. Bush: A Political and Ethical Assessment at Mid-Term,* ed. Tom Lansford and Robert P. Watson (Albany, NY: SUNY Press).
7. Samuel Kernell, *Going Public: New Strategies of Presidential Leadership,* 3rd ed. (Washington, D.C.: Congressional Quarterly, Inc., 1997).
8. Daniel E. Ingberman and Dennis A. Yao, "Presidential Commitment and the Veto," *American Journal of Political Science* 35 (1991), pp. 357–389.
9. Charles Cameron, *Veto Bargaining: Presidents and the Politics of Negative Power* (New York: Cambridge University Press, 2000).
10. See Nolan M. McCarty, "Presidential Reputation and the Veto," *Economics and Politics* 9 (1997), pp. 1–26.
11. John B. Gilmour, *Strategic Disagreement: Stalemate in American Politics* (Pittsburgh, PA: University of Pittsburgh Press, 1995).
12. Rob Portman, "For the Homeland; Congress Must Give New Department Flexibility," *Washington Times,* 30 September 2002, p. A-23.
13. Bill Miller and Juliet Eilperin, "Obscure Labor Issues Block Homeland Security Agency; Moderates to Decide Outcome of Democrats' Tangle with Bush," *Washington Post,* 23 September 2002, p. A-8.
14. David Firestone, "Threats and Responses: Congressional Action; Bush Is Thwarted on Worker Rights," *New York Times,* 25 September 2002, p. A-1.
15. David Firestone, "Traces of Terror: The Reorganization Plan; Congress Returns from Recess, and So Does the Partisanship," *New York Times,* 4 September 2002, p. A-11.
16. *Weekly Compilation of Presidential Documents,* week ending Friday, September 20, pp. 1563–1568 and pp. 1549–1554, available at http://frwebgate3.access.gpo.gov.
17. David Firestone, "Threats and Responses: Federal Reorganization; Unlikely Power Broker on 'Homeland' Plan's Fate," *New York Times,* 18 September 2002, p. A-25.
18. David Firestone, "Threats and Responses: Domestic Security; Democrats Vow to Pass New Security Agency Despite Filibuster," *New York Times,* 1 October 2002, p. A-17.
19. David Firestone, "Threats and Responses: The Senate; Democrats Try to Compromise on Domestic Security Bill," *New York Times,* 17 September 2002, p. A-21.
20. Stephen Barr, "Hunting for a Model for Homeland Security," *Washington Post,* 15 September 2002, p. C-3.

21. Norman J. Ornstein, "Homeland Security; Transition Deserves Care, Caution," *Roll Call*, 3 October 2002.
22. "Homeland Security Bill Is Stalled; Prospects Dim for Passage This Year," *Washington Post*, 2 October 2002, p. A-1.
23. Janet Hook, "After Iraq, Congress Struggles with Backlog; Politics: Key Issues Such as Energy Policy and Homeland Security Are Languishing, and Election Campaigning Will Likely Delay Any New Action," *Los Angeles Times*, 12 October 2002, p. 13.
24. Andrew Cohut, "Issues in Search of a Campaign," *New York Times*, 14 October 2002, p. A-19.
25. *Weekly Compilation of Presidential Documents*, week ending August 30, 2002, pp. 1417–1472.
26. Ibid., week ending September 27, 2002, p. 1598.
27. Quoted in David Firestone, "Threats and Responses: Domestic Security; Democrats Vow to Pass New Security Agency Despite Filibuster," *New York Times*, 1 October 2002, p. A-17.
28. Data were gathered from the on-line edition of the *Weekly Compilation of Presidential Documents*.
29. Dave Williams, "Chambliss Team Believes Race Tighter with Ad Volley; He Attacks Cleland's Stance on Bush Security Legislation," *Florida Times-Union*, 28 October 2002, p. A-1.
30. "Allow Cleland to Continue Using His Own Judgment," *Atlanta Journal-Constitution*, 29 October 2002, p. A-22.
31. Dave Williams, "Chambliss Says Timing Led to Win," *Augusta Chronicle*, 7 November 2002, p. B-5.
32. Lauren W. Whittington, "Democrats Seek Answers after Disaster in Georgia," *Roll Call*, 7 November 2002.
33. David A. Lieb, "Carnahan, Talent Clash over Patriotism, Support of the President," Associated Press state and local wire, 24 October 2002.
34. Connie Farrow, "Cheney Says Talent Is Key to Passing GOP Agenda in Senate," Associated Press state and local wire, 2 November 2002.
35. *Weekly Compilation of Presidential Documents*, week ending October 18, 2002, p. 1801.
36. Tim O'Neill and Sarah Trotto, "Voters Say Senate Balance of Power, National Issues Informed Their Choices," *St. Louis Post-Dispatch*, 7 November 2002, p. A-10.
37. David Von Drehle, "GOP Victory's Ripples Spread," *Washington Post*, 7 November 2002, p. A-1.
38. See Donald Green and Eric Schickler, "Winning a Battle, Not a War," *New York Times*, 12 November 2002, p. A-27.
39. David Von Drehle, "GOP Victory's Ripples Spread," *Washington Post*, 7 November 2002, p. A-1.
40. David Firestone and Elisabeth Bumuller, "Threats and Responses: Domestic Security; Stalemate Ends in Bush Victory on Terror Bill," *New York Times*, 13 November 2002, p. A-1.
41. John Tierney, "Threats and Responses: The Senate; Byrd, at 85, Fills the Forum with Romans and Wrath," *New York Times*, 20 November 2002, p. A-1.
42. Joseph Curl, "Bush Signs Law for Security Agency; Taps Ridge to Serve in Cabinet Post," *Washington Times*, 26 November 2002, p. A-1.
43. See Stephen Barr, "Bush's Homeland Security Team Tries to Reassure, Rally the Troops," *Washington Post*, 21 November 2002, p. B-2; Mike Allen and John Mintz, "Homeland Department May Take a Year to Take Shape," *Washington Post*, 21 November 2002, p. A-8.
44. Jeffrey Rosen, "Civil Right," *New Republic*, 21 October 2002, pp. 14–18.
45. David Johnston, "Threats and Responses: The Law; Administration Begins to Rewrite Decades-Old Spying Restrictions," *New York Times*, 30 November 2002, p. A-1.
46. Judith Miller, "Threats and Responses: Domestic Security; Report Calls for Plan of Sharing Data to Prevent Terror," *New York Times*, 7 October 2002, p. A-11.
47. Dan Eggen and John Mintz, "Homeland Security Won't Have a Diet of Raw Intelligence; Rules Being Drafted to Preclude Interagency Conflict," *Washington Post*, 6 December 2002, p. A-43.
48. Adam Clymer, "Threats and Responses: Surveillance; Senate Rejects Pentagon Plan to Mine Citizens' Personal Data for Clues to Terrorism," *New York Times*, 24 January 2003, p. A-12.
49. Audrey Hudson, "Lawmakers Seek to Limit TIA Reach; Threaten to Pull 'Big Brother' Funds," *Washington Times*, 17 January 2003, p. A-5.
50. Dan Eggen, "Proposal to Enlist Citizen Spies Was Doomed from the Start," *Washington Post*, 24 November 2002, p. A-11.
51. Audrey Hudson, "Security Loses Bid to Keep ID Technology Talks Private," *Washington Times*, 3 January 2003, p. A-3.

52. Dan Morgan, "Disclosure Curbs in Homeland Bill Decried; Information from Companies at Issue," *Washington Post*, 16 November 2002, p. A-13.
53. William Raspberry, "Embracing Big Brother," *Washington Post*, 25 November 2002, p. A-15.
54. Stephen Dinan, "Authors Defend Homeland Bill's Privacy Provisions," *Washington Times*, 16 November 2002, p. A-1.
55. Gary J. Andres, "Homeland on the Hill: The 108th Congress Should Reorganize," *Washington Times*, 19 December 2002, p. A-23.
56. Morton Kondracke, "Congress Should Heed the Other Warnings in Hart-Rudman Report," *Roll Call*, 24 June 2002. The report is available at http://www.nssg.gov.
57. "Derek Willis, "Turf Battles Could Lie Ahead in Fight to Oversee Homeland Department," *Congressional Quarterly Weekly Report*, 16 November 2002, p. 3006.
58. Mark Preston and Susan Crabtree, "Hill Confronts Reorganization: Battles Erupt over New Department," *Roll Call*, 10 June 2002.
59. David Nather and Karen Foerstel, "Proposal Presages Turf Wars," *Congressional Quarterly Weekly Report*, 8 June 2002, pp. 1505–1508.
60. Amol Sharma, "New Department, Old Issues," *Congressional Quarterly Weekly Report*, 31 August 2002, p. 2227.
61. Audrey Hudson, "Ridge Confirmation Given Priority; Hill to Move Quickly on Homeland Security Department," *Washington Times*, 8 January 2003, p. A-4.
62. Ibid.
63. Telephone communication to the office of Christopher Cox, February 4, 2003.
64. Stephen Barr, "Plenty of Tough Issues at New Homeland Security Department," *Washington Post*, 21 January 2003, p. B-2.
65. Fred Hiatt, "Truman's Rose-Colored Reforms," *Washington Post*, 15 July 2002, p. A-17.
66. See David S. Broder, "So Bigger Is Now Better?" *Washington Post*, 12 January 2003, p. B-3.

ENTRAPPED IN THE NARRATIVE OF WAR

REFLECTIONS, QUESTIONS, AND COMMENTARY

LAWRENCE C. DODD

UNIVERSITY OF FLORIDA

On September 11, 2001, as American citizens watched the World Trade Center towers collapse in real time on television, we became one in our resolve to ensure that the masterminds of the attack be brought to justice and the nation secured more fully against such criminal acts of terror. This volume now seeks to gauge how the nation and its key political institutions, Congress and the presidency, have responded to the terrorist challenge. My responsibility in concluding the volume is to reflect across the issues and questions raised by the essays and provide a commentary designed to stimulate further assessment of the overall meaning of the essays.

REFLECTIONS

What is most striking about the essays—insightful renditions on the state of American politics in the aftermath of the terrorist strike—is their overwhelming preoccupation with the narrative of war and the limited attention to concern about terrorism and terrorists. In this regard, they faithfully capture the dominant reaction of the nation and its government in the months and years following September 11. In many ways the essays could have been written at countless other moments in the nation's history, long before the fear of massive terrorist destruction was ever envisioned as a possibility. The topics include how the preparation for war transformed the president's term in office, including the following:

1. The decision processes the president pursued in going to war
2. The creation of a War Cabinet to conduct and oversee the war

3. Dissension within the War Cabinet about the decision to pursue a war strategy

4. The politics of organizing new agencies and a new department to help fight the war at home, as well as abroad

5. The role and organizational politics of Congress in face of this new concern with war and homeland security

6. How the buildup to war had impacted the 2002 off-year elections

7. The war's likely long-term impact on the president's reelection and party control of Congress

Missing from the essays is a discussion of progress in uprooting terrorist cells, the strategies for securing airports, cities, and citizens from terrorist strikes, the securing of better funded and coordinated policing structures for citizen protection, and the social, political, institutional, and constitutional consequences should terrorism establish a continuing presence within the homeland. War is the central motif—war within other homelands and against other nations. Concern for domestic terrorism is at best an occasional, fragmentary, and almost discordant subtheme—just as it has been within the nation at large.

As faithful reflections of the American reaction to 9/11, these essays suggest that something profound has happened to American politics and society in response to the terrorist strikes. The ghosts of politics past seem to have reached out, grabbed hold of the collective political psyche and entrapped us in a recurring nightmare we thought we had escaped. Concern about terrorist assaults within the American homeland appear to have morphed into preoccupation with a worldwide war not just against stateless terrorists but terrorist states.[1] The magnified fear citizens feel when flying in airplanes or working in tall buildings, and the concern that more terrorist strikes may further cripple a struggling economy, have shifted into a determination to wage war against evil worldwide, rooting out terrorism in all of its ugly guises. This transition is justified by a rhetoric so broadly encompassing that it seems to commit the nation to a long-term and aggressive foreign-policy stance, the pursuit of which could once again allow concern with war to envelop the long-term conduct of American politics and warp our balance of powers system—an experience that Americans, and American political scientists, know all too well.[2]

From the late 1930s through the early 1990s, American politics was shadowed by a war narrative—fascist aggression in Europe and Asia and then world war in response; a subsequent Cold War that greatly constrained and shaped politics for fifty years and a Cuban Missile Crisis in the midst of the Cold War that appeared to threaten the homeland with massive nuclear holocaust; a war in Vietnam in pursuit of Cold War politics that shook the nation's social and political foundations; and finally, a Persian Gulf War just as the Cold War ended that now looks like a harbinger of things to come. Amidst the war narrative, the American presidency took on imperial dimensions, the military-industrial complex feared by Dwight Eisenhower took deep root, budget deficits soared as the nation tried to finance guns and butter, and our domestic politics almost appeared frozen in time. Thereafter followed one decade—the 1990s—in which the narrative of war faded into the background and we began to imagine what politics and policy might look like as we focused full-force on domestic issues.[3] In the process, the presidency seemed less dominant and aggrandizing as an institution; Congress became more central as a driving force of policy; the economy began to recover and budget surpluses mounted; citizens moved to experiment with term limits on politicians; a partisan revolution occurred within Congress that ended the sixty year hegemony by the party in power as World War II began; and a surge of interactive talk shows arose suggesting a much more engaged populace than low election turnout seemed to demonstrate.

After just a decade freed of an overarching war narrative, scholars and the nation again appear preoccupied with war and the narrative of war as we try to understand the changing structure of American politics. Faced with a horrendous terrorist strike by a nationless band of outlaws, we are now talking about the emergence of an American president with a level of power that few had ever possessed. He has used this power to initiate a land war in the Middle East, remove the dictator his father had left in power a decade earlier, and institute a beachhead for democracy in the Muslim Middle East. He justified such action by the argument that Iraqi dictator Saddam Hussein possessed weapons of mass destruction that made him a threat to the nation's interests analogous to that of the terrorists who had struck the Trade Centers and the Pentagon. Simultaneously, while preparing for the war, the president pushed for a Department of Homeland Security to prosecute the war on the home front. Justified by the rhetoric of war, the new department was constructed in a manner and with powers that appeared to many to threaten everything from workers' rights within the department to civil rights of the American citizens whose security the department was entrusted with ensuring.

The preoccupation of the nation with war at home and abroad, rather than with vigilance against terrorism, is a stunning development, and one that few of us envisioned, I suspect, as we watched the Trade Center towers collapse and then focused on media reports that terrorists were responsible. It is also a momentous development that threatens to alter fundamental precepts that have historically characterized the nation's sense of its values and role in the world and to reshape power relations within the nation and its national government.

In addressing these developments, the enclosed essays raise fundamental questions about the nation's response to terrorism and the long-term direction that this response may be taking us. Three such questions seem paramount.

QUESTIONS AND ANSWERS

WHY DID THE NATION MOVE FROM TERRORIST STRIKES ON SEPTEMBER 11 TO THE WAR NARRATIVE THAT ENGULFED IT THEREAFTER?

The essays by James Pfiffner and Shirley Anne Warshaw suggest that the language of war came almost immediately to mind with President Bush and much of his cabinet. Moreover, this language focused not simply or primarily on the terrorist organization responsible for September 11, but on the overarching challenge posed by international terrorism to the United States and its allies. Additionally, the language employed a broad conception of terrorism, encompassing nations as well as clandestine terrorist groups. Thus any nation was considered a terrorist threat that harbored international terrorists or pursued policies—such as the creation of weapons of mass destruction—that could strike terror and destruction into the homeland of the United States or key allies.

It is self-evident that in the face of such an extraordinary experience as the devastating strikes against the World Trade Center and the Pentagon decision makers must make fast decisions about how best to respond. It is also clear that the response of President Bush and his advisors calmed and reassured the nation, and pointed it toward a clear path of action. The nation has only one president and one national government, and in times of severe crisis such individuals have and must use the great leeway given to them.

Yet nations, and particularly those of a democratic character, have substantial responsibility to assess the decisions their leaders make during crises, affirm those paths that appear justified and effective, correct perceived missteps, and learn from the overall decision processes in ways that improve the capacity to respond effectively to future crises. This is particularly the case with decisions like those made in the days and weeks following September 11. The war narrative and its fast and ready inclusion of Iraq as a target was not the only or even the most obvious response to September 11. In fact, as reported in the essay by Warshaw, Secretary of State Colin Powell was virtually incredulous that others within the president's cabinet moved so fast to articulate and embrace such a stance. Moreover, that stance, once taken, led to the reformulation of American foreign and domestic security policies in ways that had enormous long-term implications. Such developments call out for informed reassessment of the decisions and decision processes and corrective action if it is deemed appropriate.[4]

The extraordinary attention paid by scholars and public officials to the Cuban Missile Crisis and the decision processes followed by Kennedy and Khrushchev is a case in point. In the case of the missile crisis, with leaders facing almost imminent world war, days and hours mattered enormously to their capacity to find a path away from mutual destruction. As we look back at that effort, and even to some considerable extent in the days and weeks surrounding it, analysts have been concerned to determine whether the participants looked at the full range of options available, proceeded with due deliberation and caution, and availed themselves of the best information and communication possible. They have also been concerned to understand why leaders did what they did, including not just the American leaders but those in the Soviet Union.

Such efforts have generated disturbing perspectives on crisis decision making, thereby reinforcing the responsibility of a nation to review decisions and decision processes of its leaders. Thus the most widely regarded such study, *The Essence of Decision* by Graham Allison, portrays participants who entered the crisis period entranced in a Cold War narrative that focused their attention on winning the immediate standoff rather than grasping the imminent and mutual annihilation of both countries toward which such a mind-set was leading them.[5] This momentum toward disaster was magnified by organizational norms, procedures and power struggles across government departments that introduced substantial irrationality into the implementation of government strategies. Finally, key participants, including the president (who took an ill-timed political trip to Chicago amidst the crisis), were preoccupied by political power and electoral calculations that had little to do with finding the right solution to the pressing crisis and served to reinforce distorted perceptions and irrational behavior.

Analysts of the decision processes evident during the Cuban Missile Crisis suggest that early rush to judgment by participants, with such judgment colored by Cold War mind-sets, bureaucratic power struggles and political calculations, had set both nations on policy paths that would have proven devastating to them and to the world had the nations "stayed the course." In the face of this momentum, a critical moment came during the crisis when Khrushchev and Kennedy almost simultaneously came to question the appropriateness of the Cold War narrative to the crisis at hand and to recognize that it was entrapping both governments in mutually destructive behavior. The two leaders then turned their energies to convincing their advisors, their military, and their bureaucrats to pull out of the war narrative, power struggles, and political calculations and to recognize the collective threat that the crisis posed to the survival of both nations. Once safely beyond the crisis, both countries and the world at large moved toward rethinking of decision-making processes during crises, the creation of procedures to insure almost instantaneous contact between world leaders, and a renewed move toward arms control.[6]

As with the Cuban Missile Crisis, it is important for our nation and the world to grapple with the choice of strategies and justificatory arguments by leaders in the aftermath of September 11 and consider whether the processes followed and the path set at that time need to be reassessed. This is particularly true in light of the substantial deviations from traditional American policies embraced following the terrorist strike, including the move toward a foreign policy built around our (newfound) right to engage in preemptive wars against other nations if we deem them to be terrorist threats and the creation of a Department of Homeland Security with considerable authority to engage in expanded surveillance of citizens and centralized coordination of domestic policing forces. These developments, justified by the narrative of a sustained war against terrorism at home and abroad, necessarily raise a range of critical issues:

- Were a full range of alternative responses to September 11 considered, and was there a healthy debate about these responses that could have enabled the president to more fully grasp long-term implications of his short-term options?

- In the end, was the move from a focus on the criminal acts of relatively stateless terrorists and their support networks to a focus on terrorism worldwide, including the terrorist potential of nation-states such as Iraq, the only reasonable response, a sufficiently well-debated response, and the appropriate response to the terrorist threat?

- To what extent was the embrace of the war narrative, and the subsequent invasion of Iraq, a result of preexisting mind-sets of the decision makers, possibly left over from the Cold War or the Persian Gulf War, or a response to organizational power struggles and preexisting designs for war within government departments and agencies, or an outgrowth of the perceived political and electoral advantages for the president and his party—rather than a clearheaded and informed assessment of the immediate threat facing the nation and the best strategy for the nation in crafting a policy and justificatory rhetoric appropriate to that threat?

- In particular, were the war against Iraq and the subsequent effort to rebuild it the best use of our nation's resources in the effort to confront the serious threat that terrorism poses to our homeland and our national security, or would the money, time, and personnel have been better devoted to strengthening domestic security while leaving Hussein and his weapons of mass destruction to the United Nations?

- Was the articulation of the policy of unilateral and preemptive war, and the crafting of new policies for homeland security, subject to thoughtful debate within the Bush administration, or were they seen simply as necessary byproducts of the war narrative?

- As the Bush administration crafted its policy response, did it seek and encourage criticism and challenge from others, particularly from the Congress, in ways designed to allow for genuine self-correction?

- Finally, did the president himself grasp the enormity of the policy shifts he was envisioning and the long-term dynamics these shifts could unleash?

How Morally Legitimate Were the Foreign and Domestic Policies That Flowed from the Narrative of War?

With the nation posed on the brink of nuclear holocaust during the Cuban Missile Crisis, President Kennedy and his advisors considered a preemptive strike by the United States against Cuba. At the high point of that debate, Robert Kennedy, the president's brother and attorney general, argued that preemptive strikes, analogous to the Japanese strike against Pearl Harbor, violated the deepest values of the nation and should be ruled out of consideration. Robert Kennedy clearly believed that the United States had just cause to act. At issue were the moral constraints on action, and whether some actions could so violate moral standards and a nation's core principles that they were beyond the pale, actions that could undermine the ideals that the nation was seeking to honor and protect. Historians have used Kennedy's actions to underscore the point that, even when crafting strategies for war, actors can and should attend to moral and value-laden issues.

It is, of course, dangerous to draw direct analogies between one incident such as Cuban Missile Crisis and another such as September 11, particularly since decision makers were dealing in the former situation with identifiable and well-established nation-states whereas in the latter they are confronting amorphous terrorist groups with little clear linkage to nation-states and the world community. The decision processes and considerations that shaped President Kennedy's policies during the Cuban Missile Crisis could not necessarily be replicated by President Bush. But recalling Kennedy's moment of crisis does point to a question all policymakers must confront, particularly in situations where they must exercise extraordinary power.

At issue is whether a just cause justifies any and all forms of policy response.[7] Should a nation's response to a serious and heinous threat be circumscribed by moral standards and its own ideals and principles, or do some threats justify and even require our violation of our own values and sense of moral legitimacy? Clearly such questions apply to military action and war as an instrument of national policy, as illustrated by the Cuban Missile Crisis. But these questions can also apply to domestic issues such as homeland security. Thus the nation has struggled for half a century to grasp how it could have pursued the internment of Japanese citizens during World War II with little if any evidence of their involvement with the government of Japan, or how it could have endured the witch trials of the McCarthy era of the 1950s, which poisoned the nation's civil protection of all citizens. In retrospect both the Japanese internment and the McCarthy-era "red scare" look to be of dubious legitimacy, and also clearly undermined citizens' faith in the government and their willingness to trust it with domestic policing powers.

In the case of September 11, the policy response was two-pronged, focusing both on international and domestic issues. On the foreign stage, the Bush administration embraced a policy of preemptive and even unilateral strike if there were evidence of terrorist activity or of a clear terrorist threat from another nation to us or our allies. On the domestic front, the administration and the Congress embraced the creation of a homeland security apparatus, including a new cabinet department and extensive rules and procedures, that had the potential to alter the freedoms enjoyed by citizens. In the face of these developments, the pressing question is whether these policy directions fall within the moral and ethical boundaries that the nation considers to be acceptable, given our values and constitutional principles, or not.

Are these relatively benign developments, raising few fundamental moral dilemmas, or do they risk violating our most sacred values? Put a bit more pointedly, are these developments analogous in their ethical and moral overtones to the sort of preemptive strike that Robert Kennedy saw as morally repugnant during the Cuban Missile Crisis, or similar in their threats to civil liberties to the Japanese internment or the McCarthy-era red scare? If not, then the nation can move forward debating the appropriateness and effectiveness of the policies, but with little concern about ethics and morality. But if they do raise serious questions of ethics and morality, then a second question arises: Despite crossing the boundaries of behavior acceptable within our historical value commitments as a nation, are they nevertheless justified because terrorism is ultimately a more severe, diabolical, and amorphous threat than those faced in these early periods, so that moral standards and values must be loosened in the face of a more dangerous and less malleable world? With this concern then comes a third: Did Bush and his war cabinet satisfactorily confront these issues and make final decisions fully attuned to issues of prudence and moral conduct? If in fact we have embarked down a path that conceivably violates our most fundamental values and national ideals, did our leaders take us down this path through sober, systematic, and reasoned reflection on the moral issues at stake?

Finally, concern about the just pursuit of a just cause raises one last issue. In a democracy, it is the citizens who must ultimately take responsibility for the decisions made by their elected leaders, and particularly for the ongoing implementation of such decisions. That responsibility is particularly telling with respect to the conduct of the war on terrorism. The Cuban Missile Crisis took place across thirteen days, with little time for citizen input or opportunity to push for policy correction. With the Japanese internment and the McCarthy-era politics, citizens did have time to intervene and reverse course, and it is one of the great stains on the life of the nation during the twentieth century that it took so long for citizens and leaders alike to find the courage to do so. Chagrin at the slowness to challenge these earlier missteps may have been one reason why the nation was more nearly prepared to question foreign policies and domestic surveillance during the Vietnam era and to end both in due course.

The issues facing American citizens now are (1) whether they believe that unilateral and preemptive strikes against other nations are legitimate and wise responses to international terrorism, in keeping with the values and principles of the nation; and (2) whether they are convinced that the growing threat of terrorism at home justifies greatly increasing the surveillance powers of the government in the homeland. These are extremely difficult issues, and all of us can be forgiven if we blanch at the thought of grappling with them. But confront them we must.

The foreign policy logic articulated in the aftermath of September 11, and the domestic security apparatus implemented at home, are not momentary and limited actions, but developments that could fundamentally reorient our international role and domestic life long into the future. This is particularly so because they have been justified by an overarching war narrative of great power and broad scope that already has penetrated deeply into the nation's psyche, as seen in the essays in this volume, and has the potential to become the overarching political narrative of the early decades of the twenty-first century.

Repeatedly over the coming years and even decades, in election after election, we may be asked to reaffirm this narrative and its policies—or challenge, modify, reject, or reactivate it and them. However much we might wish to leave the critical decisions to leaders, in the end it is the citizens in a democracy who must take responsibility for the morality of the nation as it pursues threats to national security abroad and at home—and these moments of responsibility will come in relentless and continual fashion, and probably sooner and more consequentially than we currently anticipate. So what are the answers? Do we believe that unilateral and preemptive strikes at foreign nations are wise, legitimate, and morally acceptable policy principles, in keeping with our purpose as a nation? And are we prepared to accept incursions into our personal civil liberties, being rounded up for long-term detention if our own ethnic, gender, and age profile happens to coincide with that of suspected terrorists in some new act of terrorism? Is the threat of terrorism so severe, and so new and diabolical in nature, that values and principles that have survived for two hundred years, through civil war, two world wars and a Cold War struggle with communism now must be abrogated?

WHAT ARE LIKELY TO BE THE LONG-RUN CONSEQUENCES OF EMBRACING THE NARRATIVE OF WAR IN RESPONSE TO THE SEPTEMBER 11 TERRORIST STRIKES?

As of June 2003 there had been no substantial terrorist strikes against the American homeland, beyond the anthrax attack that came in the wake of September 11. This was no small accomplishment. In the months immediately following the collapse of the World Trade Center, American citizens had been deeply shaken by the terrorist experience, and the economy had taken a devastating hit as air travel declined and tourist spending lessened. There was genuine fear that a substantial terrorist attack during those months would provoke a long-term sense of hysteria that could do inalterable damage to national self-confidence and economic resilience. And such a strike did not seem an unreasonable possibility, given the apparent ease with which lone operatives can strike terror into the heart of a nation.

The sustained respite from domestic terrorism was a testament to the Bush administration's early and serious response to September 11 and to the willingness of the nation to rally behind such efforts with private vigilance and public support. It provided a critical breathing space that the nation needed, without which anxiety and fear might have spun out of control in the homeland. Instead, attentiveness at home, including the fast actions of an airline stewardess who helped avert another major airline disaster, forestalled domestic terrorism. Simultaneously, the massive pursuit of al Qaeda operatives and their supporters in Afghanistan threw the terrorists off-balance, and installed a regime there more responsive to the concerns of the U.S. and coalition allies.

There can be little doubt that American citizens almost universally supported these actions and saw them as effective. The president's approval ratings soared, and the Congress provided him great bipartisan support at critical moments on foreign and domestic security issues throughout this period, as Barbara Sinclair documents in Chapter 7. Nor were the scholars in this volume overly critical of these actions. Their unease was seen most particularly with respect to civil liberties. As the essays by Louis Fisher (Chapter 6) and Richard Conley (Chapter 8) show, the malaise comes not with specific and immediate actions of the government in the aftermath of 9/11, but with the embrace of the broader war narrative used to justify the actions and with the broadening array of policies and actions that came to be subsumed under the narrative.

The actual policies that the Bush administration followed in the early months after 9/11 could have been justified by a number of different policy narratives and strategic prescriptions, as the early dissent of Colin Powell within the administration indicates. Thus the U.S. and coalition actions against al Qaeda and the Afghan Taliban did not necessitate the rhetoric of world war nor the assertion of the right of unilateral preemptive strike—but could have been presented as a policing action by the world community to punish and forestall crimes against humanity. Similarly, the efforts in behalf of domestic security did not require an implicit declaration of world war and the ancillary creation of the Department of Homeland Security. In point of fact, the department was created more than a year following 9/11 and played no role in the early success of the administration in forestalling domestic terrorism.

The apprehension evident in the enclosed essays, and an apprehension I share, is that in adopting the narrative of world war, and connecting that narrative with the government's right both to preemptively invade other nations and to greatly expand domestic surveillance, the Bush administration has set in motion long-term dynamics that could have severe adverse consequences for the nation—and dynamics that may have been largely unnecessary to the uprooting of al Qaeda and the protection of the homeland. Any number of long-term consequences could flow from the war narrative and the policies subsumed under it that could prove counterproductive to national interest. For example, the right of preemptive war for one nation necessarily entails a similar right for another nation. In the current structure of the world the United States may be the only nation with the real power, particularly with the nuclear power, to successfully assert that right. But for that very reason one must expect that other nations will greatly redouble their efforts to strengthen their military and their nuclear arsenals in order to claim their dutiful rights to ensure self-protection through preemptive strikes at their perceived enemies. The end result may be a far more dangerous world, not a safer one.

Similarly, the right of expanded domestic surveillance is itself a slippery slope. Once created, one must expect a Department of Homeland Security to seek out ever-greater powers and responsibilities to justify its continued existence—a natural and ominous bureaucratic instinct that has been a major reason why Americans have been so hesitant to create such a department in the past. The last thing likely to make most Americans feel secure is more government intrusion and regulation. Moreover, in periods of domestic turmoil or political crisis, irresponsible leaders can expand and refine the concept of homeland security in quite threatening ways that U.S. citizens currently find difficult to imagine—but that the citizens of Argentina during the "dirty war" of the 1970s or Chile during the Pinochet presidency are quite familiar with. Will citizens actually feel more secure as a result of a government promise to insure homeland security, or will the very creation of such a specific government commitment lead citizens to feel more apprehensive about their freedoms and individual rights, and more leery of their government?

None of this is to suggest that such long-term and destructive dynamics were intended by the Bush administration. Rather, it is to argue that the policy narratives that frame how we understand the world and justify immediate actions—and that reassure and rally the nation in the midst of crisis—almost always have implications that are difficult for us to foresee, but that can set in motion problems and dilemmas as great or greater than those they were designed to resolve. For this reason serious attention needs to be given to the justificatory narratives that we embrace at moments of crisis. Citizens must demand that policymakers craft—or re-craft—their justificatory narratives in disciplined and foresightful ways that are true to the reality of the political world such narratives are designed to address, rather than exaggerations or magnifications of reality in ways that entrap us in new and even greater problems.

Perhaps the most powerful example of how all-encompassing a policy narrative can become, and its ability to lead a nation into disaster, lies with the magnified extension of the Cold War narrative of communist containment into every region and uprising in the world during the 1950s and 1960s, particularly its application to Vietnam.[8] The perception of the world as divided into good and evil, democrats and communists, and the consequent view that every political struggle in the world involved a victory by us or them, became so all-pervasive in the early postwar era that presidents lived in continual fear of impeachment and removal from office should they be perceived as having permitted some country or other to "fall" to the communists. This fear was exacerbated by an additional perception—the belief that nations were like dominos, with the fall of one then automatically leading to the fall of the next. In retrospect, this narrative was so powerful, and the fear that it instilled in American politicians was so deep-seated, that the nation pursued a war in Vietnam, even though the nation's leaders were not convinced that immediate national interests were at stake there. In fact, we now know that even our presidents had their troubling doubts in this regard. But in the face of their own doubts, presidents and advisors were swept along by the larger Cold War narrative that they felt almost powerless to challenge, and whose relentless unfolding then destroyed them, divided the nation, and eroded citizen confidence in government and in themselves.[9]

Just as the Cuban Missile Crisis illustrates how vital it can be for world leaders such as Khruschev and Kennedy to reassess their deep assumptions when on the edge of nuclear holocaust, the Vietnam War demonstrates how devastating it can be for a nation and its leaders to mindlessly pursue a war narrative, even in the face of their own doubts. Such narratives take on a life of their own and carry with them consequences of great potential severity. Thus, constant attentiveness to the appropriateness and longer-term implications of our policy narratives, particularly our war narratives, is a vital and even essential dimension of national life.

This is not to argue that a direct analogy can be drawn from the Cold War, the Cuban Missile Crisis, and Vietnam to the war on terrorism, Afghanistan, and Iraq. It's a different time, a different narrative, a different world. But it is to say that the broader experiences of the Cold War era carry with them lessons that later generations must attend to.

No one who lived through the Vietnam era can doubt that good leaders committed to noble ends can nevertheless become so entrapped within an overarching war narrative that they fail to see clearly the reality of specific situations and as a result make devastating mistakes, the long-term consequences of which are virtually irreversible. Ultimately the responsibility for assessing the truth about such narratives, and demanding that presidents and policymakers embrace realistic narratives that they truly believe, lies with the American public. Assessing the truth of a dominant narrative requires respectful attention to alternative perspectives, not only by leaders but by citizens.

Amidst the terrorist challenge of the contemporary period, two broad and starkly contrasting perspectives abound, hinted at in various ways within the essays in this volume. On the one hand, there are those who believe that a broad-gauged world war on terrorists and terrorist states has the potential to rid the world of both Osama bin Laden and Saddam Hussein, to cripple if not destroy al Qaeda and related terrorist organizations, to remove dangerous weapons of mass destruction from Iraq and elsewhere, and to engineer a move toward democratization and peace in the Middle East that would then reduce international terrorism while becoming a model for democratic development for much of the world. With such outcomes could come renewed national confidence and international respect. And out of them might come a more secure nation and a newly consolidated governing party—the Republicans—capable of guiding the nation forward on the domestic front with a steady hand.

In contrast, others fear that the war narrative is so self-righteous, simplistic, and moralistic in its logic, so broad and unlimited in its potential scope, and so aggressive and unilateral in its demeanor that it will inherently lead the nation to overreach in both its idealized aspirations and its policy actions. Rather than leaving us safer internationally, it could leave us a more vulnerable and isolated nation amidst an increasingly conflictual and hostile world in which old friends and allies would be as afraid of us—or even more afraid of us—as they are of international terrorism. Instead of leaving us feeling more secure at home, it could leave us coping with the enormous economic, social, and civil-libertarian costs of war and unilateralism and unable to focus energy and collective effort on domestic needs and homeland vigilance. And instead of yielding a new and confident partisan regime at the head of national affairs, able to unite the presidency and Congress in a new era of cooperation and policy responsiveness, it could shatter the emerging Republican order, so that for a second time in forty years a tragically erroneous war would upend our domestic politics and leave the nation adrift and its political and partisan institutions unhinged from safe mooring.

Naturally, there are nuances, middle positions and alternative assumptions that individual analysts stress as they contemplate the future. Nevertheless, amidst such qualifications distinctly different visions of the appropriate national response to terrorism are clearly evident. This division, moreover, comes not as a result of the failure of the Bush administration in responding effectively in the immediate aftermath of 9/11. It comes, rather, in assessments of the appropriateness of the narrative of war as the foundation of the nation's long-term response to terrorism, and in differential assessments of where that narrative will take us over the next decade or so—whether into a world of renewed international safety, domestic security and political clarity, or into a world of vulnerability and isolation on the international scene, insecurity and social disarray on the home front, and partisan meltdown, interinstitutional warfare and governing crisis within the domestic political sphere.

Each of us must clarify for himself or herself which of these alternative perspectives—or their nuances variations—seems the most compelling assessment of our current conditions. Much rides on our judgment, including not just which candidate or party wins the presidency or Congress, but also what type of nation and world leader we will become in subsequent decades, how the character of our political and economic life will develop, and what the structure of international politics will look like. Faced with such momentous choice, one final consideration seems particularly paramount.

CONCLUDING COMMENTARY

War is generally justified as a route to peace, and certainly that may well be true. But judging from the history of the twentieth century, it is a long and elusive route that has generated very little peace. In recent years scholars in the United States have espoused the notion of "the democratic peace"—the idea that democracies seldom if ever fight each other, so that the spread of democracies brings international peace.[10] I wonder.

History will surely conclude that the past sixty years or so have been a great age of democracy on the international scene—an era when democracies proliferated, when the most powerful nations in the world collectively were its major democracies, and when the international community itself was governed to some remarkable extent through quasi-democratic institutions such as the United Nations. Yet in fact this age of democracy has been almost entirely consumed by the narrative of war, rather than the reality of peace. This recognition raises two questions: (1) Is the rush to the narrative of war itself somehow built into the logic of democratic politics—a logic in which leaders preemptively embrace such rhetoric when the opportunity arises in order to secure their own political advantage and avoid the difficulties of domestic problem-solving—with the only requirement being a nondemocratic autocrat on whom national aggressions and fears can be projected? And (2) How long can democracies flourish when their politics are overshadowed by the narrative of war and the distortions—as in the reliance on executive power—such narratives introduce to domestic politics, public policy, constitutional structures, and the international order?

As we grapple with the three core questions raised by the essays in this volume, we also seriously need to grapple with these two deeper and more troubling questions as well. The power to evoke war is an awesome one, and no one envies democratic presidents and legislative leaders who at times must act for their citizens in pursuing such a course and overseeing its conduct. Yet it is equally important—and momentous—for leaders to bring war to an end and eschew its ready embrace to steer a course to peace in so far as possible.

Clearly, some wars have to be fought, particularly in settings where the international community affords no procedures for ensuring regional or world security through other means. But are all wars inherently justified, so long as they are conducted against authoritarian regimes with unsavory leaders? Wars have costs and tradeoffs, and not just in economic terms or lives lost. They also have the capacity to warp the values of a nation, to cripple civil liberties and democratic institutions, and to distort the constitutional order and the power relations among institutions. In addition, wars and the narratives associated with them have the capacity to distort and mask the true nature of reality, limiting the clarity of our perceptions with respect to other nations, our own national interests, our domestic challenges, and the erosion of our democratic processes and liberties. The decision to go to war is an immensely consequential one—not just another alternative on our repertoire of policy options, but a qualitatively different type of policy decision that can undercut the very freedoms and institutions in whose name we fight. Thus war and the narrative of war must be embraced with the utmost caution, and with due regard to genuine necessity, the multiple trade-offs involved, and the severity of the potential consequences.

Perhaps a worldwide war on terrorism is necessary, and perhaps the invasion of Iraq will prove to have been a vital part of that effort.[11] Similarly, perhaps the right of unilateral preemptive invasion and expanded governmental powers of domestic surveillance are essential in an era of terrorism. I leave these issues open, acknowledging that I lack the necessary information and breadth of perspective to answer them in a confident and definitive manner, though I do have my own judgment. But what does seem self-evident—and particularly so if in fact a worldwide and expansive war on terrorism is truly the only route to a long-term and democratic peace—is that great attention needs to be given to how to secure democratic liberties and ensure continued democratic resilience in the face of the narrative of war.

The longer the narrative of war persists, and the more reliant on war our economics, our political calculations, our national unity, and our social fabric become, the more difficult it will be to find a sound political compass and peaceful democratic path once war recedes. Already we have a history of over sixty years that were almost entirely overshadowed by war and the narrative of war. And now we have a new war narrative, and one with no endgame in sight—a narrative whose ready embrace and sustenance seems to owe in no small degree to its familiarity and proven political potency.

How does a nation spend seventy years, eighty years, a hundred years, entrapped in the narrative of war—war against fascism, war against communism, war against terrorism—and emerge with its liberties and values and democratic institutions and election processes and propensity for peace unscathed? What special protections can it engender to protect, secure, and nurture them? And can it eventually transition to the narrative of peace, and adjust to the difficulties of governing amidst sustained peace, after a century of war? Having repeatedly used the narrative of war to rally and unite the nation's citizens, and in the process having struck the heroic pose of war leader and defused domestic opposition by portraying a world of black and white, good and evil, will leaders voluntarily forsake such a tempting and self-serving narrative and readily choose to embrace and sustain a democratic peace? And perhaps most at issue—will citizens ever demand that they do so? Or in an age of extraordinary military superiority by the United States, minimal American causalities, and televised military triumph does the public simply find war such an exhilarating, vicariously intoxicating and cathartic experience that it prefers life amidst the narrative of war and foreign domination to coping with the complexities, nuance, and moral confusions that come with peace and domestic vigilance?

If in truth a war on terrorism is the only way to deal with the vulnerabilities of a terrorist age, and if this war is going to be a long one, then we do truly need to begin debating what a century of war means for the capacity of a democracy to rediscover the politics of peace. Entrapped in the narrative of war once again, we need to work with redoubled energy to remember and value the politics of democracy at peace—and to debate how best to rekindle it. The essays in this volume, written after a ten-year hiatus in war as the nation was moving to embrace yet a new one, bring to the fore just enough concern for the politics of peace to remind us not only of the vital responsibility presidents have amidst crisis. They also underscore the vital role of dissent within the cabinet, the value of active congressional oversight, the need to attend to civil liberties, particularly in a time of crisis, the responsibility for an attentive and well-informed citizenry to attend closely to leaders' words and deeds, and the reliable compass provided to a nation in crisis by its bedrock values and civic beliefs. Entrapped as we are in the narrative of war, such scholarly work serves as a beacon light reminding us of the domestic requisites of a democratic peace.

NOTES

1. Bob Woodward, *Bush at War* (New York: Simon & Schuster, 2002).
2. Arthur M. Schlesinger, Jr., *The Imperial Presidency* (Boston: Houghton-Mifflin, 1973); John White, *Still Seeing Red: How the Cold War Shapes the New American Politics* (Boulder, CO: Westview Press, 1997).
3. Lawrence C. Dodd, "The New American Politics," in *The New American Politics,* ed. Bryan D. Jones (Boulder, CO.: Westview Press, 1995).
4. For one such reassessment by a leading conservative commentator, see Clyde Prestowitz, *Rogue Nation: American Unilateralism and the Failure of Good Intentions* (New York: Basic Books, 2003).
5. Graham T. Allison, *The Essence of Decision* (Boston: Little Brown, 1971).
6. Steven Weber, "Interactive Learning in U.S.-Soviet Arms Control," in *Learning in U.S. and Soviet Foreign Policy,* ed. George W. Breslaner and Philip E. Tetlock (Boulder, CO.: Westview Press, 1991).
7. Robert W. Tucker, *The Just War: A Study in Contemporary American Doctrine* (Baltimore, MD: Johns Hopkins Press, 1960); for a probing assessment of the applicability of the "just war" doctrine to terrorism, arguing that war can be a necessary step in constraining such developments as worldwide terrorism, see Jean Bethke Elshtain, *Just War against Terror: The Burden of American Power in a Violent World* (New York: Basic Books, 2003).
8. Daniel Ellsberg, "The Quagmire Myth and the Stalemate Machine," *Public Policy* 16 (spring 1971), pp. 217–274.
9. For a particularly poignant analysis of the way in which the Vietnam War intersected with the effort of Lyndon Johnson to move forward on civil rights and domestic social reform, tragically upending his own emotional health, his closest political friendships, his reform agenda, his party, and the nation, not to mention Vietnam itself, see Robert Mann, *The Walls of Jericho: Lyndon Johnson, Hubert Humphrey, Richard Russell, and the Struggle for Civil Rights* (New York: Harcourt Brace, 1996); and for a more complete focus on the nation's experience with Vietnam, see Robert Mann, *A Grand Delusion: America's Descent into Vietnam* (New York: Basic Books, 2001).
10. Bruce M. Russett, *Grasping the Democratic Peace* (Princeton, NJ: Princeton University Press, 1993).
11. For a helpful perspective on the issue of Iraq, less partisan and more balanced than most analyses in the aftermath of the war, see Kenneth M. Pollack, "Saddam's Bombs? We'll Find Them," *New York Times,* 20 June 2003, p. A-25.

INDEX